3124300 568 3478

D1163149

Television Series of the 1950s

Television Series of the 1950s

Essential Facts and Quirky Details

VINCENT TERRACE

ROWMAN & LITTLEFIELD
Lanham • Boulder • New York • London

Published by Rowman & Littlefield
A wholly owned subsidiary of The Rowman & Littlefield Publishing Group, Inc.
4501 Forbes Boulevard, Suite 200, Lanham, Maryland 20706
www.rowman.com

Unit A, Whitacre Mews, 26-34 Stannary Street, London SE11 4AB

Copyright © 2016 by Rowman & Littlefield

All rights reserved. No part of this book may be reproduced in any form or by any electronic
or mechanical means, including information storage and retrieval systems, without written
permission from the publisher, except by a reviewer who may quote passages in a review.

British Library Cataloguing in Publication Information Available

Library of Congress Cataloging-in-Publication Data

Names: Terrace, Vincent, 1948–
Title: Television series of the 1950s : essential facts and quirky details /
    Vincent Terrace.
Description: Lanham : Rowman & Littlefield, [2016] | Includes index.
Identifiers: LCCN 2015038755| ISBN 9781442261037 (hardback : alk. paper) |
    ISBN 9781442261044 (ebook)
Subjects: LCSH: Television programs—United States—Plots, themes, etc. |
    Television programs—United States—Dictionaries.

∞™ The paper used in this publication meets the minimum requirements of American
National Standard for Information Sciences—Permanence of Paper
for Printed Library Materials, ANSI/NISO Z39.48-1992.

Printed in the United States of America

Contents

Acknowledgments

The author would like to thank James Robert Parish for his assistance on this project.

Introduction

Once upon a time—back in August 1931—Columbia Broadcasting System (CBS)'s experimental television station W2XAB presented the first known American variety TV series, *Half-Hour on Broadway*. Shortly after, in the same month, the first identified U.S. dramatic TV series, *The Television Ghost*, premiered, followed by the initial domestic television comedy series *Ned Wayburn's Musical Comedy Show*. Virtually nothing is known about these early shows, as they aired live and the programs no longer exist. (There was also little or no documentation [reviews, ads] regarding these early experiments.) Imagine what nostalgic information these pioneering CBS programs contained, and—if they were still viewable today—what trivia treasures they may have possessed.

This book is like a time machine back to an era, the 1950s, when commercial television was still in its infancy. It was also a period when TV programs telecast in that era still exist today. Through the viewing of such actual episodes, that lost trivia information has been uncovered and is presented in this volume in as much detail as possible based on what offerings have survived.

This is *not* a book of opinions or essays about specific television programs; it is a narrative of the facts associated with each of the programs that are included here. Readers will discover a wealth of fascinating information that, for the most part, cannot be found anywhere else. In some cases, the factual data detailed herein is the only such documentation that exists currently on these bygone shows.

While all the basic information available about each television series has been included (e.g., story line and cast), the bulk of each entry focuses on the trivia aspects associated with each of the programs examined. This includes such data as street addresses, names of pets, telephone numbers, character facts, program facts, and other items you may have once known but have long since forgotten.

Whether the titles in this book ring a bell of recognition or are totally unknown to you, readers will find a new perspective regarding old-time TV with this first in a series of volumes that will also explore other decades of American television fare: the 1960s, 1970s, 1980s, 1990s, and 2000s.

Each of the alphabetically arranged entries was compiled by acquiring and watching its available episodes. In some cases, only a handful of segments exist today or were obtainable for viewing, and thus not all entries are equal in presentation of information. However, each entry is as complete as possible based on accessible material.

Did you know, for example, that Amos McCoy (*The Real McCoys*) could not read or write but had "a taste for dirt" when it came to planting crops? (knew what should be planted where) or that on *The Many Loves of Dobie Gillis*, the "G" in the offbeat character named Maynard G. Krebs stood for Walter? How about Ralph and Alice Kramden's apartment electric bill (on *The Honeymooners*) being only 39 cents a month? Or that Ralph would buy Alice a TV set only "when they invented 3-D TV?" And on *I Love Lucy*, were you aware that Ricky originally performed at Manhattan's Tropicana Club? (later the Club Babalu). And on *Richard Diamond, Private Detective*, Sam, Diamond's answering service provider, operated the Hi Fi Answering Service? These are but a few of the many thousands of fun and intriguing trivia facts contained in this volume.

All told, it's a totally different perspective on a past era of American TV, one that will bring back fond memories or enlighten those too young to remember what U.S. TV was really like in its infancy.

The Abbott and Costello Show

(Syndicated, 1952–1954)

Cast: Bud Abbott, Lou Costello, Hillary Brooke, Sidney Fields (Themselves), Gordon Jones (Mike the Cop), Joe Besser (Stinky), Joe Kirk (Mr. Botchagalupe).

Basis: Out-of-work actors (Bud Abbott and Lou Costello) seek a means of employment (with Bud finding work for Lou) until they can make a show business comeback.

BUD ABBOTT AND LOU COSTELLO

Address: The Fields Rooming House at 214 Brookline Avenue in Hollywood.

Rent: $7 a week.

Telephone Number: Alexander 4444 (also given as Alexander 2222).

Jobs (Bud): Professional loafer (one who makes bread, not one who sleeps all day, like Lou believes).

Jobs (Lou and Bud): Whatever could make them money (including: salesman for the Susquehanna Hat Company on Flugel Street, door-to-door vacuum cleaner salesmen, waiters at Brodie's Seafood Restaurant, roller skate salesmen ("Abbott and Costello Cheap Skates"), wallpaper hangers, pest exterminators, pet store owners, and drugstore soda jerks.

Favorite Way of Making Money: Pawning what they have at Harry's Hock Shop.

Lou's Catchphrase: "Heyyyyy Abbott!" (which he yells when he needs Bud's help).

Character: Former vaudeville, radio, and feature film comedians who are now out of work (a specific reason is not given why they are suddenly out of show business, and they apparently have little chance of revitalizing their careers). Lou, born in Paterson, New Jersey, claims he has to support his sister and three nieces.

"We've got to raise money" could be considered Bud's catchphrase as he continually seeks to find Lou a job to raise the money they need to pay their rent. Bud and Lou appeared on the TV game show *Hold That Cuckoo,*

1

wherein Lou performed a stunt before the cuckoo sounded and won the grand prize—a box of bubble gum. If Bud and Lou encounter a situation where a friend (or stranger) is in trouble, Bud always remarks, "Costello will get you out of this." They also attempted to become police officers but flunked out of rookie school.

Although Lou is an adult with child-like tendencies, he loves to play games with his pal Stinky Davis, a 30-year-old "kid" who dressed as a child and liked to play games with Lou like cops and robbers, football, and hopscotch. Lou also fancies himself as a private detective and is a graduate of the Junior G-Man Correspondence School; he also carries a cap pistol with him at all times.

HILLARY BROOKE

Character: A beautiful woman who lives across the hall from Bud and Lou. While Hillary is generally seen as Lou's girlfriend, she handles a number of other roles that ignore her relationship with Bud and Lou (actually whatever a scene calls for—from secretary to hospital nurse). Hillary is the owner of the B-Bop-Bop Ranch in Texas (where Bud and Lou attempted to become ranch hands) and a haunted castle at Goblin's Knob (which she inherited from her Uncle Montague and where Lou, Bud, and Hillary attempted to find the castle's hidden treasure). Her regular series job appears to be a secretary-receptionist. When Hillary calls on Lou, she brings him cream puffs.

SIDNEY FIELDS

Character: The easily exasperated owner and landlord of the Fields Rooming House. Sidney wants only a peacefully run rooming house and has posted a number of rules tenants must follow: "No cooking cabbage in the apartment; no door slamming; no babies; no pets; and no loud music playing after 9:30 p.m." Unintentionally, Lou sees to it that Sidney never gets that desired peace and quiet with his antics.

While Sidney Fields plays primarily the landlord, he also plays numerous other roles, most notably relations to Sidney: Professor Melonhead, the judo expert, and Claude Melonhead, the lawyer, and Judge Melonhead.

BINGO THE CHIMP

Character: The chimpanzee that Lou adopted when working at a pet shop. Bingo, six years of age, dresses like Lou (trademark checkered jacket and gray hat) and eats 50 pounds of bananas a week "with a side order of popcorn." He and Lou alternate bubble bath nights, and at the dinner table, all that Bud asks is for Bingo to behave himself and eat "like a human being." Lou has traced Bingo's lineage and has learned that he was born in the

Belgian Congo (where his father was a mighty gorilla) and that his mother now works in a circus.

OTHER CHARACTERS

Mike Kelly, better known as Mike the Cop, is the neighborhood foot patrol officer continually plagued by Lou's antics; Mr. Bothagalupe is the Italian neighborhood entrepreneur, a street vendor (from vegetables to ice cream) simply trying to make an honest dollar in difficult times.

Adventures in Paradise
(ABC, 1959–1962)

Cast: Gardner McKay (Adam Troy), Weaver Levy (Oliver Wendell Key), James Holden (Clay Baker), Guy Stockwell (Chris Parker).

Basis: A schooner captain's adventures (Adam Troy, owner of the *Tiki*) as he transports passengers and cargo around the South Pacific.

ADAM TROY

Place of Birth: Connecticut.

Education: Yale University, Class of 1954 and a member of the Omega Fraternity.

Ambition: Hopes to one day own his own ranch (but for the moment he says, "Not right now").

Blood Type: A-B negative.

First Sea-Related Job: Skipper of a barge in Pusong.

Current Job: Captain of the *Tiki*, a 60-foot schooner that anchors in the Papeete Harbor in Tahiti. The *Tiki* has two masts and five sails (two large, three small) and a temperamental engine that Adam and his crew call "The Lady." The schooner's transmitter, with the call letters KRQ, cost Adam $750; he also has a jeep (in Tahiti-based episodes with the license plate 3134 A). To guide him during long sea voyages, Adam follows the constellation called the Southern Cross ("Find those stars and you'll never lose your way in the South Pacific").

OTHER CHARACTERS

Oliver Wendell Key first served as Adam's mate, cook, and lawyer (as Adam says, "He handles all the deals"). Clay Baker, born in Tennessee, replaced Oliver in second-season episodes, while Chris Parker replaced him in final-season episodes. When Chris signed on, Clay became the innkeeper of the Bali Miki, a hotel originally owned by Trader Penrose (played by George Tobias). Clay renamed the inn the Bali Miki Baker and became famous for two exotic drinks he created: Tahitian Madness and the Polynesian Rainmaker ("Two of these," he says, "and

4 THE ADVENTURES OF OZZIE AND HARRIET

you'll swear it rained"). Before the inn became a featured aspect of the series, it was called the Hotel Dujour. Kelly (Lani Kai), who doubled as Clay's lounge singer, and Bulldog Lovey (Henry Slate) also served as Adam's shipmates in various episodes. Bulldog, who claimed that Adam lived by a code ("There are certain things he will do and there are certain things he won't do"), was a master at predicting when night would fall simply by looking at the sky ("I can give you the exact hour and minute, but don't hold me to the seconds").

Note: To provide story lines other than Adam transporting cargo, Adam often became involved in the problems of his passengers. When police help was required, Inspector Marcel Bouchard (played by Marcel Hillaire) of the Tahitian Policia was most often called in. The program's official title is *James A. Michener's Adventures in Paradise.*

The Adventures of Ozzie and Harriet
(ABC, 1952–1966)

Cast: Ozzie Nelson, Harriet Hilliard Nelson, David Nelson, Ricky Nelson, June Nelson, Kris Nelson (Themselves).

Basis: A look at the lives of "America's Favorite Family," the Nelsons: parents Ozzie and Harriet and their children David (16) and Ricky (12), who live at 1822 Sycamore Road in the town of Hilldale.

Ozzie (full name Oswald George Nelson) was born in Bergen County, New Jersey, on March 20, 1906 (in real life, Ozzie was born in Jersey City, New Jersey). He attended Richfield Park High School and was a quarterback on the school's football team. It was also at this time that Ozzie dated a girl named Penelope Briggs (according to the episode "Ozzie's Old Team Mate"). Ozzie had intended to become a lawyer, but his love for music (especially singing and playing the saxophone) led him to organize his own dance band in the late 1920s. As the band became more and more successful, he abandoned his chances of becoming a lawyer.

In 1932, while performing in New York City, Ozzie met Harriet Hilliard, the 23-year-old daughter (born in 1909) of a show business couple, and hired her as the band's singer. They dated, fell in love, and married in 1935. In another episode, Ozzie mentions it was in college that he and Harriet met (but no mention was made of the band). They eventually became the parents of two children: David (in 1936) and Ricky (in 1940). With two children to raise, Harriet gave up singing with the band to concentrate on becoming a housewife.

In real life, Ozzie and Harriet began a radio series called *The Adventures of Ozzie and Harriet* (1944–1954), wherein Ozzie still had ties to his band while

Harriet raised David and Ricky. Prior to adapting their radio series to television, Ozzie produced a feature film called *Here Come the Nelsons* (1952), which supposedly served as an introduction to the Nelson family, but its concept was not brought over to the actual TV series. Here Ozzie and Harriet are no longer associated with the band, and Ozzie has an actual job—as an executive with the H. J. Bellows and Company advertising agency. When the first episode of the TV series begins, there is no introduction to the characters, and Ozzie (with no mention of the job he held in the movie) is assumed to be retired, but his prior occupation is unknown. Two episodes reveal that Ozzie was a bandleader and is now retired: "Ricky, the Drummer" (April 10, 1957) and "The Sea Captain" (October 7, 1959). Ozzie admits that he has too much free time on his hands, and his efforts to find something to do often involve him (and his family) in some sort of mischief.

Ozzie, a member of The Men's Club, is a man who seems to take a back-seat to everything. He often wears a cardigan sweater, is very mellow, and has a stammering personality (often hesitant in speech and a bit absentminded). Harriet, on the other hand, is a take-control type of woman who manages to help Ozzie overcome the precarious situations he often becomes involved with. She is a member of the Women's Club (also called the University Women's Club). Ozzie believed in strong family values and preached that to his children. Ricky and David were typical sitcom kids, always finding mischief but always finding help in solving their problems from their parents. They did hold jobs (in 1952) delivering newspapers for an unnamed publication. While music was not a major part of the show, Ozzie and Harriet did perform a song when situations permitted it (like a PTA show). As the children grew, each picked up on what their father had originally intended to become: a lawyer.

Both David and Ricky attended Hilldale High School and State College (also called State University). David, the first to graduate, became a lawyer with the firm of Dobson and Kelly; Ricky followed, first as an apprentice, then as a lawyer. Love also entered the lives of David and Ricky. June Blair was David's girlfriend (and later wife). After marrying in 1961, David moved out of the Nelson home and into an apartment with June while attending law school. For Ricky, love came in 1963 in the form of Kristin Harmon (in real life, the daughter of Heisman Trophy–winning football player Tom Harmon). Kristin and Ricky also married—both in real life (when Kristin became pregnant) and on TV (they became the parents of Tracy, perhaps best known for her TV roles on *Square Pegs* and *Father Dowling Mysteries*).

Life changed for the Nelson family in 1957 when Ricky, who played the drums, became a high school heartthrob when he sang the song "I'm Walking" (in the episode "Ricky, the Drummer"). Not only was Ricky's singing incorporated into episodes, but occasional songs by Ozzie and Harriet were also

The Nelson Family: Ricky, Ozzie, Harriet, and David. © ABC ABC/Photofest

featured. At this same time, Harriet would appear before the closing theme to promote Ricky's current album releases and/or upcoming movies.

OTHER CHARACTERS
Ozzie's friends: Thorny (Don Defore), Joe Randolph (Lyle Talbot), Herb Darby (Parley Baer), and Doc Williams (Frank Cady). Wally Dipple (Skip Young) is Ricky's friend; Ginger (Catherine Salerno) is Wally's girlfriend; Connie (Constance Harper) is David's secretary; Ralph Dobson (Francis De-

Sales) and Don Kelley (Joe Flynn) are the senior law partners. In a flashback sequence in the episode "The Miracle," Ricky plays his father as youngster and David plays Ozzie's older brother, Al. The program is widely known as *Ozzie and Harriet* and was broadcast for a short time in 1960 under the title *The Adventures of the Nelson Family*.

In 1973 (to 1974) Ozzie and Harriet returned to television in the syndicated series *Ozzie's Girls* (although the pilot aired on NBC). Here Ozzie and Harriet are now living at 1822 Sycamore Street in the town of Hilldale. Their sons, David and Ricky, have moved out, and to fill a void in their lives, they advertise in the *Campus News* for someone to rent their sons' former room. College coeds Susan Hamilton (Susan Sennett) and Jennifer MacKenzie (Brenda Sykes; her character later became Brenda MacKenzie) answer the ad. The girls pay the difference between what it now costs the Nelsons to run the house as opposed to their just living alone. The school Brenda and Susan attend is called the "Campus" or the "College." Brenda is an Aquarius, sophisticated, and neat. Susan is a hippie type and disorganized. She is a Pisces and plays the guitar. Her father calls her "Charlie" (her mother calls her father, whose name is George, "Jackson"). Ozzie is a Pisces and Harriet a Moonchild. Lenore Morrison (Lenore Stevens) and her daughter, Alice (Joie Guerico), are Ozzie's neighbors.

The Adventures of Superman
(Syndicated, 1952–1957)

Cast: George Reeves (Clark Kent/Superman), Phyllis Coates, Noel Neill (Lois Lane), Jack Larson (Jimmy Olsen), John Hamilton (Perry White), Robert Shayne (Inspector Bill Henderson).

Basis: Kal-El, the last known survivor of the doomed planet Krypton, assumes the identity of Clark Kent and, with his abilities of flight, speed, and strength and in the guise of the mysterious Superman, battles the evils of his adopted city, Metropolis.

CLARK KENT

Home Planet: Krypton (saved from its destruction [being pulled into its sun] when his father placed him as an infant in an experimental rocket ship and programmed it to land on Earth).

Birth Parents: Jor-El (Robert Rockwell) and Lara (Aline Towne).

Earth Parents: Eben (Tom Fadden) and Sarah Kent (Dina Nolan), a childless farm couple who found the rocket when it landed (on April 10, 1926), adopted the infant, and named him Clark Kent.

Earth Home: Smallville, Kansas (a farming community), in Metropolis U.S.A.

Occupation: Reporter for the *Daily Planet,* a crusading newspaper.

Metropolis Residence: Apartment 5H of the Standish Arms Hotel.

Telephone Number: West 3-0963.

Character: As Clark Kent, Superman possesses strength, speed, the ability to fly, X-ray vision, and an immunity to harm. To conceal his true identity, Clark appears as a mild-mannered, somewhat wimpy reporter (seemingly to always disappear when trouble brews). This allows him to change into his Superman costume (which he apparently wears under his work clothes), discard his eye glasses, and bring criminals to justice. His red, white, and blue costume was made by Sarah from the blankets that were originally wrapped around him as an infant (it is never stated how Sarah was able to cut and sew the blankets to make the costume when they are indestructible).

Weakness: Kryptonite, green remnants from Krypton that provide a negative charge (Superman is positively charged) and deplete Superman of his powers (too long an exposure can kill him; lead can shield Superman from its effects). A series of articles written by Clark about crime in Metropolis were made into the feature film *Czar of the Underworld.* In his apartment, Clark has a human-like plastic head for his hat he calls "Sam." Stuart Randall played Clark as a boy.

LOIS LANE

Place of Birth: The small town of Clifton-By-The Sea.

Occupation: Investigative Reporter for the *Daily Planet.*

Address: Apartment 6 A at 453 Metropolitan Avenue.

Car License Plate: ZN 18683.

Character: Lois is a young woman who often places her life at risk by venturing into situations she is not totally prepared for. She wants to get the stories that make the headlines and often finds herself being saved by Superman. Lois suspects that Clark is really Superman, but she can't prove it (as Clark always disappears when there is trouble and Superman then arrives on the scene; as she says when Clark makes an excuse to get away, "Looking for a hole to hide in, Clark?").

JAMES "JIMMY" BARTHOLOMEW OLSEN

Place of Birth: Metropolis.

Home: McDougal Place where he resides with his never-seen mother.

Occupation: Cub Reporter (then photographer) for the *Daily Planet.*

Character: Not as brave as Lois; more of a follower than a leader (as he will accompany Lois and also find himself in harm's way).

Relations: Louisa Horne, Jimmy's aunt (Sarah Padden).

PERRY WHITE

Occupation: Editor of the *Daily Planet.* Perry was a top-notch crime reporter, then the mayor of Metropolis before becoming editor.

Mobile Phone Number: MX 31962.

Catchphrase: "Great Caesar's ghost!" (which he says when he gets upset; the phrase refers to Julius Caesar).

Character: Perry is a member of the American Magician's Society and often remarks that he can do a better job in acquiring the stories than some of the reporters he has working for him. Jimmy has a knack for calling Perry "Chief," which upsets Perry, and he continually tells him, "Don't Call Me Chief!"

Relations: Mabel Albertson as Kate White, Perry's sister; Lane Bradford as Chris White, Perry's nephew.

DAILY PLANET FACTS

The building (with the street number 5045) is located next to the Thomas Drug Store (in close-up scenes and establishing shots, the building is actually Los Angeles City Hall). The building is characterized by a metal model of the planet Earth that can be seen through the front doorway in the lobby. Copies of the paper sell for five cents, and Metropolis 6-0500 is its phone number.

Note: Black and white episodes feature a steam locomotive in the opening sequence. Color episodes use stock footage of a diesel engine owned by Southern Pacific Railroad (its orange and red color scheme indicates that it is the Southern Pacific Daylight passenger train).

The Amos 'n' Andy Show
(CBS, 1951–1953)

Cast: Alvin Childress (Amos Jones), Spencer Williams Jr. (Andrew H. Brown), Tim Moore (George "Kingfish" Stevens), Ernestine Wade (Sapphire), Amanda Randolph (Mama), Jane Adams (Ruby Jones).

Basis: The mishaps that befall three African American men living in Manhattan: Amos Jones, Andrew H. Brown, and George "Kingfish" Stevens.

AMOS JONES

Place of Birth: Marietta, Georgia.

Occupation: Co-owner and driver for the Fresh Air Taxi Cab Company of America, Inc.

Address: An apartment at 134th Street and Lexington Avenue.
Spouse: Ruby (maiden name Ruby Taylor).
Bank: The New Amsterdam Savings Bank.
Lodge: The Mystic Knights of the Sea.

ANDREW H. BROWN

Place of Birth: Marietta, Georgia.
Occupation: Co-owner and president of the Fresh Air Taxi Cab Company of
    America, Inc.
Address: A one-room apartment on 134th Street and Lexington Avenue.
Status: Single.
Most Famous For: His romantic involvement with Madame Queen.
Favorite Activity: Sleeping.
Bank: The Lenox Avenue Savings Bank.
Weakness: Gullible; easily taken advantage of.
Lodge: The Mystic Knights of the Sea (of which he is the entertainment chairman).

GEORGE STEVENS

Place of Birth: Harlem (in New York City).
Occupation: Con artist.
Address: An apartment at 134 East 14th Street.
Spouse: Sapphire.
Mother-in-Law: Mama.
Nickname: Kingfish (he is the "Kingfish" of the lodge [the Mystic Knights of the
    Sea] in which he, Amos, and Andy are members). The lodge is located at
    127th Street and Lenox Avenue.
Favorite Pigeon (person to con): Andy.
Favorite Activity: Being lazy.

PROGRAM INFORMATION

It began in 1933, when friends Amos Jones and Andrew H. Brown chose to
leave Georgia and seek a better life in New York City. With only $340 in sav-
ings and hoping to start their own business, they met Kingfish and soon found
themselves as the owners of a decrepit taxi cab (no roof, missing one door) when
Kingfish conned Andy into buying the cab. Amos, the levelheaded, clear thinker,
made the best of the situation by repairing the cab and beginning their company.

It was also at this time that Amos met Ruby Taylor at a Sunday church
social and fell in love. They dated and married shortly after. Andy is simply not
the brightest of beings. He believes virtually everything he hears (especially from
Kingfish) no matter how absurd it may sound. He considers himself a ladies'
man and finds nothing but trouble being one. While not specifically stated,
it could be assumed that his romantic woes began when he met the fabulous,

flamboyant Madame Queen (Lillian Randolph), the woman who swept him off his feet and later sued him when he broke his promise to marry her (as marriage is not on Andy's agenda).

George's obsession with money (and not having to work to acquire it) began when he was a youngster. At a family christening, George noticed that his Uncle Clarence freely gave $500 to the child's parents after the ceremony. George saw that money was easily acquired and figured that he too could make money by being clever. George began his new life by conning fellow students at school and has carried on this tradition ever since. He is the proud owner of a worthless lot in New Jersey (which he feels is the second mistake he made, as he can't unload it. He bought it in 1932 for $1,000, "figuring to make a fortune when New Jersey spread into New York"). The first mistake he claims was marrying Sapphire (in 1931), an always nagging woman who constantly belittles George for not getting a real job. George knows he is henpecked, and his worries have also gotten worse when Sapphire's equally annoying mother, Mama, moved in with them. George "tries" to find work and please Sapphire, but "there ain't no jobs around for a man like me." George has deduced that with his savings account, checking account, and Christmas Club account, his net worth is $9. Sapphire helps support the family with a job at the Superfine Brush Company and is treasurer of the neighborhood Women's Club of Lexington. One of the few pleasures George has is lunching with Amos and Andy at the Beanery, the diner located next to the Mystic Knights lodge.

OTHER CHARACTERS
Algonquin J. Calhoun (Johnny Lee), the totally inept lawyer whom Andy hires to help him out of legal entanglements (as Algonquin once told a client who was sentenced to the electric chair, "Don't sit down"). Lightnin' (Nick O'Demus) is the slow-moving cab company janitor who doubles as the Mystic Knights' janitor. He calls Andy "Mr. Andy" and George "Mr. Kingfish." The series is based on the radio series of the same name created by Freeman Gosden and Charles Correll.

Andy's Gang
(NBC, 1955–1958)

Cast: Andy Devine (Andy).
Basis: A revised version of *Smilin' Ed's Gang* (see entry) wherein children are
  entertained with songs, stories, and adventure serials.

Movie actor Andy Devine, the genial host, first appeared to say, "Hi ya kids, it's Andy's Gang." Andy, joined by the studio audience (his gang), would then sing the theme: "I got a gang, you got a gang, everybody's gotta have a gang; but there's only one gang for me—good old Andy's Gang."

Retreating to a large easy chair onstage (in the clubhouse), Andy would begin the program with "Andy's Story Time." As Andy opened a rather large book of stories and began reading a chapter, a previously filmed sequence would be shown that most often related the adventures of "Gunga, the Elephant Boy." The tales, set in Bakore, India, related the exploits of Gunga (Nino Marcel) and his friend Rama (Vito Scotti) as they performed dangerous missions for the Maharajah (Lou Merrill, then Lou Krugman).

Additional segments included Grandie the Talking Piano (voice of June Foray) and Midnight the Cat and Squeaky the Mouse (here a cat, voiced by June Foray, and a mouse would perform a musical number). The most beloved segment, however, was Froggie the Gremlin (a rubber toy frog that caused havoc by interfering with a guest's efforts to teach the gang a fact about life).

The conclusion of the Froggie segment also meant the end of our Saturday morning at Andy's Clubhouse. Andy appeared one last time to say, "Yes sir, we're pals and pals stick together. And now don't forget church or Sunday School. And remember, Andy's Gang will get together right here at this same time next week. So long fellows and gals."

Annie Oakley
(Syndicated, 1954–1957)

Cast: Gail Davis (Annie Oakley), Brad Johnson (Lofty Craig), Jimmy Hawkins (Tagg Oakley).

Basis: A young woman of the Old West (Annie Oakley) risks her life to uphold the law in Diablo County.

Diablo County is a small but growing town in the Arizona of what appear to be the early 1900s (an exact time is not specified). When first seen, Annie Oakley is the guardian of her younger brother, Tagg, and being cared for by her uncle, Luke McTavish (Kenneth McDonald), the town sheriff (who is dropped from the series shortly after). While other girls had dreams of marrying, Annie was different and spent her spare time learning how to shoot, trick ride a horse, and follow in the footsteps of her Uncle Luke. The death of her parents in an Indian raid changed all that, as Annie soon became like a mother to Tagg, and began risking her life, as a town sheriff seemed to be out of the question. But Diablo is a town besieged by evil (mostly outlaws), and, with her skills as a cowgirl, Annie uses her abilities to help the town deputy, Lofty Craig, maintain the peace (although the concept originally established of Annie abandoning her dream had not been followed through).

Annie is not a young woman to walk away from trouble. She will do what it takes to keep her town safe but never shoots to kill; her skill with a gun has taught her that guns can be used to teach a lesson (like shooting one out of an opponent's hand) rather than taking a life. Annie appears to live in town with Tagg but also seems to own a ranch that she inherited from her parents. Target and, later, Daisy are Annie's horses; Forest is Lofty's horse; Pixie is the horse ridden by Tagg. Tagg also had a pet frog (Hector) and a rabbit (Mr. Hoppity, who lived on a game preserve Annie called "Annie's Ark").

Judy Nugent played Lofty's niece, Penny; and Nan Martin, a remarkable Gail Davis look-alike, played Annie's outlaw double, "Alias Annie Oakley." Fess Parker played Tom Conrad, editor of the town newspaper, the *Diablo Courier* (the role is later played by Stanley Andrews as Chet Osgood, editor of the *Diablo Bugle*). Other townspeople of note were Tom Jennings (played by William Fawcett), the postal clerk; Gloria Marshall (Sally Fraser), owner of the Diablo General Store; Curley Dawes (Roscoe Ates), the telegraph operator; George Lacey (Stanley Andrews), owner of the Diablo Hotel; and the Diablo County schoolteachers: Marge Hardy (Virginia Lee), Mary Farnsworth (Wendy Drew), and Deborah Scott (Nancy Hale).

In the original unaired pilot film, titled *Bulls Eye*, Billy Gray played the role of Tagg Oakley.

Bachelor Father

(CBS, ABC, 1957–1962)

Cast: John Forsythe (Bentley Gregg), Noreen Corcoran (Kelly Gregg), Sammee Tong (Peter Tong).

Basis: Bachelor attorney Bentley Gregg struggles to rearrange his swinging lifestyle when he becomes the guardian of his 13-year-old niece Kelly after her parents are killed in an automobile accident. The Greggs are cared for by Bentley's houseboy, Peter.

Address: 20006 Tower Road; later 1163 Rexford Drive in Beverly Hills.

Phone Number: Crestview 6-4599.

Family Dog: Jasper.

BENTLEY GREGG

Occupation: Private-practice corporate attorney.

Business Address: Canyon Road (later given as Office 106 in the Crescent Building on Crescent Drive in downtown Los Angeles).

Education: California State University, Harvard Law School.

Quirk: Likes to wear brown suits, especially in the courtroom (although he says he is also partial to the color blue).

Character: Suave and sophisticated ladies' man with a compulsion to date only the most beautiful girls in town. Golf and tennis are his favorite sports, and he is known for his smooth, romantic conversations with women (Kelly calls him "the greatest general in the romancing department"). Bentley claims that it was in grammar school when he realized "that girls weren't soft boys" and became "the Romeo of grade school" (he became a teenage ladies' man in high school, and by the time he reached college, he had become an expert on women). While he likes to have a beautiful woman by his side, he fears marriage ("The toughest thing about being a bachelor is remaining one").

Bentley's Secretaries: J. D. Thompson played his first secretary, Vickie, in the pilot. She was replaced first by Alice Backus (as Vickie), Shirley Mitchell and then Jane Nigh (as Kitty Devereaux), Sue Anne Langdon (as Kitty Marsh), and finally Sally Mansfield as Connie.

KELLY GREGG

Age: 13 when the series begins.

Background: The daughter of Bentley's brother and wife (names not given). This is contradicted in a later episode when Bentley states that he never had a brother (thus making Kelly his sister's child). It also contradicts the original pilot film (*New Girl in His Life*), wherein Kelly has the last name of Green (being the daughter of Bentley's sister and brother-in-law).

Education: Beverly Hills High School (cheerleader; writer of the advice column "Dear Kelly" for the school newspaper; math is her favorite subject), California State College.

After-School Hangout: Bill's Malt Shop (later the Campus Snack Bar).

Dress Size: 8.

Character: Charming and always smartly dressed (never experienced the tomboy phase). Pink is her favorite color. For one so young, she is well versed on the opposite sex (watching her Uncle Bentley "operate" has made her choosy about boys, and she is looking to date ones who have been cast in the shadow of her uncle).

Jobs: At 15, Kelly worked as a door-to-door salesgirl selling Disolv-O (a spot remover that damaged clothing) to supplement her weekly allowance of $8. She was the manager of a high school band called the Rockets and a member of the Lucky 13 Club and the Pathfinders Troop. She also worked briefly for her uncle as his secretary. In an attempt to make money, Kelly, Peter, and her friend Howard Meechim formed "Meechim, Gregg and Tong," a catering business they ran from her home (dinners were $3 a plate). With Jack Benny being her favorite comedian (she has a picture of him on her bedroom wall next to Tab Hunter), she became president of the Beverly Hills chapter of the Jack Benny Fan Club.

Hopes: Kelly had aspirations first to be a journalist and then a lawyer. She also modeled briefly for Brodney Bieber Originals when she envisioned herself becoming a model.

Love Interest: ABC episodes find Kelly falling in love with Warren Dawson (Aaron Kincaid), the young lawyer who joins Bentley's practice.

Friends: Ginger (Bernadette Withers) and Howard Meechim (Jimmy Boyd). Ginger is first introduced as Ginger Farrell (1957–1958) with Catherine McLeod playing her widowed mother, Louise. Whit Bissell and Florence MacMichael next played her parents, Bert and Amy Loomis (1958–1961), with Del Moore and Evelyn Scott as her parents, Cal and Adelaide Mitchell, in the final season. As for Howard, only his older sister, Elaine, was introduced (Joan Vohs). Both Howard and Ginger attend the same schools as Kelly, with Howard as Kelly's on-and-off-again boyfriend. Howard mentions that he grew up "with a lot of sisters" and that his father didn't pay much attention to him. He looks upon Bentley as his father—no matter how much trouble he causes him.

PETER TONG
Occupation: Houseboy. He calls Bentley "Mr. Gregg" and Kelly "Niece Kelly."
Expertise: Gourmet cook (has dinner ready each evening at 7:00).
Education: Attends night school to improve his knowledge of America. It is not clearly stated, but it appears that Peter was born in China but grew up in San Francisco's Chinatown.
Catchphrase: "Walla Ballou."
Character: Feels like part of the family and helps Bentley raise Kelly. He mutters in Chinese when he gets upset, is a member of the Purple Dragons Lodge, and is very fond of a woman named Suzie—who works at the local supermarket (which Peter frequents often to see her). Peter has a knack for falling for (and losing money in) get-rich-quick schemes. His favorite TV series is *Bart Bellamy, M.D.*, and his most treasured possessions are his recipes.
Peter's Relatives: Victor Sen Yung as Cousin Charlie, "The Beatnik of the family" (as Peter calls him). He is a schemer and supposedly owns a laundry (although he is always in need of money and finds Peter an easy mark to scam for it). Cherylene Lee as Blossom Lee, Peter's niece; Beulah Quo as Peter's Aunt Rose; Beal Wong as Peter's Grandpa Ling, a 70-year-old who knows only two words of English—"Hello, Joe" and "Nice"; and Alan Jung as Peter's Cousin Lee.

Note: The pilot film, *New Girl in His Life*, aired on G.E. Theater, and the series' original title was proposed as *Uncle Bentley*.

Beulah
(CBS, 1950–1953)

Cast: Ethel Waters, Hattie McDaniel, Louise Beavers (Beulah), William Post Jr., David Bruce (Harry Henderson), Ginger Jones, Jane Frazee (Alice Henderson), Clifford Sales, Stuffy Singer (Donny Henderson), Percy "Bud" Harris, Dooley Wilson, Ernest Whitman (Bill Jackson), Butterfly McQueen, Ruby Dandridge (Oriole).

Basis: The house at 213 Lake Street is home to Harry Henderson; his wife, Alice; their son, Donnie; and Beulah, an African American maid who, despite the problems she has, solves those of the family she considers her own.

Beulah is a member of the Ladies Auxiliary Sewing Circle and is looking for a husband ("I'm in the market for a husband," she says, "but they don't sell husbands in markets"). She is a cook, maid, laundress, and housekeeper (as she considers herself). And can she dance? "When I hear the beat right, I just take off." She calls Harry "Mr. Harry" and Alice "Miss Alice."

Harry, a lawyer with the firm of Henderson and Associates, collects stamps, enjoys playing golf on Saturday, and has a prize rosebush in the front garden. In college, Harry claims he was quite the ladies' man and was called "Hot Lips Harry." He also attempted to make extra money by raising chinchillas. Alice, who has aspirations of becoming an actress, is a member of the local bridge club and head of the local recycling program. She was popular in college and mentions that the boys referred to her as "a trim little craft" (while the term is not explained, it most likely refers to the sexy lines of a ship or car, as they are referred to as "she").

Harry and Alice met in high school, dated, and bonded at their first prom together (a reference is not made that they attended the same college). Ever since their marriage, George has longed for a portable barbecue, and Alice shops at Potter's Department Store. Alice is very proud of how she and Beulah care for the house—so much so that *Flash* magazine chose the Henderson's as "The Typical American Family."

Donnie, who enjoys hiking and catching frogs, races his soapbox racer, the "Fire Streak," down the 36th Street hill. He was born in 1942, is captain of his football team, and is a Junior Fire Fighter, and a sandwich is the only thing Beulah knows that will cure Donnie when he is sad.

Beulah's boyfriend, Bill Jackson, owns Jackson's Fix-It-Shop and eats at Slippery Joe's Diner (when he isn't mooching a meal in Beulah's kitchen). He and Beulah appear to be close, but Bill is the not marrying kind, and Beulah's endless efforts to make him see that she would make the perfect wife are also a part of the series. Seeing that Beulah is a great cook, Bill suggests that they go in business together, and they attempt to run a diner (by converting a former streetcar) and calling it "The Ding Dong Diner."

Oriole, Beulah's scatterbrained girlfriend, "knows everything about nothing," and, as Beulah says, "She is as simple as she looks" (as Oriole speaks without thinking first and when she has something to say, she is usually the only one who knows what she said). The series is also known as *The Beulah Show.*

Madge Blake appeared as Alice's mother, and Ruth Robinson played Harry's mother.

Note: Based on the 1945–1946 CBS radio series *The Marlin Hurt and Beulah Show*, wherein a white man (Marlin Hurt) played Beulah, the black maid to white businessman Marlin Hurt (Himself). The series was revised by ABC in 1947 as *Beulah* with a white man (Bob Corley) playing Beulah. When CBS picked up the series (1947–1952) as *The New Beulah Show*, Hattie McDaniel, Louise Beavers, and Amanda Randolph played the title role.

The Bickersons
(Syndicated, 1951)

Cast: Virginia Grey (Blanche Bickerson), Lew Parker (John Bickerson), Lois Austin (Clara Gollup), Sam Lee (Barney Gollup), William Pullem (Dr. Hersey).
Basis: A peek into the lives of a seemingly happily married couple (Blanche and John) who thrive on arguing.

Blanche and John Bickerson live at Apartment 22 at 123 Englewood Drive, and John says, "We should have been married by the Secretary of War, not a justice of the peace," after celebrating his eight-year wedding anniversary. Blanche is the typical housewife struggling to make ends meet on what little money John earns as a vacuum cleaner salesman for Household Appliances. John and Blanche share their humble little home with a cat (Nature Boy) and an unnamed gold fish and canary and also have one thing in common: they love to bicker about everything and anything.

John always appears to be in need of money (as he says, "I'm so broke that I pick fights with Indians [referring to a scalping] because I can't afford a haircut," "I sew sleeves on Blanche's old drawers and wear them for sweaters," and "I cut down Blanche's old girdles to make suspenders"). Blanche claims that "John doesn't act human until he has his morning coffee and is the only man in town who eats duck eggs and reindeer milk" (where Blanche acquires such "delicacies" is not revealed).

If something around the apartment breaks down and needs fixing, John refuses to replace it or send it to a repair shop—"I'd rather fix it myself than give some crook two bucks to do what I can do." To be honest, John tries, but, as Blanche says, "We have an electric orange juice squeezer that John hooked up to the vacuum cleaner to replace the burned-out motor. It now sucks up the orange juice and spits the pits in your face."

Sleeping with John is also a challenge for Blanche. John is a chronic snorer and is so loud that the neighbors often call to complain. "It's like sleeping with a one man band. . . . Now I know what it is like to sleep at Cape Canaveral," Blanche says.

John's only pride and joy appears to be the one bedroom slipper he has. Blanche and her sister, Clara, bought a raffle ticket and won a pair of slippers. They split the prize, and John wound up with the right slipper. John keeps the slipper under his pillow—"It's the only slipper I have and I have to protect it with my life."

When it comes to Blanche's cooking, John doesn't hate it, he just doesn't understand it (for example, deviled pancakes, two-foot-long rhubarb pies, powdered frog legs, and possum broth). While Blanche has an explanation for the rhubarb pies ("I couldn't find a shorter rhubarb), John can't also explain why Blanche gets "dizzy spells every five minutes that last a half hour." Since Blanche often has little spare money to spend, she borrows it from the money John saves for his life insurance policy (she tells the company to pay the premium "by deducting what they will pay her when John drops dead").

Clara, Blanche's older sister, is married to Barney and lives next door at 121 Englewood Drive. Clara, like Blanche, is struggling to make ends meet on what little money Barney wins at gambling. He hangs out at the United Nations Pool Hall and has installed a doorbell that plays the opening trumpet song that signals the start of a horse race.

Dr. Hersey is "the quack," as John calls him, who treats the various illnesses the Bickersons encounter. His greatest challenge is to solve John's chronic snoring. He has thus far prescribed two aspirins and a jigger of bourbon every night. John is six months behind on the aspirin and two years ahead on the bourbon.

Blanche and John keep what little money they have in the sugar bowl in the kitchen (which also contains what could be the very first conceived notion of a refrigerator, what was then called an icebox—a monstrosity with six doors). Murphy's Bar and Grill is John's favorite hangout. Prior to their cat Nature Boy, John and Blanche had a pet feline called Joy Boy (according to John, the cat committed suicide after he caught him in the liquor cabinet—"The cat got caught in a ball of string and hung himself").

Mentioned but not seen were Blanche's mother and Blanche's sister Hottie (who has 12 children and lives in Idaho). Lew Parker later teamed with Betty Kean and reprised *The Bickersons* via guest shots on various variety shows.

Blondie

(Syndicated, 1957)

Cast: Pamela Britton (Blondie Bumstead), Arthur Lake (Dagwood Bumstead), Stuffy Singer (Alexander Bumstead), Ann Barnes (Cookie Bumstead), Florenz Ames (J. C. Dithers), Lela Bliss, Elvia Allman (Cora Dithers), Hal Peary (Herb Woodley), Lois Collier, Hollis Irving (Harriet Woodley).

Basis: A pretty, levelheaded housewife (Blondie) struggles to contend with the problems that arise from her mishap-prone husband (Dagwood).

Blondie Davenport is a young woman (depicted in the comic strip on which the series is based, as a gold digger seeking a rich husband). Dagwood Bumstead is an apprentice architect with the J. C. Dithers Construction Company. Blondie and Dagwood are strangers who meet, coincidentally, on different blind dates set up by friends of theirs. While Dagwood was not too happy with the straight-laced girl he was set up with, he could see that Blondie did not care for the man she was with. While Dagwood is considered a bumbling fool and has difficulty making decisions, his attraction to Blondie changed him (for the instant), and he pursued the girl he fell in love with at first sight. Blondie, however, did not feel the same way, as he was not the rich man she was seeking. But Dagwood's persistence changed Blondie's way of thinking, and the two fell in love and decided to marry. They eloped to a town called Sherman Grove and were married by a justice of the peace. (Dagwood has since lost their marriage license. He accidentally grabbed the license when he went on a hunting trip and lost it—but he bagged three ducks.)

It is years later when the series begins, and Blondie and Dagwood live in a house with the street number 4224 and are the parents of Alexander, called "Baby Dumpling," and Cookie, and six dogs (Daisy, "a purebred mongrel" and her "five children"). Dagwood apparently can't help being mishap prone, and Blondie and the kids accept that—"We all adore you Dagwood, even if you are dumb at times," says Blondie. Dagwood becomes nervous over virtually everything but especially when it comes to his boss, Julius Caesar (J. C.) Dithers. When J. C. says "Emergency," Dagwood answers like a faithful Saint Bernard and drops whatever he is doing to rush to the office. While Dagwood has risen from his apprentice standing, he is now "sort of a vice president—it comes and goes." When he blunders, it goes, and he is fired, but when his blundering turns out for the best, he is back in J. C.'s good graces and has his job back. Birthday celebrations are something special in the Bumstead home. On Dagwood's special day, Blondie gets him something she needs for the house or something the kids want (over the years, Dagwood has gotten a washing machine, a dollhouse, a baseball bat and glove, and a sewing machine).

Blondie, so called because of her blonde hair (her actual first name is not mentioned), is very pretty and sensible. While background information is not mentioned for other family members in available episodes, Blondie does have a bit of history. She was born in New York City during the Great Depression. She grew up in a poor family who struggled to provide the best life they could for her under the extreme circumstances. It was most likely Blondie's hard upbringing that set her on a path to becoming a gold digger in later life.

She attended Howard High School and was a good student but never pursued a better education as times improved. She was set on marrying money and pursued that goal, only to be sidetracked by meeting and falling in love with Dagwood. She is a good mother and wife to Dagwood and never shows signs of regret for marrying him.

Dagwood and J. C. are members of the Loyal Order of the Caribou Lodge; J. C. has an antique gun collection that his wife (Cora) feels is a waste of money (he buys his guns at Miller's Sports Shop). Dagwood is famous for his yell— "Blooooondieeee"—when something goes wrong and he needs her help (as it is most often she who solves his mishap dilemmas).

The series is based on the comic strip by Chic Young, and most people readily associate Penny Singleton and Arthur Lake as the stars of the 1930s and 1940s series of motion pictures as Blondie and Dagwood. In 1952, the first attempt was made to bring the comic strip to television (although it was based more on the radio series of the same title) in an unaired pilot called *Blondie* that starred Jeff Donnell (Blondie) and Jason Harvey (Dagwood). Two years later, another pilot called *Blondie* was produced that starred Pamela Britton (Blondie), Hal LeRoy (Dagwood), Stuffy Singer (Alexander), Mimi Gibson (Cookie), Robert Burton (J. C. Dithers), Isabel Withers (Cora Dithers), Robin Raymond (Tootsie Woodley, Blondie's neighbor), and Lucien Littlefield (Mr. Beasley, the mailman). Herb Woodley, Tootsie's husband, was mentioned but not seen.

The second and last series appeared in color on CBS in 1968 with Patricia Harty (Blondie), Will Hutchins (Dagwood), Pamelyn Ferdin (Cookie), Peter Robbins (Alexander), Jim Backus (J. C. Dithers), Henny Backus (Cora Dithers), Bobbi Jordan (Tootsie Woodley), and Bryan O'Byrne (Mr. Beasley).

THE BOB CUMMINGS SHOW. SEE *Love That Bob*

Bonanza
(NBC, 1959–1973)

Cast: Lorne Greene (Ben Cartwright), Pernell Roberts (Adam Cartwright), Dan Blocker (Hoss Cartwright), Michael Landon (Little Joe Cartwright).

Basis: A father (Ben Cartwright) and his three sons (Adam, Hoss, and Little Joe) battle to operate and protect their ranch, the Ponderosa, during the 1880s.

BENJAMIN "BEN" CARTWRIGHT
Date of Birth: 1825.
Place of Birth: Jonns Common, Massachusetts.

Typical Dress: A taupe shirt with a brown leather vest and gray pants. He also wore a cream-colored hat and an occasional green scarf.

Original Career: Sailor (third officer on the *Wanderer*, a ship captained by Morgan Stoddard, the father of the woman he loved, Elizabeth Eloise Stoddard). After several years at sea (beginning when he was age 20), Ben quit to open a chandler's shop in Boston. At one point, Ben was a major with the 116th Militia, but it is difficult to place because there are no flashback sequences regarding it.

Later Career: Owner of the Ponderosa, a 1,000-square-mile timberland ranch in the Comstock Lode Country in the Nevada Territory near Virginia City. The ranch is named after the large Ponderosa pine trees native to the land. Ben is also the owner of a riverboat (the *Dixie*, which operates on nearby Lake Tahoe) and has invested in a railroad (the High Sierra Shortline). He was also on the Board of Directors of the Golden State Marine Bank and Trust Company and was head of the Virginia City School Board. The Sierra Freight and Stage Lines deliver mail and freight to Virginia City. The Overland Stage provides passenger service from town to town; the *Enterprise* is the town newspaper. The Cartwright's frequent the Silver Dollar Saloon in Virginia City.

First Wife: Elizabeth Stoddard (Geraldine Brooks), the daughter of sea captain Morgan Stoddard. Ben married Elizabeth in 1841, but a year later, after giving birth to Adam, Elizabeth died due to complications from the birth.

Second Wife: Inger Borgstrom (Inga Swenson). It is 1847, and Ben had given up his chandler business to journey west to begin a new life in California. In St. Joseph, Missouri, Ben befriends Inger, the owner of the general store. They become close when Inger saves the life of five-year-old Adam, who had developed a high fever. Ben and Inger marry a year later, and Inger, believing in Ben's dream that a better life lies ahead in California, encourages him to continue to follow it. With other pioneers believing as Ben does, Ben becomes the wagon master and takes on the responsibility of bringing settlers to a new land. During the hazardous trek through Nevada, Inger gives birth to a son they name Eric Hoss. Shortly after, during an Indian attack, Inger is killed. Ben abandons his dream forever and settles in Virginia City, Nevada.

Third Wife: Marie DeMarne (Felicia Farr). After having established the Ponderosa, a ranch hand is killed while attempting to save Ben's life. Ben, feeling obligated to tell his widow, Marie, what has happened, journeys to New Orleans. Ben's stay is longer than expected, and a love soon develops between him and Marie. They marry in 1856 and return to the Ponderosa ranch. Marie becomes a vital part of Ben's life, helping design the house in which they live but also presenting him with his third son, Little Joe

Clockwise from upper left: Michael Landon, Pernell Roberts, Lorne Greene, and Dan Blocker. *NBC/Photofest © NBC*

(in 1857). But, like his prior wives, tragedy strikes when Marie is thrown from her horse and killed. A story-line contradiction arises in a later episode when Joe claims that his mother was named Felicia and that she and Ben met on a business trip.

Hobby: Collecting firearms.

Horse: Buck.

Character: Ben has a strong sense of justice and is well respected throughout the territory. He believes everyone should be paid a fair wage and treats his ranch hands well, offering them $30 a month plus a bunk and meals. He passed away in 1903.

Relatives: Guy Madison as Ben's nephew, Will Cartwright; Bruce Yarnell as Ben's Cousin, Muley Jones; and Mitch Vogel as Ben's adopted son, Jamie.

ADAM CARTWRIGHT

Mother: Elizabeth Stoddard (Ben's first wife).

Date of Birth: 1842.

Place of Birth: Boston, Massachusetts.

Middle Name: Milton (reflects Ben's favorite writer, John Milton).

Typical Dress: A black shirt, pants, and hat and occasionally a yellow trail coat.

Abilities: Fast on the draw; good business sense; considered by Ben as having
    good "horse sense, (ability to select the right horses), better than anyone
    else in the territory."

Horse: Sport.

Relaxation: Enjoys reading, singing, dancing, and playing the guitar.

Romantic Interests: Ruth and Laura. Ruth left Adam to help an Indian tribe save
    their people. Laura Dayton was a widow with a young girl who, although
    in love with Adam, became attracted to Adam's cousin Will and ran off
    with him.

Character: Adam is well educated and the most sensitive of the three Cartwright
    brothers. He had architectural knowledge and was said to have built the
    house in which he and his family lived (contradicting what was said about
    Ben's third wife, Marie, who was said to have designed the house). In 1965,
    Pernell Roberts chose to leave the series to better establish himself as an ac-
    tor onstage and in films. As Adam grew older, he became disillusioned with
    the West and left the Ponderosa to further his education (in New York and
    then abroad). It was in England while studying architecture that he married
    and had a son (Adam Cartwright Jr.). It was also said that Adam left to go
    to sea (somewhat following in his father's footsteps).

HOSS CARTWRIGHT

Real Name: Eric Cartwright (nicknamed Hoss by his Swedish mother, Inger.
    Although Inger lived only long enough to see Hoss as in infant, she knew he
    would become a big, friendly man, and Hoss reflects that image).

Date of Birth: 1848.

Place of Birth: Nevada.

Mother: Inger Borgstrom.

Height: 6 feet, 4 inches tall.

Weight: 270 pounds.

Catchphrase: "Dabdunit" (which he says when he gets upset or angry).

Typical Dress: A white shirt, brown pants, and brown suede vest with his trade-
    mark white 10-gallon hat.

Temporary Jobs: Sheriff of Virginia City, Nevada, and Trouble, California.

Favorite Activity: Eating (he felt he would perish without meals prepared by the
    ranch cook, Hop Sing [Victor Sen Yung]). He did, however, dislike cheese.

Horse: Chub.

Character: Hoss was a big man with a powerful punch and a big, friendly smile. He was feared for his strength but had a heart of gold and often gave of himself to help others. He had a habit of bringing home hopeless cases and trying to reform them. Spring was a bad time for Hoss, as he would come down with severe case of what Ben called "Spring Fever Clumsiness" (which Ben "cured" with a mixture of molasses and sulfur). Because of his size, Hoss handled all the heavy chores around the ranch. Hoss was also sensitive and shy around women. He lost his life in 1881 while attempting to save a woman from drowning.

LITTLE JOE CARTWRIGHT

Full Name: Joseph "Joe" Francis Cartwright, and the youngest of Ben's sons.
Date of Birth: 1857.
Place of Birth: Nevada.
Nickname: Little Joe. Early in the series, Joe claims he was called "Little Joe because Hoss is so big." Later, he says, "that's what I get for being the youngest member of the family."
Mother: Marie DeMarne.
Height: 5 feet, 4¾ inches.
Typical Dress: A gray shirt with tan pants and hat and a green corduroy jacket.
Horse: Cochise.
Romantic Interest: Alice (played by Bonnie Bedelia). Little Joe and Alice married, but Alice later died in a fire.
Character: Little Joe has jet-black hair and was as handsome as his older brother Adam. He was the only left-handed Cartwright and also had an eye for the ladies but was short-tempered and too fast to use his fists (which often got him into trouble). He was fond of horses, enjoyed playing practical jokes, and often attempted to make money through harebrained schemes. He had a half brother on his mother's side named Clay Stoddard. In the 1988 TV movie *Bonanza: The Next Generation*, it is learned that Little Joe married a woman named Annabelle and that they had a son named Benjamin "Benji" Cartwright. During the Spanish-American War, Little Joe became a member of Teddy Roosevelt's Rough Riders. He was listed as missing in action in 1899 and was presumed killed.

Note: The four regulars were each considered a star, and to reflect this, their credits were rotated each week in the opening theme to allow for equal billing. Although *Bonanza* is thought to be the first western series to be broadcast in color, the assumption is wrong, as *The Cisco Kid* (1951) and *Judge Roy Bean* (1955) preceded it. An attempt was made to revive the series in a syndicated television movie pilot, *Bonanza: The Next Generation* (March 16, 1988). John Ireland is Aaron Cartwright, the late Ben's brother and the new head of the Ponderosa ranch; Barbara Anderson is Annabelle Cartwright, the wife of the late Little Joe; Michael Landon Jr. is Benji Cartwright, Little Joe's son; and Brian A. Smith is Josh Cartwright, the late Hoss's illegitimate son.

Boston Blackie
(Syndicated, 1951–1953)

Cast: Kent Taylor (Boston Blackie), Lois Collier (Mary Wesley), Frank Orth (Inspector Faraday).

Basis: A former safecracker (Boston Blackie) turned private detective uses his knowledge of the underworld to apprehend criminals.

BOSTON BLACKIE

Expertise: Opening safes, picking locks, picking pockets, relieving people of money or jewelry.

Address: The Brownstone Apartments at 1103 Hampton Drive in Los Angeles.

Favorite Eatery: Andy's Luncheonette (also called Andy's Lunch Room).

Pet Dog: Whitey (has the ability to sense danger and come to Blackie's aid; he also barks when he hears the word "bone" mentioned).

Character: Described as "friend to those who need a friend, enemy to those who make him an enemy." Although he claims to be reformed, Blackie follows no set of rules and often resorts to his old ways to accomplish a goal. His attire makes him appear like a hood of the era, he has little respect for anyone (except his girlfriend), and he is quick to use his fists or gun if the situation warrants. He is also a ladies' man, although he has curtailed this aspect of his life since meeting Mary (after a beating that sent him to the hospital).

MARY WESLEY

Occupation: Nurse at Wilshire Memorial Hospital in Los Angeles.

Address: 712 Walden Avenue.

Character: A gorgeous young woman who truly loves Blackie but constantly worries about him "because he won't." Mary is very independent and rather gutsy for a woman at this time on TV. While she appears very feminine, she can handle herself in a rough situation (mostly when assisting Blackie), and it is not unusual to see her getting punched, bruised, or knocked out. Blackie is very protective of Mary and becomes very jealous if anyone "makes goo goo eyes" at her. "Before you get any ideas," he would tell an admirer, "Miss Wesley is my girl. Got it!" At times, Mary is not too sure, as she worries about his roving eye for beautiful women (he tells her, "If I didn't have a roving eye for beauty, I couldn't appreciate you").

INSPECTOR FARADAY

Position: Homicide Inspector with the Los Angeles Police Department

Character: Not the brightest of inspectors but one who is dedicated to his job. Blackie and police officers are not exactly on the best of terms, but somehow Blackie trusts him, as he can always manipulate him into thinking just the opposite when he resorts to his former trade. While Blackie could be arrested for what he does (never follows the book), he leads Faraday to believe he is helping him rather than the actual truth—he is helping Faraday.

Bourbon Street Beat
(ABC, 1959–1960)

Cast: Richard Long (Rex Randolph), Andrew Duggan (Cal Calhoun), Van Williams (Kenny Madison), Arlene Howell (Melody Lee Mercer), Nita Talbot (Lusti Weather).

Basis: Case investigations of Rex Randolph and Cal Calhoun, the owners of the New Orleans–based Randolph and Calhoun—Special Services, a private detective agency.

Agency Address: Next to the old Absinthe House, a nightclub on Bourbon Street in the French Quarter of New Orleans.

Telephone Number: Express 7123.

REX RANDOLPH

Character: An Ivy League man and native to New Orleans, Rex, the son of wealthy business executive parents, was born in New Orleans in December 1927. He loves to cook, and since Rex's hobby was a part of the show, a book called *Recipes from Bourbon Street Beat* was released in 1959. Rex will not give up on a case until he uncovers the who, where, and how of a crime. Rex originally ran a company called Randolph and Jelkins—Special Services. When his original partner, Sam Jelkins, disappears while investigating a case in a town called Pelican Point, Rex begins an inquiry. He befriends Police Lieutenant Calhoun ("people call me Cal"), and together they solve the mystery, and Cal decides to relocate to join Rex. "I kissed Pelican Point good-bye," and the company sign is changed to Randolph and Calhoun.

CAL CALHOUN

Character: Cal (no other first name given) was born in 1923 and raised in the bayou country where his parents worked as sharecroppers. Cal wanted a life of excitement and joined the police force after graduating from college. He is knowledgeable in many areas but is rather untidy compared to Rex's neat and orderly ways. Cal believes that clutter is an asset, as it gives him an edge when it comes to investigating a case (as criminals are often untidy and leave clues behind).

KENNETH "KENNY" MADISON

Character: The firm's part-time investigator. He is from an oil-rich Texas family and is attending Tulane University, where he is studying to become a lawyer. While he doesn't need the money, he works for Rex for the experience he hopes to acquire in apprehending lawbreakers.

MELODY LEE MERCER

Character: The firm's attractive receptionist, secretary, and file clerk. She was born in Shreveport, Louisiana, and was Miss U.S.A. in the 1958 Miss Universe Pageant. Melody Lee was previously the runner-up as Miss Sazu City in the Miss Mississippi Pageant. She claims she lost "because the judges were northerners." When Melody Lee took the job, "I knew there would be gunplay and such," and she "puts up with Rex and Cal and all the violence." She hopes to one day become a detective and is thrilled when she is asked to do investigative work on a case. She likes to be called Melody Lee and not Melody ("I don't like it when people leave off part of my name").

LUSTI WEATHER

Character: A beautiful singer and dancer at the Racquet Club in the French Quarter. She also plays the bongo drums and says, "The bongos keep my torso from becoming more so" (as she likes to wear revealing outfits). She often exposes too much skin and is not only suspended but also "busted by the police," says Cal. Rex calls her Lusti Love, and she has such colorful, unseen friends as Sunset Strip and Midnight Frenzy. Lusti also has a language all her own (for example, "magnesia" is amnesia, and "hot shot on the rock" is a martini). Lusti also yearns to be a detective and enjoys helping Rex and Cal. It is at this time that Melody Lee becomes extremely jealous— "I'll show that female Sherlock Holmes who does the detective work around here," says Melody Lee, who often plunges unthinkingly into a case, only to be rescued by Lusti in the end.

OTHER CHARACTERS

The Baron (Eddie Cole), the leader of the jazz group that plays nightly at the Absinthe House (in the pilot episode, they are seen playing and singing the show's theme song), and Beauregard O'Hanlon (Kelton Garwood), the painter who runs an art objects business next to the Absinthe House called Beauregard O'Hanlon's World Renowned Treasure Chest.

Bronco
(ABC, 1958–1960)

Cast: Ty Hardin (Bronco Layne).

Basis: A spin-off of *Cheyenne*. Bronco Layne is an ex–Confederate army captain who wanders from town to town fighting injustice in the post–Civil War West.

Bronco was born in Texas ("down around the Old Panhandle," and "there ain't a horse that he can't handle; that's how he got his name"). His father and grandfather were "rebels," and Bronco continued in that tradition by serving with the Texas Confederates. His gun, a Colt .45, has an inscription that reads "Courage Is the Freedom of Honor," and his pocket watch plays the song "Deep in the Heart of Dixie." Inside the watch, there is a picture of Redemption McNally (played by Kathleen Crowley), the one and only girl Bronco ever loved (they grew up in Texas together). Bronco also has a pet cat, Elmira (who hates chili), that he found abandoned during the Civil War battle of Elmira.

After serving the Confederacy, Bronco returned to his hometown to become business partners with his friend Enrique "Rickie" Cortez (played by Gerald Mohr) in the Layne and Cortez General Store. Since he was a child, Bronco disliked staying in one place for too long and developed a taste for the wanderlust. When the business began to bore him, Bronco left town "to go where the grass may be greener." He departs without Elmira (whom he gives to Enrique) and without his gold pocket watch (which he gave to the chief of an Indian war party to save his and Enrique's lives when they crossed Indian territory).

Undercover agent, frontier scout, post office undercover agent, miner, wagon train captain, deputy, and army scout were some of the jobs held by Bronco as he traveled across the West. Although he preferred to avoid trouble, Bronco refused to stand by and see others abused. He was fast with a gun and tough with his fists (as the theme says, "You've never seen a twister, mister, till someone gets him riled").

In the window of the Layne and Cortez Store, there is one very special item: Bronco's gold watch (which Enrique acquired from a drifter who bought it from that Indian chief). There is also a sign next to the watch: "Will Owner Please Claim." Bronco never did.

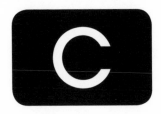

Captain Midnight
(CBS, 1954–1956)

Cast: Richard Webb (Captain Midnight), Sid Melton (Ichabod "Icky" Mudd),
Olan Soule (Aristotle "Tut" Jones).

Basis: A man of mystery, known only as Captain Midnight, battles evil as head
of the Secret Squadron, an organization that is ready at a moment's notice
to go anywhere to help people in trouble.

CAPTAIN MIDNIGHT

Real Name: Jim Albright.

Headquarters: A secret mountain retreat.

Plane: The *Silver Dart.*

Character: Virtually no information is stated other than how Captain Jim Albright acquired the name of Captain Midnight. At the height of World
War II, the Allies were in terrible danger of being defeated by the enemy.
In an Allied bomb shelter in France, a man (Jim), whose name the general in charge does not want to know, enters the shelter. The man is told,
"Only two people in the world know the mission to which you have been
assigned—myself and the president of the United States. The odds are 100
to 1 against you. If you fail tonight, it will be the end for all of us. If you
succeed tonight, you will have started a long and dangerous task that may
require a lifetime to complete [protect the world from evil]." The Captain's
assignment is to exterminate Ivan Shark, the most dangerous criminal in
the world (a traitor who has cost the lives of many Allies). As the Captain is
about to leave, the general tells him, "Henceforth, until you complete your
task, you will not be known by your true name. What name you will be
known by rests in the hands of fate." "Sir," the Captain says, "If I have not
returned by twelve o'clock, you will know I have failed."

The hours that follow are a desperate wait for the General and his associate. The clock is nearing midnight, and there is no sign of the Captain. The General believes he has failed until, at 15 seconds before midnight, the faint sounds of a plane are heard. "Listen to that," the General tells his aide. "We're saved, and it's just twelve o'clock. To me he will always be known as Captain Midnight."

As the General mentioned, it may require a lifetime for the Captain to complete his mission, and following the war, Captain Midnight retreated to a secret mountain location and formed the Secret Squadron to help him in his quest to safeguard the world. Members of the Secret Squadron (identified by the initials SQ and a number, for example, SQ 7) are people dedicated to the cause of freedom and democracy.

While Captain Midnight oversees the Secret Squadron, he also actively participates in missions with the help of his close friends, Icky and Tut (there is no information as to how they know the Captain or became a part of the squadron). Icky is the Captain's mechanical genius and Tut his scientific adviser. Icky is a bit superstitious and carries a rabbit's foot for luck ("I'm packin' a little insurance"), and after he is introduced to someone by the Captain, he says, "That's Mudd with two d's."

PROGRAM INFORMATION

Secret Squadron members contact the Captain by sending a telegram (which is received by the Captain at headquarters by a special receiving unit). "Squadron members never send unimportant messages," says the Captain. Each squadron member also possesses a microfilm of pertinent information that enables the captain to determine who is right for a specific assignment. Viewers could become members of the Secret Squadron by mailing in coupons found under the lids of the show's sponsor, Ovaltine (chocolate milk–flavored crystals). Those who responded would receive a decal and patch identifying them as SQ members plus a special pin for decoding the secret message given at the end of each episode. Secret Squadron uniforms are simple (military gray) outfits with the insignia of the *Silver Dart* on shirt pockets and helmets. The program is based on the radio series of the same title but ran on television for only 39 episodes when Ovaltine, the owner, canceled the popular show due to a lack of sales (apparently, kids were removing coupons from the jars but not buying the product). Because Ovaltine reserved the right to the character name, the program was syndicated as *Jet Jackson, the Flying Commando* (with voice-over dubbing used to delete Captain Midnight for Jet Jackson).

Captain Video and His Video Rangers
(DuMont, 1949–1955)

Cast: Richard Coogan, Al Hodge (Captain Video), Don Hastings (The Video Ranger).

Basis: In a futuristic time, a mysterious man, known only as Captain Video, retreats to a secret mountain headquarters on the planet Earth and establishes The Video Rangers, an organization of young people dedicated to his cause of battling evil wherever it exists and becomes a threat to the lives of innocent people.

CAPTAIN VIDEO

Character: Called "The Master of Space" and "Hero of Science," Captain Video is said to be operating in the 22nd century (years range from 2149 to 2155). While information is quite scarce (fewer than 40 episodes are known to exist), it is learned that the Captain chooses only the best candidates from his Video Ranger training academy to become actual Video Rangers. Captain Video first pilots a rocket ship called the *X-9*, then the *Galaxy*, and finally the *Galaxy II*. He is attired in a military uniform (with a lightning bolt across the chest) and always appears stern and all-military. The Video Ranger, just as stern, had his first assignment aboard a ship called the *Cormorant*. He used the catchphrase "jumpin' jets." While Captain Video does operate from his "Secret Mountain Retreat," there is a governing force on Earth at the time (the Federation) which is based on the 144th floor of the Public Safety Building in Planet City. It appears that Captain Video takes orders first from Commissioner Bell (Jack Orsen), then his replacement, Commissioner Carey (Ben Lackland), members of the governing Space Council.

Whether communicating with the Space Council or with the Video Ranger, Captain Video uses the code 398. While Captain Video is a daring crusader, he has also applied his scientific abilities to create such devices as the Atomic Collector Screen (prevents dangerous atomic particles from striking the Earth from outer space), the Atomic Rifle (emits a powerful blast of energy that is capable of destroying stone), and the Cathode Gun (incorporates highly complex technology to emit a paralyzing ray). The Cosmic Vibrator enables sound waves to disrupt the path of approaching comets (or other space debris), the Optical Astro Viewer allows viewing the deep regions of space from rocket ships, and the Pocket Radio is a pre–transistor radio type of device that allows remote audio communication.

Villains captured by Captain Video (or other law enforcers) are sentenced to penal colonies established on the moon. Interplanetary travel (by Copter Cabs) has been accomplished, especially between Earth, Mars, Venus, Torion, Nemos, Cosmos, and Layra. Planets such as Saturn, Uranus, and Pluto have unsuitable atmospheres and have yet to be colonized. The Captain mentions that the first attempt to land on Jupiter occurred in 1990 and that in the early 21st century, an intergalactic sporting event called the Rocket Meet was introduced as an Olympic Games event.

Life for Captain Video is not devoted solely to his scientific discoveries. He has vowed not to rest until he captures Dr. Pauli (Bram Nossen, Hal Conklin, Stephen Elliott), an evil being who rules from his man-made metallic planet he calls Dr. Pauli (from which he plans to rule the universe). (Dr. Pauli later rules from Planet 1-X-7, the home of Queen Karola [Natalie Core]). Like Captain Video, Dr. Pauli is a scientific genius but uses his abilities for his own diabolical means. He has invented the Cloak of Invisibility (which enables him to remain unseen when wearing it) and has established the Asteroidal Society, a group of super villains who do Dr. Pauli's bidding. In a twist of events, one of Dr. Pauli's creations, the evil robot Tobor (Dave Ballard) becomes a force for good when Captain Video captures it and re-programs it for good.

PROGRAM INFORMATION

The program premiered on DuMont's local New York station, WABD, Channel 5, on June 27, 1949, under the title *Captain Video* with the captain (Richard Coogan) serving as the host of a program of 1930s theatrical western films that were shown in segments each week (Monday through Friday). As the DuMont network began to grow, the *Captain Video* format was revised to make the Captain a crime fighter known as "The Guardian of the Safety of the World" and given an assistant, the Video Ranger (Don Hastings). It is difficult to determine when the words "And His Video Rangers" were added to the title, as the prenational (1953) *TV Guide*, *TV Forecast*, lists the program only as *Captain Video*, and it most likely occurred in the fall of 1949, when the new TV season began. In 1951, Al Hodge took over the role of the Captain. In 1953 (to 1955), DuMont added a Saturday morning version of the daily program titled *The Secret Files of Captain Video*, wherein stories were complete in themselves as opposed to the serial-like daily episodes. The daily series ended on March 28, 1955, but continued locally in New York as *Captain Video*, wherein the Captain (Al Hodge) played host to theatrical cartoons. On September 25, 1955 (to August 16, 1957), Captain Video became a segment of the DuMont network's *Wonder Time* program, which ran from noon to 6:00 p.m. Sandy Becker served as the host with Al Hodge as Captain Video, showcasing cartoons and theatrical documentaries.

Early episodes that were broadcast live had the Captain situated in a futuristic-like room where he oversaw the activities of the Video Rangers (the characters seen in the theatrical films that were showcased). The Captain brought viewers their activities via the Remote Carrier Delayed Circuit TV (his code to them was KRG-L6). While the program did have an occasional, local New York sponsor, most pre-network episodes were platforms for public service announcements geared to children (the Captain would introduce them as a "Video Ranger Message"). Fred Scott, who later played Video Ranger Rogers, announced and narrated.

Captain Z-Ro
(Syndicated, 1952–1955)

Cast: Roy Steffins (Captain Z-Ro), Bobby Trumbull, Jeff Silvers, Bruce Haynes (Jet), H. M. Chamberlain (Micro).
Basis: A mysterious man, known only as Captain Z-Ro, travels through time and space to keep history on track.

Captain Z-Ro is a scientific genius who has invented a time machine that enables him and his assistant, Jet (a young boy), to view the past via the machine's telescreens. The Captain's presence is known to only a very few people, and his laboratory is located in a mountainous, remote section of the planet. When a decision is made to view the past (usually the Captain's way to prove to Jet that something he read about in a history book actually happened), the following procedure occurs: (1) The chosen era is divided into longitude and latitude and programmed into the time machine's computer. (2) The voltage is set (for example, at 8.4). (3) The Electro Generator is set (for example, at 8.993). (4) The Isotron Output is programmed (for example, at 4.712). (5) The Trillatron is set (for example, at 12.1195). (6) The Lectric Chamber is readied. (7) Jet hands the Captain the Cycle Reactor, "which cracks the fourth dimension and ejects us back into time." (8) With the Lectric Chamber now active, beeps are heard, and the computer searches all the coordinates that have been programmed into it. When the search has been completed, a special television screen allows the Captain and Jet to see an event from the past.

The Captain also has the ability to change the past. If, while viewing a past event, the Captain sees that someone that is meant to set history is in danger, he can go back to that exact moment and change what is about to happen to set history on the path to which it has been recorded. To do so, the Captain enters the Lectric Chamber while Jet sets the Specter Wave Length. Within seconds, the Captain begins to dematerialize and disappears from view. Symmetrical impulses are then transmitted over time, and the Captain reappears in the programmed era. To assist, the Captain uses his Pararay Gun (which paralyzes its subject for 60 seconds) and gives him the needed time to make the necessary changes so that history will not be altered. When he has accomplished his mission, the Captain says, "All right Jet, take me back." Jet then reverses the Symmetrical Impulses, and the Captain returns to the present.

The Captain, a research explorer in space and time, has a rocket ship called the *ZX 99*. The Video Plate aboard the ship is a round picture-like TV tube that allows the Captain to view outer space. The Gravity Generator regulates the gravity inside the ship (on their first flight, the Captain, Jet, and their assistant, Micro, were floating halfway to the ceiling before they realized they needed to activate it). The *ZX 99* travels at the rate of five miles per second, and when one of the team is about to embark on a mission, the Captain says, "Spaceman's luck." A "Z" is worn slightly off center on the Captain's uniform and on his helmet. A "Z" in a circle is worn on each sleeve cuff. In some episodes, a robot named Roger assists the Captain and Jet.

"Be sure to be standing by when we again transmit you to this remote location on the planet Earth when Captain Z-Ro and his associates will conduct another experiment in time and space" (the program's closing).

The Cases of Eddie Drake
(DuMont, 1952)

Cast: Don Haggerty (Eddie Drake), Patricia Morison, Lynn Roberts (Dr. Karen Gayle), Theodore Von Eltz (Lieutenant Walsh).

Basis: The investigations of Eddie Drake, a detective with a remarkable affinity for crime and violence.

EDWARD "EDDIE" DRAKE

Occupation: Private detective and owner of the Drake Detective Agency in New York City.

Address (Business): 130 West 45th Street in Manhattan.

Address (Home): An apartment on West 67th Street.

Telephone Number (Business): 346-1621.

Car License Plate: 3C-26-53.

Character: Honest, personable, and quite intelligent. He had studied to become a lawyer but rejected that after a short period as a prosecutor. (He found that the wheels of justice often favor the criminal and that the innocent are the ones that suffer and felt he could accomplish more in the investigative aspect, where he could go by his own rules and not get disbarred while doing it.) While Eddie relies on walk-ins as clients, he does get referrals from an agency called Jenny's Bail Bonds (the cases that start off simple enough but eventually turn violent and deadly). Eddie is quick with his fists and will not hesitate to use a gun if the situation warrants.

DR. KAREN GAYLE

Occupation: Private-practice psychiatrist.
Education: Princeton University.
Address (Office): 64 Park Avenue.
Address (Home): 11 Paulding Drive.
Telephone Number (Office): 346-7112.
Character: A beautiful woman with an uncanny interest in crime and criminal activity. She considers herself "a student of all the abnormal behavior of the human mind." She is anxious to write a book on criminal behavior and has approached Eddie as a different type of client—one who assists him so she can get firsthand knowledge—"I want to know all about criminals. What they do, how they act, and why they do the things they do." She now considers Eddie her personal library, although she also finds herself actively involved in solving crimes. She does, however, object to one thing—the violence—and wishes Eddie "could guarantee me a minimum of shooting." She and Eddie are also friendly with Homicide Bureau detective lieutenant Walsh, and each helps the other (with Karen also acquiring the police thinking that comes along with each case).

Cheyenne
(ABC, 1955–1963)

Cast: Clint Walker (Cheyenne Bodie).
Basis: A young man's journey across the American frontier of the 1860s as he seeks a place to settle down and call home.

CHEYENNE BODIE

Horse: Brandy.
Ability: Fast on the draw; won't back down from a fight.
Game of Chance: Poker.
Trait: Strong, quiet man who will stand up for anyone who cannot stand up for himself.
Heritage: Learned in the ways of both the white man and the Indian.
History: A wagon train, traveling through Wyoming Territory on the third day of the ninth month of the Indian calendar (September 12; this calendar has

13 moons each year with 28 days in each month), is attacked by Cheyenne Indians. Chief White Cloud (Richard Hale) spares the life of an infant boy and raises him as his son. The boy, whom White Cloud claimed "was so quiet and solemn that he must have the brain of a wise grey fox," was given the name Grey Fox. On the day of his 12th birthday, Grey Fox chose to go the way of the white man and took the name Cheyenne Bodie. He left his tribal home ("south where the river winds at the foot of the hills") and set out on his own. No further information is given regarding Cheyenne's past, although another episode claims Cheyenne was taken captive by the Indians when he was 10 years old and at the age of 18 "walked away [from the Cheyenne tribe] with their blessings."

Mission: Looking for a place to settle down; dedicated to helping the army build up the land and establish a peace treaty with his blood brothers (Cheyenne can read smoke signals and is trusted by Indian chiefs).

Weapons: A hunting knife is on the left side of his holster; a gun is on the right side.

Dream: To find a place to settle down and call home (he is hoping to buy a ranch and raise horses).

Jobs: Cheyenne held many jobs, including ranch hand, cavalry scout, army undercover agent, deputy, trail boss, and wagon train guide.

Commando Cody, Sky Marshal of the Universe
(NBC, 1955)

Cast: Judd Holdren (Commando Cody), Aline Towne (Joan Albright), William Schallert (Ted Richards), Richard Crane (Dick Preston).

Basis: A government agent, known to the public as only Commando Cody, battles evil wherever it exists.

At the government's insistence, Commando Cody must wear a black mask (like the Lone Ranger) at all times to protect his true identity (while his actual name is not revealed, he is apparently an ingenious inventor, as he has created the Rocket Flying Suit, which enables him to fly through space). Cody does carry a gun and is called "The Sky Marshal of the Universe." He operates from secret headquarters in an apparent Old West town called Graphite. The organization for which Cody works is not revealed. It is headed by a Mr. Henderson (Craig Kelly), and Cody works with fellow agents Joan Albright and Ted Richards (Ted is later replaced by Dick Preston). Cody, Joan, and Ted communicate with each other through their identification patches (which contain miniature two-way radios and operate on a frequency assigned only to Commando Cody). The Rocket

Flying Suit, which Cody wears over his gray suit, incorporates a silver helmet and a backpack that contains two rockets for power. The front panel of the suit has controls for On/Off, Up/Down, and Slow/Fast. Like Superman, Cody needs to take a running start and then jump before he is able to soar. When longer flights need to be taken, Cody incorporates a spaceship (not named) that is equipped with a ray gun that can fire bullets or a heat-seeking ray that can target the enemy when they are out of normal firing range. Other than their ability as scientists, nothing is revealed regarding Joan and Ted. (They were originally teamed with Cody to help him adapt atomic power for rocket ship propulsion. Cody took the concept one step further and developed a situation where he could compress the power of atomic energy and control its abilities via the Rocket Flying Suit.) Commando Cody was not a superhero. He was depicted as having no special powers, and the only weapon he carried was an ordinary gun.

PROGRAM INFORMATION

Episodes (12 were produced) run like a theatrical serial of the 1940s, and very little is done to explain what happens. As the story opens, it is revealed that Commando Cody has perfected the Cosmic Dust Blanket to protect the Earth from the evil ruler Retik (Gregory Gray), an extraterrestrial who plans to conquer the universe. He needs to first conquer the Earth and use it as his staging platform to conquer other planets. Dr. Varney (Peter Brocco) first assisted Retik; he was replaced in episode 4 by Baylor (Lyle Talbot). How Retik arrived on Earth or how he acquired Earthlings as accomplices is not shown. Cody's battle against Retik and his deadly inventions (Hydrogen Hurricanes, the Magno Force Ray, Radioactive Gas, the Magnetic Drag Ray, and the Refraction Field Force) forms the basis of the only story line presented.

The program is based on three Republic theatrical serials: *King of the Rocket Men* (1949), *Radar Men from the Moon* (1952), and *Zombies of the Stratosphere* (1952). Tris Coffin played Jeff King, the director of security for Science Associates and creator of the Rocket Flying Suit, who was known as the mysterious Rocket Man. By the second serial, Commando Cody (George Wallace) replaced the Rocket Man character. The final serial continued the Commando Cody character with Judd Holdren playing him as Larry Martin. Aline Towne as Joan Albright was introduced as his assistant (both of whom appeared in the TV version).

THE DANNY THOMAS SHOW. SEE *Make Room for Daddy*

A Date with Judy
(ABC, 1951–1953)

Cast: Patricia Crowley, Mary Linn Beller (Judy Foster), Frank Albertson, Judson
 Rees, John Gibson (Melvyn Foster), Anna Lee, Flora Campbell (Dora Fos-
 ter), Gene O'Donnell, Peter Avramo (Randolph Foster), Jimmy Sommers
 (Oogie Pringle).
Basis: Events in the life of a bubbly teenage girl named Judy Foster.

JUDY FOSTER
Parents: Melvin and Dora Foster.
Brother: Randolph Foster.
Boyfriend: Oogie Pringle.
Address: 123 State Street.
Age: 16.
Height: 5 feet, 5 inches.
Weight: 106 pounds.
Dress Size: 3.
Measurements: 34-26-32.
Education: City High School (currently a sophomore).
Catchphrase: "Oh butterflies" or "Oh caterpillars" (which she says when some-
 thing goes wrong).
Allowance: $2 a week.
After-School Hangout: The Coke Parlor; later, Pop Scully's Soda Fountain.
Character: Judith "Judy" Foster is a very pretty girl who is called "the cutest date
 in town." Although the town has no official name, the local movie theater is
 the Bijou, and the *Gazette* is the only newspaper. Judy has a knack for find-

ing mischief and has a firm belief that her family doesn't understand her: "I think the people who are related to me are unsympathetic and full of a lack of understanding. Every time I offer something constructive and valuable in the way of something concrete, I get stepped on before the germ of my idea ever gets a chance to bud into blossom."

OTHER CHARACTERS

Melvyn and Dora Foster: On the day Judy was born, they said, "Our house would always be open to anyone she [Judy] wants to bring into it. Her friends will be our friends. Her dates will be our dates." What they hadn't counted on were "the kooks" Judy would have for friends. Melvyn owns the Foster Canning Company and met Dora in college. He was in a fraternity and belonged to a band. To impress Dora, he "and the boys" would stand beneath Dora's dorm room window and sing a song he wrote especially for her—"A Rendezvous with Dora" ("I've got a rendezvous with Dora, not Jenny Belle or Flora; digga-digga-do, 23 skiddoo. I've got a rendezvous with Dora"). Dora and Melvyn married after graduating from college, and Dora is content as a housewife. Melvyn mentioned that his favorite movie star is Hedy Lamarr.

Randolph Foster: Judy's 12-year-old brother. He has an allowance of 75 cents a week and loves Boris Karloff and Humphrey Bogart movies. He is not as mischievous as Judy (more wisecracking) and tries to help Judy out of jams when he can—for her allowance money.

Oogie Pringle: Judy's boyfriend and the object of her endless efforts to improve him and make him the man of her dreams. Oogie drives a hot rod and is in a band called the High School Hot Licks (they play at school dances three times a year). Oogie too wrote a song for the girl he loves, one he titled "I've Got a Date with Judy" ("I've got a date with Judy, a big date with Judy, oh geepers and gee, I've got a date with Judy and Judy's got one with me"). Judy and Oogie first met when she ran him over with her tricycle.

In some episodes, the locale is called "The Town," "The City," or "Our City." In one episode, Cincinnati was mentioned as being the nearest big city.

December Bride

(CBS, 1954–1959)

Cast: Spring Byington (Lily Ruskin), Frances Rafferty (Ruth Henshaw), Dean Miller (Matt Henshaw), Harry Morgan (Peter Porter), Verna Felton (Hilda Crocker).

Basis: Events that spark the life of a lively 60-year-old widow (Lily Ruskin).

Lily Ruskin is a 60-year-young widow who lives at 728 Elm Street in Westwood, California, with her married daughter, Ruth Henshaw, and Ruth's husband, Matt. "The street is lined with palm trees," says Matt. "One block over is Palm Street which is lined with elm trees." In later episodes the house is located at 728 North Palm Drive.

Lily writes an advice-to-the-reader column for the *Los Angeles Gazette* called "Tips for Housewives" (she also had a second column called "Let Yourself Go"—about doing only what you want to do). She is also the treasurer of the Westwood Cultural Club. Lily was born in Philadelphia (as was Ruth), and when her husband passed away, she sold her home and came to live with Matt and Ruth. Her fondest memory of the home was the century-old grandfather clock that had been handed down from generation to generation; it now resides (with its broken chiming mechanism) with her, Matt, and Ruth. Lily involves herself with reader problems and claims, "If Romeo and Juliet had written to me, they would be alive today." Her best friend is Hilda Crocker.

"I'm an ordinary guy, wear ordinary clothes, and live in an ordinary house. In fact, I'm just what I appear to be—a perfectly normal guy except for one thing: I like my mother-in-law. In fact everybody likes her, especially eligible bachelors," says Matt about himself and Lily. Matt, an architect for Coricon Company and Associates (later the Gordon Architectural Firm; also called Gordon and Company), designed the house in which they live (he also received honorable mention for a project in the August 1955 issue *of Architect's Journal*). Matt and Ruth met in Philadelphia (where Matt would have dinner every night at Lily's home). When they wed, they had $60 to their name (they have been married five years when the series begins). Matt loves to smoke cigars, but Ruth will not let him: "Some men can look distinguished smoking cigars; you look like a walrus with one tusk." Ruth shops at a grocery store called Harry's Market (which she has nicknamed "Old Grouchy's"). Her passion is to squeeze fruit before she buys it, but store policy forbids squeezing the fruits and vegetables. "Ordinarily I don't mind," Ruth says, "but when I buy tomatoes, I like to squeeze tomatoes." One day, Ruth's dream came true. "For three years I wanted to reach out and say I'll take this one and that one. Well, today I got even with Harry. When I finished shopping I gave him a $20 bill. When he turned his back to put it the cash register, I squeezed ten tomatoes as fast as I could, but only bought one. I feel wonderful!" Ruth is also very civic minded and, as Matt says, becomes overly involved in projects and needs rescuing by him and Lily.

Much of the comedy stems from Lily's conversations with next-door neighbor Pete Porter. Pete is married to the never-seen Gladys, "a tyrant and total boss over Pete." "I'm not hen pecked," Pete says, "I'm buzzard pecked. I wear the pants in my family. Even though Gladys makes them I still wear them." Pete is an insurance salesman for the Delta Insurance Company, and although he constantly insults Gladys, he does love her. They also have a never-seen daughter named Linda. When the series *Pete and Gladys* was spun off from *December Bride* in 1960 (to 1962), Harry Morgan revived the role of Pete with Cara Williams brought on to play Gladys; Linda was not a part of the new series.

Arnold Stang appeared as Marvin, Pete's brother-in-law; Isabel Randolph was Hilda's cousin, Emily; Sandra Gould was Hildy's niece, Frieda Manheim; and Sandor Szabo played Frieda's husband, Carl Manheim, a singing wrestler called "The Singing Sheik."

Decoy
(Syndicated, 1957–1958)

Cast: Beverly Garland (Casey Jones).
Basis: New York City policewoman Casey Jones's investigations into crimes in and around Manhattan.

PATRICIA "CASEY" JONES
Occupation: Plainclothes policewoman (sometimes seen in uniform) with the Police Department of New York City (the term N.Y.P.D. had not yet come into use).
Age: 31 (born in October 1926)
Badge Number: 300.
Salary: $75 a week.
Office: Room 307 (at the Police Woman's Bureau).
Address: 110 Hope Street (also given as 36 Gramercy Park).
Telephone Number: Murray Hill 3-4643.
Character: Attractive, alluring (when she wants to be), and tough. Called "A Dame Copper" by thugs, Casey can (and does) take a beating like her male counterparts (seeing Casey with a bruise or disheveled hair and clothing is not unusual). She is also somewhat of a loner and totally devoted to her job, putting in long hours, covering dangerous cases (in seedy neighborhoods), and often doing what she should not do—entering a situation without backup. For Casey, her first job was quite demanding (going undercover at a carnival to bust a money-laundering and stolen-property ring). After four days and no results, she felt she was just wasting taxpayer's money (although her two-piece harem costume, where she posed as a hula dancer at the carnival, was quite provocative for the time). Being a policewoman appears to allow her a special privilege: the option of quitting a tough case or sticking with it. Beverly Garland is television's first profiled policewoman in a series, "presented as a tribute to the Bureau of Police Women, Police Department, City of New York" (as seen in the opening theme).

Dennis the Menace

(CBS, 1959–1963)

Cast: Jay North (Dennis Mitchell), Herbert Anderson (Henry Mitchell), Gloria Henry (Alice Mitchell), Joseph Kearns (George Wilson), Sylvia Field (Martha Wilson), Gale Gordon (John Wilson), Sara Seegar (Eloise Wilson), Jeannie Russell (Margaret), Billy Booth (Tommy).

Basis: The chaos that results when a mischievous young boy (Dennis Mitchell) attempts to help people he feels are in some sort of trouble.

DENNIS MITCHELL

Parents: Henry and Alice Mitchell.

Address: 627 Elm Street in the town of Hilldale (9th District).

Pets: Sam (a frog), Herman (a guinea pig), George (a duck), Freddy (a rabbit).

Catchphrase: "Hel-looooo Mr. Wilson!" (refers to his neighbor; he also calls him "Good Old Mr. Wilson," as he considers him his best friend).

Allowance: 25 cents a week.

Club: The Tree House Club (with his friend Tommy), the Explorer's Club.

Favorite Color: Red.

Activities: Star pitcher and captain of his grammar school baseball team (originally a member of the Pee Wee League baseball team); member of the school basketball team; ringing doorbells to see if they work; creating havoc in the neighborhood.

Jobs: Washing Mr. Wilson's car; collecting empty bottles for the deposit money; delivering circulars; selling soda (like a lemonade stand); dog washing business (with his friend Tommy) for 25 cents a dog; turning an old washing machine into a business ("The Dirty Clothes Cleaner").

Hobbies: Model airplanes, rocket ships (dreams of becoming an astronaut), bowling (where his highest score is 68).

Dislikes: Girls ("Girls are no fun. They can't play catch because they can't throw. You can't hit 'em because they're a girl and the first thing you know you wind up playing house").

Achievement: Made Goodwill Ambassador to Washington, D.C., to plead for a petition to declare his state's Hickory Mountain a national forest. Aptitude tests reveal he has the ability to become an engineer.

Good Luck Charm: A rabbit's foot.

Favorite Board Game: Parcheesi.

Favorite TV Show: The space series *Captain Blast*.

Favorite Movie Character: Pete the Penguin.

Most Prized Possession: His bug collection.

Character: As mischievous as Dennis is and no matter how much he tries to help others, his intentions most often result in some kind of good thing happening. He has a bad habit of leaving his toys in the driveway, on the back porch, in the living room—or other places where they shouldn't be. He and his friend Tommy Anderson (born on the same day as Dennis) produced a neighborhood newspaper about Mr. Wilson they called "The Mr. Wilson Paper." In first-season episodes, Ron Howard played Dennis's friend Stewart. When Dennis is in trouble, he eats ice cream. Early episodes feature Dennis carrying a slingshot in his back pants pocket.

HENRY AND ALICE MITCHELL

Character: Very little information is given. Alice (maiden name Perkins) and Henry married in 1950. He and Alice apparently grew up in Hilldale, and Henry proposed to Alice during a backyard barbecue at her parents' home (where her mother "baked one of her delicious apple pies"). Alice had worn "the dress I was always crazy about," and that apparently prompted Henry to ask Alice to marry him. Prior to meeting Alice, Henry served time in the navy and graduated from college as an engineer (he acquires a job at Hall [later Trask] Engineering; later promoted to manager of the engineering department). Henry smokes a pipe and relaxes playing golf and fishing. Alice, a member of the Ladies' Committee, claims that she owns one antique—an end table in the living room. Henry sums up Dennis's activities as "Good intentions, bad results." For Alice, it is "He's quite a wire. If his energy could be run through a wire he could light up New York City." She also claims that Dennis gives her "sick headaches." While Alice is a loving mother and housewife, she has one bad habit—playing matchmaker to her single friends. Yellow Roses are her favorite flower. Henry Norell appeared as Henry's employer, James C. Trask.

Relations: James Bell as Charlie Perkins, Alice's father, called "Grandpa" Perkins, and Kathleen Mulqueen as Henry's mother.

GEORGE WILSON

Address: 625 Elm Street.

Car License Plate Number: OL 2-317.

Pet: Fremont (a dog).

Spouse: Martha.

Hobbies: Coin collecting, stamp collecting, gardening, bird watching, painting, chess.

Affiliations: National Bird Watchers Society, the State Society of Bird Watchers, the Lookout Mountain Bird Sanctuary, the Northside Bird Watchers, the Garden Club, chairman of the Community Chest.

Catchphrase: "Great Scott!" (which he says when something goes wrong).

Suit Size: 44.

Stock Holdings: 100 shares of the Buzzard Mountain Mining Company.

Character: While his age is not stated (early 60s), George has retired from business (the Kramer Business Machines Company; he is retired four years when the series begins) and tries to live a peaceful life despite the constant intrusions from next-door neighbor Dennis. To help him survive his encounters with Dennis, George has created his own "Nerve Tonic" that calms his nerves when he takes a teaspoon full. As a child in school, George won a copy of *Treasure Island* in an elocution contest. George considers his 1907 $10 gold piece his most valuable coin and has won several blue-ribbon prizes for his gardening skills (including his roses, dahlias, and sweet potato vines). He is also very particular about his goldfish pond in the backyard.

Relations: Nancy Evans as June Wilson, George's sister; Elinor Donahue as Georgiana Ballinger, George's niece; and Mary Adams as Helen Forbes, George's sister.

JOHN WILSON

Occupation: Magazine writer; author of the Jane Butterfield advice-to-the-love-lorn column for the local newspaper, the *Daily Chronicle*. Temporary job as the Official City Cat Catcher (rounds up stray cats who prey on birds).

Spouse: Eloise.

Address: 425 Elm Street (purchased the house from his older brother, George, after he and Martha moved).

Car License Plate: SZ 214 (later BG 55Z).

Education: Bedford University.

Hobbies: Stamp collecting.

Character: Rather grumpy and stubborn and, like his brother, constantly plagued by Dennis. He smokes a pipe, was called "Tubby" as a kid ("I was chubby"), and wrote a book about his eccentric uncle called *My Uncle Jed* (published by the Winfield Publishing Company; his second book was titled *The Land We Love*). John served with the navy during World War II and calls the magazine for which he writes "my magazine" (although he mentions it as the *National Journal* in one episode). He believes "Dennis is a magnet. Every time I start a project Dennis comes by." On a grammar school aptitude test, John was qualified to become a butcher.

Relations: Edward Everett Horton as Ned Matthews, John's uncle; Verna Felton as Emma, John's aunt; and Allan Hunt as Ted Wilson, John's cousin.

MARGARET

Character: The girl with an unrelenting crush on Dennis (although he totally ignores her and refers to her as "that dumb old girl" or "dumb old Margaret"). Margaret is very smart (has a high IQ), is a school cheerleader, and mentions wanting to become an atomic scientist when she grows up. She is almost always seen pushing her doll carriage and considers her dolls, Pamela, Francine, and Gwendolyn as "the children." She is forever asking Dennis to play house (which Dennis constantly refuses to do—unless he needs something from her). She attends dancing school, and her catchphrase is "Dennis! Dennis!" (when she calls him).When first introduced, Margaret had the last name of Wade; she is later called Margaret Moore.

OTHER REGULARS
Charles Lane as Lawrence Finch, the stingy owner of Finch's Drug Store; Willard Waterman as Mr. Quigley, the owner of Quigley's Market; Will Wright as Mr. Merivale, the owner of Merivale's Florist Shop; Mary Wickes as Esther Cathcart, the "old maid" desperately seeking a husband (most notably, the neighborhood policeman, Sergeant Theodore Mooney, played by George Cisar); Irene Tedrow as Lucy Elkins, George's neighbor (her cat: Tinkerbell).

Dick Tracy
(ABC, 1950–1951)

Cast: Ralph Byrd (Dick Tracy), Angela Greene (Tess Trueheart), Joe Devlin (Detective Sam Catchem), Pierre Watkin (Pat Patton), John Harmon (Blackstone Springem), Dick Elliott (Officer Murphy).
Basis: Detective Dick Tracy's relentless pursuit of justice in a city riddled with crime and dangerous criminals.

RICHARD "DICK" TRACY
Occupation: Homicide detective with the 12th Precinct (the town or city not identified, although it is assumed to be New York City). The precinct is also called "Headquarters."
Car Code: 15.
Address: 3904 Orchid Drive (appears to be in a suburban neighborhood).
Spouse: Tess Trueheart.
Character: Described as "fair, honest and will never waste a bullet" (and he is one to use his gun often and says, "I always hit what I aim at"). Tracy is a thorough investigator and constantly relies on tips from his many informants to solve crimes (he also claims that he has to think like a criminal in order to outsmart them). People often say, when Tracy is on a case, "He's just not from police headquarters, he's from homicide." The famous two-way wrist radios developed in the comic strip are seen as the way Tracy communicates with his partner and the police chief.

TESS TRUEHEART

Character: A woman who is not only beautiful and an excellent cook but also a wife who wishes she were a super criminal "because then I might get to see something of Mr. Dick Tracy" (as Tracy's cases often require long hours and even less time to spend with Tess). While Dick does enjoy Tess's homemade meals, he often finds himself snacking on hamburgers or hot dogs when on a case.

OTHER CHARACTERS

Sam Catchem, aptly named for his uncanny ability to capture criminals, is Tracy's partner; Pat Patton is the police chief at "Headquarters"; Blackstone Springem is the corrupt criminal attorney (known for springing even the worst offenders); Officer Murphy is the jovial, overweight station house cop. The program is based on the comic strip created by Chester Gould.

DOBIE GILLIS. SEE *The Many Loves of Dobie Gillis*

The Donna Reed Show
(ABC, 1958–1966)

Cast: Donna Reed (Donna Stone), Carl Betz (Alex Stone), Shelley Fabares (Mary Stone), Paul Petersen (Jeff Stone), Patty Petersen (Trisha).

Basis: Incidents in the lives of a doctor (Alex Stone), his wife (Donna), and their children (Mary and Jeff).

Setting: The town of Hilldale.

Address: 453 Elm Street.

Telephone Number: Hilldale 4-2936 (later given as Hilldale 7281 and Hilldale 8842).

Family Pet: A dog called Boy (on the DVD release of the 1961–1962 season, Paul Petersen mentions the dog was named Cocoa). In a second-season episode, they also have a cat named Harry.

DONNA AND ALEX STONE

Character: Donna is a dedicated wife, loving mother, and all-around problem solver. (She says she handles problems "with love, kindness and nagging." Alex does it as the situations warrant: "The only thing we can do as parents is to give our children a set of values and when they have to make a choice between what is right and an easy victory, we can only hope that those values will guide them.") Donna, maiden name Mullinger, was born on a farm and became a nurse after graduating from high school. It is first mentioned that Alex and Donna met in high school (as Alex said, "I would carry her [Donna's] books"). It is next said that Donna met Alex when he was an intern (and she was a nurse). Alex later claims he and Donna first met when his friends Bill and Dorothy Sayers married. Dorothy wanted all her friends to "know the bliss of married life" and invited her friends to a dinner party. Donna, Alex says, "just happened to drop by that evening." Donna, however, contradicts that story by saying Alex saw a picture of Donna taken with Dorothy and insisted on meeting her. Bill and Dorothy threw a dinner party and invited Alex, and it was there that he met Donna.

Alex eventually became a pediatrician and interned at the Children's Hospital. He also served a hitch in the army (stationed at Fort Dix) during World War II. Alex has an office in their home but later moves into a medical building office when the opportunity arises (1961). He is also on staff at Hilldale Hospital, and prior to the move, Donna would assist him with patients. Donna is a member of the Garden Club, WIVES (Women Independent Voters and Entertainment Society), the PTA, and the Children's Clinic Charity and is a volunteer salesgirl at the hospital's gift shop. She attended Blaine University (an all-girls college), where she was a cheerleader and had the nickname "Donniepie." In high school, Donna had a dream "of becoming the world's greatest actress" and is the type of woman who will wear a previously worn dress to an important occasion ("I've only worn it a few times before," she says). Donna professes that she spends most of her time in the kitchen and considers it her "office." She also enjoys growing roses in the backyard. Her biggest obsession is the auction of unclaimed freight at the railroad warehouse—something she looks forward to attending each year. She also makes money for charity by selling her homemade pickles ("Pickles for Charity") for 50 cents a jar and attempted a dog-grooming business called "The Poodle Parlor." Alex says that one of the advantages of being a doctor "is being able to come home late without his wife suspecting lipstick on his collar."

MARY

Age: 14 (when the series begins).

Education: Hilldale High School, then Fairburn College (where she is a member of the Delta Sorority House). The college is four and two-tenths miles from her home.

Character: Mary is typical of the girls of her day: stylish, attracted to boys, good at school, and struggling to overcome the problems of adolescence and over what to wear for dates and dances. Although very pretty, Mary dislikes being told by her dates how pretty she is or how intelligent she is (she finds it boring and will never date those boys again). Mary has aspirations to become a fashion designer, and her biggest problem appears to be making decisions. She prefers to wear Abalone shade nail polish (but will settle for Iceberg if it is sold out). As a preteenager, Mary was a member of *The Mickey Mouse Club* television program (of which, in real life, Paul Petersen was a Mouseketeer; Shelley appeared in the *Mickey Mouse Club* serial *Annette*, starring Annette Funicello). She enjoys gardening (especially growing the annual flower Bachelors Buttons) and was a singer with a band in high school (which led to her performing the song "Johnny Angel" [about a teenage girl's feelings about a boy who doesn't know she exists] in the episode "Donna's Prima Donna"). Mary wears a size 8 dress, plays tennis, dances at the Round Robin, has meals (with dates) at the Blue Lantern, and hangs out at Kelzey's Malt Shop. Mary loves to talk on the phone, and her nylons and lingerie "hog the bathroom" (as Alex says). Alex sometimes calls Mary "Baby," while Mary calls Donna "Mama," "Mother," and "Mommy" (she always calls Alex "Daddy").

JEFF

Age: 11 years old when first introduced (he weighed ten and a half pounds at birth).

Education: Hilldale High School (but also seen as Central High School). He played Elroy in the school play "Mistress of Galloway" (with his girlfriend, Angie [Candy Moore], as Sheila Galloway).

Character: Jeff is the typical little brother and a pain in the neck to his sister (Mary considers him "the disgrace of the family," but Jeff can't figure out why). He is a member of the Explorers Club and, in the episode "To Angie with Love," sang the song "She Can't Find Her Keys." Jeff worked as a newspaper delivery boy (for the Hilldale *Sentinel*) and was a member of the Acme Boilers basketball team (jersey number 9), the Friends of Outer Space, and the Bobcats football team. He was also the umpire for Angie's softball team, the Hilldale Starlets. His favorite TV series are *Gunbutt* (sponsored by Happy Gum, "the all-purpose chewing gum") and *Johnny Sapphire* (which instilled in him the desire to become a private detective). As a kid, he had a hand puppet named Bongo and a pet mouse named Herman. Jeff has perfect musical pitch (can identify any note) and was editor of his grammar school newspaper. He was also depicted as very mischievous during the show's first two seasons (as Alex said, "Jeff is a master of devising excuses for getting out of trouble"). He enjoys playing golf with (and caddying for) his father. Jeff and his friend Morton Smith (called Smitty; played by Darryl Richard) hang out at Hotenmeyer's (the local soda fountain). Jeff also wrote the newspaper article "Don Drysdale—A Hero to His Fans, a Friend to His Friends" to commemorate his trip to Chicago and meeting the Dodgers baseball player. In later episodes, Janet Landgard plays Jeff's girlfriend, Karen (it is mentioned that Angie has moved and that Jeff has been lax in writing to her).

TRISHA

Character: Became a regular in 1962 when she "adopts" the Stone family. Alex, Donna, Mary, and Jeff are playing touch football in the park when eight-year-old Trisha, seemingly homeless, joins them. When the game ends, she follows them home—"Because you're my family." They soon discover that her parents are deceased and that she is living with her uncle Fred Hawley and being cared for by a nanny (due to Fred's constant traveling). When Trisha expresses a desire to remain with the Stones, Fred makes an arrangement with Alex and Donna to let her remain. Trisha sleeps with Mary in her room and enjoys helping around the house (her character is not as prominent as Mary and Jeff, and thus there is very little information on her).

Note: In the French-dubbed version of the series (*The Family Stone*), Shelley Fabares is called Marie (and noted as such in the closing credits). In addition to the songs performed on the program by Shelley and Paul, two additional songs were produced but not used: "Quarantine" by Paul Petersen and "Just So Jimmie Can See" by Janet Landgard.

Dragnet
(NBC, 1951–1957)

Cast: Jack Webb (Sergeant Joe Friday), Barton Yarborough (Officer Ben Romero), Barney Phillips (Sergeant Ed Jacobs), Herb Ellis, Ben Alexander (Officer Frank Smith), Dorothy Abbott (Ann Baker).

Basis: Intense investigations of a detective (Joe Friday) into cases of robbery, homicide, car theft, and kidnapping.

SERGEANT JOSEPH "JOE" FRIDAY

Place of Birth: Los Angeles (as Joe says, "I work here. I carry a badge").

Occupation: Homicide detective with the Los Angeles Police Department (said to be located at 1335 Georgia Street).

Badge Number: 714.

Address: 4646 Cooper Street, Apartment 12.

Car License Plate: 58 0216.

Car Code: 1-K-8-0 (although it also sounds like A-D-K and 80-K).

Catchphrases: "My name is Friday. I'm a cop" and "Just the facts, ma'am."

Romantic Interest: Ann Baker.

Character: A no-nonsense detective with virtually no sense of humor. He is totally dedicated to his job and goes beyond the call of duty to solve each crime, especially when "I sometimes get a notebook full of notes and a crime lab full of evidence but nothing to tie them together. I just have to put them together." Joe joined the police force in 1940 when he became a rookie at the Los Angeles Police Academy. His diligence quickly moved him up the department ladder and he was soon made a plainclothes detective and then a Homicide Bureau sergeant (which he is seen as when the pilot film aired on December 19, 1951, as a segment of the anthology series *Chesterfield Sound-Off Time*). Joe's intense investigations and attention to detail were profiled, and terminology used by Joe—M.O. (method of operation) and R.I. (records and identification) became part of the general language.

JOE'S PARTNERS
Before Officer Frank Smith, a married man with a family, became Joe's steady partner, Joe had been teamed with two other officers: Officer Ben Romero and Sergeant Ed Jacobs. The characters of Joe Friday and Ben Romero were seen on TV and heard on the radio version of the series. On December 19, 1951, shortly after the pilot film aired, Barton Yarborough (Ben Romero) died of a heart attack. Over the next three weeks, the episodes filmed with Barton aired. In the fourth episode, "The Big Sorrow," Joe mentions that Ben had passed; it is also at this time that Joe shows signs of compassion. The fifth episode found Joe being teamed with Ed Jacobs and finally Frank Smith.

Ben Alexander and Jack Webb. *NBC/Photofest © NBC*

Note: The show's famous theme song, composed by Walter Schumann, is known as "Dragnet," "The Dragnet March," and "Danger Ahead." When first syndicated, the program title became *Badge 714.*

Duffy's Tavern
(Syndicated, 1954)

Cast: Ed Gardner (Duffy), Alan Reed (Clifton Finnegan), Pattee Chapman (Miss Duffy), Veda Ann Borg (Peaches La Tour).

Basis: A rather sleazy con artist (Archie) manages a bar with his financial gains more important than those of his employer (Duffy).

On Third Avenue, in a shabby section of Manhattan in New York City, stands Duffy's Tavern, a friendly neighborhood bar where "the elite meet to eat" and where, with a beer, the free lunch costs 15 cents. Archie runs the bar for the never-seen Mr. Duffy and says the tavern is not difficult to find, especially if you are on Park Avenue: "Go into the street. You will see a lot of them dames with the new look—long dresses. Well, just keep going east 'till you see knees." The Feinschmecker Brewery of Greater Staten Island services the tavern (Duffy orders the Weehawken Lager Beer Nectar). On rainy nights, the tavern loses business—"Who wants to go out and lay in the gutter" (referring to its normal intoxicated customers). Archie stipulates that at Duffy's Tavern, "we have ethics. We don't roll [rob] customers until they're drunk." The safe is a hole in the wall, and "the books are a little unbalanced." A large three-leaf clover is painted on the window above the door to the tavern.

Archie (no last name given) answers phone calls with "Hello. Duffy's Tavern . . . Archie the Manager speaking, Duffy ain't here." Although Mr. Duffy is never seen, Archie does talk to him over the phone to tell him how business is going. Archie attended P.S. 4 Grammar School and has known Duffy for 15 years (they despise each other). Archie's only thought is to con someone out of money and he considers himself an expert in medicine ("For four years I watched *Dr. Kildare* movies") and a crack lawyer ("For ten years I worked for Muelbacker, Bushwacker, Millstone, and Briggs painting the ipsos on the factos").

Peaches LaTour, a gorgeous stripper at the Burlesque Palace (later called the Bijou Burlesque), is Archie's girlfriend. She sees only the good in Archie and accepts him as he is. Archie claims that a girl like Peaches deserves to be treated to the best, like dinner at the Stork Club (but that happens only when he has the money—"which ain't often"). Clifton Finnegan is Archie's childhood friend, "a sub-normal chowder head; a dope; a low grade moron" (and those are his good points!). But, as Archie says, "You have to forgive him. When he was born, the baby doctor was a little near-sighted and Finnegan got slapped on the head." Although he is simpleminded and Archie does see him as a patsy, he also says to beware if Finnegan gets angry: "He'd throw a termite on a lame man's wooden cane." Finnegan mentioned that he would never marry because of what happened to his parents—"They became a mother and father." Archie, on the other hand, never married "because I wanted my wife to have everything—money, a mansion, a big car, a yacht. But I ain't found the right dame yet." Finnegan mentioned that he collected cigar bands as a hobby.

Miss Duffy, whom Archie calls "Mother Nature's revenge on Peeping Toms," is Duffy's daughter, who works as the cashier at the tavern and is desperately seeking a husband. She freely gives out her phone number (Murray Hill 5-8000) to anyone she has the opportunity to meet. "Unfortunately," Archie says, "her phone ain't never rung." Miss Duffy, like Archie, has only one name. When she calls her father, she says, "Poppa, this is your daughter, Miss Duffy." She also introduces herself to people as Miss Duffy. Charley (Jimmy Conlon) is Archie's elderly friend, a waiter at the tavern; Second Story Jackson (Herb Vigran) is Archie's old schoolmate (both flunked out of kindergarten together) and leads the life of an incompetent thief.

Father Knows Best

(CBS, NBC, 1954–1960)

Cast: Robert Young (James "Jim" Anderson Sr.), Jane Wyatt (Margaret Anderson), Elinor Donahue (Betty Anderson), Billy Gray (James "Bud" Anderson Jr.), Lauren Chapin (Kathleen "Kathy" Anderson).

Basis: An insurance salesman (Jim Anderson) and his wife (Margaret) contend with the antics of their children: Betty, Bud, and Kathy.

Setting: The town of Springfield.

Address: 607 South Maple Street (a white frame house) in the town of Springfield.

Telephone Number: Springfield 2274 (later Springfield 4657 and Poplar 5-400).

Town History: Springfield was founded in 1857 by pioneers Jonas and Agatha Wentworth.

JIM ANDERSON

Occupation: Insurance salesman and manager of the General Insurance Company (also called the Cavalier Casualty Insurance Company; he occupies Office 201).

Sedan License Plate Number: 2K46 475

Character: Jim is known for his ability to resolve family problems, although he often uses psychology to make his children solve their own problems. Jim is seen smoking a cigarette in the first episode only and enjoys reading (although constantly interrupted) the newspaper (the *Springfield News*). He and the former Margaret Merrick were married on the 20th (no month given), and each year they donate $25 to the Children's Home Society. In high school, Jim sponsored a "Most Kissable Lips Contest" (of which Margaret says she won). Jim began working at the age of 14, driving a truck for Hotmeyer's Feed and Grain. His first car was a Model-T Ford for which he paid $5. He plays the piano and as a kid raised an albino gopher. Jim's specialty is annuity policies. In 1960, Jim was awarded the Gold Key when he was voted "Father of the Year" by the city council and later served as the head of the Safe Driving Program.

Relations to Jim: Susan Oliver as Milly Anderson, Jim's brother's (Wilbur's) daughter.

MARGARET ANDERSON

Character: Margaret Portia Merrick was born in the town of Lemon Falls (a short distance from Springfield). She enjoys being a housewife and mother and normally lets Jim deal with the children's problems (as the children appear to have more confidence in their father to help them when they get in trouble). She rarely takes time for herself and is totally devoted to her family. Sketchy information is given regarding how Jim and Margaret met. It is first said they met in college (State University; also called Springfield College). Margaret was a sophomore and Jim a senior (Class of 1931; later said to be

Jim Anderson (Robert Young) reads to his family. Clockwise from upper left: Betty (Elinor Donahue), Bud (Billy Gray), Margaret (Jane Wyatt), and Kathy (Lauren Chapin). *NBC/Photofest © NBC*

Class of 1933). It is next mentioned they were high school sweethearts and married in 1937 in her parents' home in a simple ceremony, as they couldn't afford a church wedding. Margaret was a member of the Iota Theta Sorority House, and Jim would serenade her by playing the song "Juanita" (the only one he knew) on his banjo. At the annual family reunions, Margaret is charged with bringing the homemade baked beans to Lemon Falls; she is also a member of the Women's Aid Committee and the Women's Club of Springfield.

Relations to Margaret: William Hudson as Tom, her cousin, and Lillian Powell as Iona, her cousin.

BETTY ANDERSON

Education: Springfield High School, then Springfield Junior College (where she is on the debating team). The Hovel, also known as Hanno's Place, is the campus eatery and hangout; later, the hangout is the Campus Malt Shop. She held a job as a grocery store (Hixon's Country Market) salesgirl for Peachy Peaches canned peaches and was a camp counselor at Indian Springs Summer Camp.

Character: The eldest of the children and the smartest (she hopes to become a teacher). Betty is called "Princess" by Jim and was chosen by *Hollywood Photoplay* magazine as the girl who most resembles movie star Donna Stewart (Elinor Donahue in a dual role; her picture was submitted by the Women's Club of Springfield). Betty says, "Anything you want to know, just ask father." Unlike other family members who have official first names, Betty is only known as Betty. Elinor Donahue personally related the fact (as Betty was the name of Robert Young's wife, who was always called Betty). When Betty felt it was time to spread her wings, she moved into an apartment (number 3) with her girlfriend Jean (Donna Jo Gribble) at the Wellington Arms only to find that she missed the family and returned to the nest hours later. "Bewildered" and "Dream of Romance" are the lipstick shades she enjoys using the most. In 1960 episodes, she is seen displaying an interest in photography (including developing the pictures she takes) and was crowned the 1960 Campus Queen and the Flower Queen of Springfield Junior College. A vocational test taken by Betty indicated that she should pursue a job as an engineer (which she did during spring break and signed up with the county surveying crew).

BUD ANDERSON

Character: James Anderson Jr., called Bud, is the middle child (born in 1941). He attended Springfield High School, then Springfield Junior College. He has a fascination with cars and hopes to become an engineer (although this is a recurring theme; one 1960 episode finds Bud stating that he intends to become an insurance salesman like his father. He even acquires a job with Arthur Higgins, an insurance salesman, when Jim suggests that it would be better if he started with someone else and then worked his way into his father's office). He is a member of the Beavers baseball team. Jobs (that are said to be his first) vary by episodes—from grill cook at Snow's Drug Store to paperboy for the *Springfield News* to gas station attendant (at Shepherd's Service Station) to grocery store box boy. He wears a size 8½ shoe and calls Betty "Tallulah." Bud attempted to play the piano and then the accordion and finally mastered a musical instrument—the bongo drums. As a member of the high school football team, Bud, a kicker (jersey number 66), was called "The Hope of Springfield High." He also has a reputation as "The Classroom Casanova." Bud's jalopy license plate is 3X 4535 (later HGR 143). When Bud gets scared or upset, he hides in the basement; his homing pigeons are Charlie and Mabel.

KATHLEEN LOUISE ANDERSON

Education: Springfield Elementary School, then Springfield High School.

Character: Called Kathy, she is the youngest of the children and called "Kitten" by Jim (Margaret calls her "Angel"; Bud calls her "Squirt," "Shrimp," and "Shrimp Boat"). She has a plush teddy bear (named Bear) and a favorite doll (Genevieve), receives an allowance of 35 cents a week, and was a member of the Maple Street Tigers. She is also a member of the Little Squaws of America Troop (later a Girl Scout) and member of the Pocahontas Tribe, District 19. She enjoys ice skating (at the Snow Palace), and in one episode she had a kitten named Fluffy. Greer Garson (who guest starred in one episode) is Kathy's favorite actress, and her greatest desire is to visit Hawaii. Mr. Quigley is the name Kathy gave to an injured sparrow she found and nursed back to health.

Fibber McGee and Molly

(NBC, 1959–1960)

Cast: Bob Sweeney (Fibber McGee), Cathy Lewis (Molly McGee), Barbara Beard (Teeny), Addison Richards (Dr. John Gamble), Harold Peary (Mayor Charles La Trivia).

Basis: A tolerant wife (Molly) and how she copes with the never-ending trouble caused by her husband, Fibber, an expert liar.

"Can I watch the fight, Mister, can I?" are the words often spoken by an adorable nine-year-old girl named Teeny. Teeny lives next door to Fibber McGee and his wife, Molly, a married couple who love each other but constantly argue over everything, mainly the predicaments that result when Fibber does what he does best: embellish the truth as often as possible.

Fibber and Molly live at 79 Wistful Vista in the town of Wistful Vista. Fibber is an amateur inventor and has earned a reputation as "the world's greatest liar" (he doesn't mean to lie, but circumstances always force him to do so). Molly is totally honest and devoted to him. Fibber believes he is a man of stone (until he meets a man with a chisel), can tackle any job (until he tries), and can resolve any problem (if he puts his mind to it). Fibber finds that stretching the truth seems to work best for him—until he gets in so deep that additional lies cause additional problems and the famous verbal arguments when Molly has to come to his rescue.

Fibber claims, "The McGees' may not be in the blue book, but we're in the phone book." Fibber is a member of the Wistful Vista Men's Club and the president of the Chamber of Commerce. His past history dates back to the days of vaudeville, where he performed with Fred Nitney in an act called "Nitney and McGee, the Two Likeable Lads." Fibber's favorite meal is a buffet supper ("He goes around the table like Seabiscuit [famous racehorse] on a fast track"), and lemon meringue pie with spumoni ice cream is his favorite dessert. Everyone, including Molly, calls Fibber "McGee" (Fibber is rarely mentioned). Molly buys her dresses at Polly's Department Store.

John Gamble, called Doc Gamble, is the town physician (about Fibber, he says, "I took an oath to tend the sick and I have never known anyone sicker"). Charles La Trivia, the mayor, is called La Triv by Fibber, and Teeny lives at 81 Wistful Vista. The series is adapted from the long-running radio program of the same title.

The Gale Storm Show (Oh! Susanna)

(CBS, 1956–1959; ABC, 1959–1960)

Cast: Gale Storm (Susanna Pomeroy), ZaSu Pitts (Elvira Nugent), Roy Roberts (Captain Simon Huxley).

Basis: A beautiful young woman (Susanna Pomeroy) finds both romance and mishap as the social director of a cruise ship that sails from New York Harbor to Southampton in England and vice versa.

SUSANNA POMEROY

Place of Birth: Los Angeles.

Age: 36.

Los Angeles Address: 6 Melrose Avenue.

Present Address: 11 Randolph Street in Manhattan.

Education: Hillside Grammar School, California State High School (where she was a cheerleader and member of the swimming team), University of California (where she was a member of the Alpha Ro sorority).

Degree: Bachelor of fine arts.

Current Occupation: Social director aboard the luxury liner SS *Ocean Queen* (owned by the Reardon Steamship Lines).

Talents: Singer and dancer.

First Job: Selling lemonade in front of her home.

Character: Susanna's jobs aboard ship include giving dance lessons and teaching deck tennis, arranging shuffleboard matches, arranging bridge (card) games, performing songs in the entertainment lounge, and doing whatever else is necessary to keep passengers occupied and happy. Susanna is a bright, cheerful, and bubbly woman who also hopes that she will meet the man of her dreams during one of her cruises. She is also a bit mishap prone, and her efforts to help passengers overcome a problem often get her into trouble with the ship's captain, Simon Huxley, "for butting in." Susanna mentioned that once a year, "I treat myself to a bottle of perfume that costs $30 an ounce."

OTHER REGULARS

Elvira Nugent, called "Nugey," is the ship's beauty shop manicurist (later, she is a salesgirl in the souvenir shop). She shares a cabin with Susanna and is just the opposite in personality: shy and timid and always becoming involved in Susanna's antics. In some printed sources, Nugey has the first name of Esmeralda (Elvira is mentioned in episodes).

Simon Huxley, the ship's captain, is quite stern and becomes easily angered when Susanna upsets the ship's routine (as he says, "I know your aim is not to go through life destroying me; it just works out that way"). Simon joined the navy after college and acquired the job with Reardon Steamship Lines after his discharge. He objects to giving his employees bonuses ("It destroys morale among the other crew members") and was honored with a bust of John Paul Jones for his work by the Anglo Globetrotters.

Cedric (James Fairfax) is the British steward; Eugene Reynolds (Rolfe Sedan) is the ship's physician.

The George Burns and Gracie Allen Show
(CBS, 1950–1958)

Cast: George Burns, Gracie Allen, Harry Von Zell, Ronnie Burns (Themselves), Bea Benaderet (Blanche Morton), Hal March, John Brown, Bob Sweeney, Fred Clark, Larry Keating (Harry Morton).

Basis: Life with a show business couple (George Burns and Gracie Allen) as seen through George's eyes as he shares his experiences living with a scatterbrained wife.

GEORGE BURNS AND GRACIE ALLEN

George (levelheaded) and Gracie live at 312 Maple Drive in Beverly Hills. George addresses the audience to establish a story and then permits viewers to see what progresses through Gracie's involvement in the situation. George and Gracie met in vaudeville during the later 1920s, and on their first date, George gave Gracie flowers (which she pressed between the pages of a book called *A Report on the Sheep Herding Industry*). In 1930, they eloped and were married in Cleveland (Jack Benny, George's friend, was a witness). They lived at the Edison Hotel in New York City before relocating to California to star in their first radio series.

George was born on the East Side of New York and got into show business when he was seven years old in a musical act called "The Pee Wee Quartet." He later became a singer in an act called "Brown and Williams" ("I was Brown"), then in an act called "Harrigan and Friend" ("I was Friend; Harrigan was a seal"). He next ventured into a dancing act called "Goldie, Fields and Guy" ("I was Guy"). The next stint in his thus-far-less-than-illustrious career was an act called "Burns and Gary" ("I was Gary"); this was followed by an act wherein he partnered with Charlie Lowe, a comic who stuttered. It was while in an act with Jack Benny ("Benny and Burns") and staying at a cheap boardinghouse in Chicago that George met Gracie Allen, the daughter of the landlady, who yearned to get into show business. George fell in love with Gracie and to be close to her devised an act called "Burns and Allen"—wherein George could do his favorite thing, sing, while playing straight man to Gracie as she presented her weird observations on life. The act was a hit, and George and Gracie became famous (as George relates. "In order to have a successful act you have to have something special. I do. Gracie. Without her I'd be selling ties"). Gracie claims that her father is younger than her husband ("I met my husband when he was 30; I first saw my father when he was 24") and sews up the button holes on George's shirts "so no one will know the buttons are missing." Gracie also has a system for avoiding misspelled words: she never uses that word again ("That's why I don't make the same mistake twice").

Gracie believes everything she reads and takes things literally. She has a true knack for complicating things that are seemingly simple and loves "nice things like antiques." She pickles vegetables with bourbon (believing they need to get drunk [pickled]). Gracie wrote an article for *Look* magazine called "My Life with George Burns" (wherein she says that George is her husband and she doesn't think of him as a man; she also had to type two copies of the article. She tried using carbon paper—"but it's black and you can't see what you type on it").

George loves to smoke cigars and carries three cigars with him at all times in his inside jacket pocket. He believes he is a great baritone (but no one else apparently does). He is a member of the Friars Club and famous for "The Pause," which he developed for Gracie's responses to his questions. George tries to discourage salesmen from visiting the house: "You heard of the play *Death of a Salesman*? Well trying to sell something to Gracie is what killed him." Gracie has a collection of hats that visitors leave behind when they try to talk with her but become so confused that they rush to get out and forget to take their hats. George mentioned that his first girlfriend was Ruby Van Eaten.

Gracie's stories about her family are the subject of many skits. Her mother, who lives in San Francisco (telephone number Market 1-0048), attended her and George's wedding but cried through the whole ceremony because she had to miss the premiere of the Rudolph Valentino movie *The Sheik* (which would place her and George's marriage three years earlier than George mentioned). Her Uncle Harry is a forger who spends much of his time in San Quentin Prison. Hazel, Gracie's sister, is only two-thirds married ("Only she and the minister showed up; the groom couldn't get away from his wife"). Gracie's sister, Mamie

Kelly (Sarah Selby), is the one apparently normal member of the family (not scatterbrained) and the mother of three very pretty daughters (Jerri James, Lynn Plowman, and Kelly Oppenheim, who are credited as "The Kelly Kids"). Gracie also receives letters from her sister Betsy, and Gracie's activities include being a member of the Beverly Hill Uplift Society (raises money for worthy causes) and the Book Review Club. Their son, Ronnie, a teenage ladies' man, attends UCLA and appears in later 1950s episodes of the series.

"I just came in [to the house] and I'm already confused," says Harry Von Zell, George's announcer, who often finds himself as George's pawn in an effort to solve the crisis Gracie has created or add to it when the story line needs some uplifting. George's original announcer, Bill Goodwin, was a ladies' man and flying enthusiast (he owned "a twin seat yellow plane").

BLANCHE AND HARRY MORTON
George and Gracie's neighbors, living at 314 Maple Drive. Harry is first an insurance salesman, then a real estate salesman, and finally a certified public accountant (Blanche was his secretary before they married). Blanche does not think George deserves a wife like Gracie and feels that revealing her age is unladylike (Harry says "that it is a secret known only to her and her twin brother"). Harry is also a bit confused by George and Gracie's marriage but, unlike Blanche, rarely questions it. He also says he is not interested in pretty girls—"I gave that up when I married Blanche." Harry and Blanche have been married for 13 years (1950) and have been George's neighbors for 12 years. Harry is a graduate of Dartmouth and will drink only one alcoholic beverage—blackberry cordial. Harry considers himself the lord and master of the house and insists that when he comes home from work, Blanche have dinner ready for him.

The hedges seen in the front window box at the Burns's home were planted by Gracie (she trims them with George's electric razor). Early episodes are sponsored by Carnation Evaporated Milk, which confused Gracie—"How can they get milk from carnations?"

The Great Gildersleeve
(Syndicated, 1954–1955)

Cast: Willard Waterman (Throckmorton P. Gildersleeve), Stephanie Griffin (Marjorie Forrester), Ronald Keith (Leroy Forrester), Lillian Randolph (Birdie Lee Coggins).

Basis: Radio series adaptation about Throckmorton P. Gildersleeve, a bachelor caring for his orphaned niece (Marjorie) and nephew (Leroy) in the town of Summerfield.

THROCKMORTON P. GILDERSLEEVE

Place of Birth: The small town of Wistful Vista.

Address: 1467 Vista Drive.

Education: Wistful Vista Grammar School, Wistful Vista High School.

Occupation: Owner of the Gildersleeve Girdle Works Company ("If You Want the Best of Corsets Its Gildersleeve's").

Present Residence: The town of Summerfield.

Present Address: 217 Elm Street.

Present Occupation: Town water commissioner.

Nickname: Gildy and Throcky.

Lodge: The Jolly Boys (Gildy is president; meetings are called "Jolly Boys Night"; their slogan: "All for One and One for All").

Character: A carefree bachelor and ladies' man enjoying life in Wistful Vista when tragedy strikes the family: his sister and husband are killed in a car accident. With no other relatives, their children (Marjorie and Leroy) are placed in Throckmorton's custody, and he is appointed administrator of his brother-in-law's estate, the Forrester Automotive Agency. Throckmorton takes over the agency and later petitions the court to legally adopt Marjorie and Leroy. He decides to sell his girdle company and makes Summerfield his permanent home (after being appointed water commissioner by the mayor). Gildy, as he is most often called, compares his luck with women to streetcars: "If one streetcar goes by, another one will be along in a few minutes. The tracks are loaded." He also says, "When you want women you can't have 'em; when you don't want 'em you can't get rid of them." While Gildy has an eye for the ladies, they also have an eye for him. His romantic encounters (and headaches dealing with them) are Leila Ransom (Shirley Mitchell), the southern belle; Katherine Milford (Carole Matthews), a nurse at Summerfield Hospital's maternity ward; Amy Miller (Marian Carr), a member of the Summerfield Ladies' Poetry Club; and Lois Kimball (Doris Singleton), the librarian (who lives at 181 Oak Street). At 217 Elm Street, one will see a house with apple trees, butterflies, flowers, and a green lawn and hear chirping birds. In the back, near the garage, is an area that Gildy avoids, as he has yet to clear the mess that has accumulated with the un-wanted items the family has tossed there. Birdie Lee is Gildy's housekeeper; Floyd Munson (Hal Smith), the town barber, and Mr. Peavy (Forrest Lewis), owner of Peavy's Pharmacy, are friends of Gildy. Bessie (Barbara Stuart) is Gildy's secretary.

MARJORIE AND LEROY FORRESTER

Marjorie, 15 years old (when the series begins), attends Summerfield High School. She calls Gildy "Unkie" and rarely causes problems for him. She sometimes wishes for a larger allowance ("There is not much you can do on $1.50 a week these days"), as she is starting to become interested in boys and needs more appropriate "young woman" clothes: "He [Gildy] still thinks of me as a little girl." She is a member of the school's cheerleading team, hangs out (after school) at Peavy's, and attends movies with her friends at the Bijou Theater.

Leroy, 10 years old, attends Summerfield Elementary School and receives an allowance of 75 cents a week (although he too complains, he always finds ways to increase his income—from turning in empty bottles for their deposit to conning his uncle into giving him more money when he needs it). Leroy is a bit mischievous, and Gildy believes he takes more after him than his father. While the Leroy character is based on the radio character, here he is not the same wisecracking character who is always getting yelled at by Gildy (who would always yell "Leroy!") but a much toned down, much less mischievous young boy. He calls Gildy "Unk."

Gunsmoke
(CBS, 1955–1975)

Principal Cast: James Arness (Matt Dillon), Amanda Blake (Kitty Russell), Milburn Stone (Doc Adams), Dennis Weaver (Chester Goode), Ken Curtis (Festus Haggen), Buck Taylor (Newly O'Brien), Glenn Strange (Sam), Burt Reynolds (Quint Asper).
Basis: A marshal (Matt Dillon) and his efforts to maintain the peace in Dodge City, Kansas, during the 1860s.

The Atchison, Topeka, and Santa Fe Railroad services the area in and around Dodge City, Kansas. Boot Hill is the cemetery; the Dodge House is the hotel, and the Longbranch Saloon is the local watering hole. There is also Ma Smalley's Boarding House and the Marshal's Office on Front Street. Matthew "Matt" Dillon occupies that office—a tough but honest U.S. marshal who earns $100 a month. Matt has a horse named Marshall (with two l's) and pays $35 for a saddle; the office wall has six rifles chained together in a rack, and the famous coffee pot with the rust stain seen in the closing theme over the credits is next to his desk. Matt is fast with his guns but not always quick to use them. He will shoot to kill only if circumstances force his hand. Matt would like outlaws to surrender rather than fight because he believes a fair trial is a just means of deciding fate. Matt is a bachelor (never been married) and enjoys a drink at the Longbranch Saloon.

Chester Goode first served as Matt's deputy (1955–1961). He walks with a limp (his right leg) and calls Matt "Mr. Dillon." Chester carries a shotgun with him and enjoys eating lunch with Mr. Dillon at Delmonico's Café.

Kathleen Russell, called Miss Kitty, owns the Longbranch Saloon and is a woman of the Old West who rose above other females in that she owns her own saloon. Kitty, an auburn-haired beauty, shares a platonic relationship with Matt. Kitty appears at times to be all business and had a hard life; she struggled to succeed in a world where women were never meant to be anything more than dressmakers, wives, or saloon girls. Kitty broke the mold and now fiercely defends her livelihood. Kitty and Matt never kissed; they were more in admiration of each other as opposed to being lovers. Matt's first kiss appeared in the episode of September 24, 1973 ("Matt's Love Story"), wherein a widow ("Mike" Yardner,

Marshal Matt Dillon (James Arness), Miss Kitty (Amanda Blake), Doc (Milburn Stone), and Chester (Dennis Weaver). *CBS/Photofest © CBS*

played by Michael Learned) found and nursed back to health the wounded marshal (suffering from amnesia after being ambushed by a murder suspect).

Galen Adams, affectionately called "Doc," is the town's lone physician (he drives a horse and buggy). Matt appears to be his best customer, as Doc is seemingly always digging a bullet out of him. Doc is well educated and has opinions about everything. He can be only as helpful as 1870s medical knowledge will allow, and his prognosis is often, "We'll have to wait and see." Doc is a bachelor, and his office is on Front Street. He enjoys a drink at the Longbranch, and when puzzled or talking, he has a tendency to grab his ear or nose.

Festus Haggen is the deputy marshal to Matt (replaced Chester, who "brewed a mean pot of coffee"). Festus is from a backwoods family and uneducated (although he does have what today would be called street smarts). He is very loyal to Matt, whom he considers his best friend. Festus is a bachelor who also takes whatever odd jobs he can find to make money. He rides a mule named Ruth.

Newly O'Brien is the town gunsmith (later studies to become a doctor); Sam is the Longbranch bartender; Quint Asper is the town blacksmith.

The Halls of Ivy

(NBC, 1954–1955)

Cast: Ronald Colman (Dr. William Todhunter Hall), Benita Hume (Vickie Hall).

Basis: Life among the faculty and students at the mythical Ivy College in Ivy, U.S.A.

WILLIAM AND VICTORIA HALL

Occupation (William): President of Ivy College.

Occupation (Victoria): Wife (formerly a London stage star).

Address (William and Victoria): One Faculty Row.

Telephone Number: Ivy 4-0042.

Nickname (William): Toddie (as called by Victoria).

Character: William was a student at Ivy College and became an instructor there after graduating. He lived in a boardinghouse across the street from Faculty Row (where he rented a top-floor room with kitchen privileges; female visitors were permitted only so far as the front downstairs parlor). As time passed, William became an assistant professor and found new accommodations on the opposite side of Faculty Row, where he now had a sitting room, a bedroom, and bath and hot-plate privileges but "no wild parties" ("which in those days [1940s] consisted of more than two people laughing at the same time").

In 1950, when William became a full professor, his life would change forever. During that summer, he chose to return to the land of his birth (England) for a vacation and met Victoria "Vickie" Cromwell, a celebrated stage star (he attended her performance of "Give Them Tears" and returned 25 additional times before he had the courage to approach her). Victoria began her show business career at the age of 15 in a variety act called "Pinarro and Cromwell—Those

Funny People." They worked in a variety of clubs in London's East End and received more boos than laughs. Victoria never ate before a performance and was always nervous before a final curtain.

William and Victoria dated, fell in love, and married shortly after. She returned to America with him, and they moved into that lonely apartment William had been renting (and which she called "a Charles Addams mansion" [referring to the creepy Addams Family comic, later turned in the TV series *The Addams Family*]). It was now a home for Vickie ("I never had a home of my own. It was hotel rooms and flats or living out the backs of dressing rooms"). They later moved onto Faculty Row in a house reserved for the president of Ivy College. The school's motto is "And ye shall know the truth and the truth shall make you free."

OTHER CHARACTERS
Alice (Mary Wickes), the Halls' housekeeper; Clarence Wellman (Herb Butterfield), the chairman of the board of Ivy College (Sarah Selby appears as his wife; he was also the editor of the school's newspaper the *Ivy Bulletin*); Professor Warren (Arthur Q. Bryan), an instructor at Ivy ("Teaching," he says, "hardly ever pays off in money. And it hardly ever pays off in glory. I can myself name ten baseball players and ten burlesque queens, bless 'em, for every teacher you can bring to mind. It's the pride in the job that makes us stick with it"). It is also a good bet to avoid accepting an invitation for coffee from Warren: "In all the world no one concocts as nauseating a cup of coffee as I do."

Ivy College is a small university, rich in tradition and dedicated to giving its students the best education possible. An annual Christmas tradition, depending on the amount of snowfall, is for students to build a snowman in front of the home of each faculty member. The more affection the students have for a professor, the larger the snowman they build.

Have Gun—Will Travel
(CBS, 1957–1963)

Cast: Richard Boone (Paladin), Kam Tong (Hey Boy), Lisa Lu (Hey Girl), Olan Soule (Mr. McGinnis).

Basis: A mysterious man, known only as Paladin, and how he helps people requiring the services of a fast gun for hire.

"Have Gun—Will Travel. Wire Paladin, San Francisco" reads the calling card of a man known only as Paladin, who operates out of the Hotel Carlton in San Francisco (1860s). Paladin is a connoisseur of the arts. He has box seats at the opera house, enjoys fine food (he even has his own recipes), and has an eye for the ladies. He smokes expensive cigars (he carries a spare one in his boot), collects chess pieces (especially the knight), and is lucky at gambling. He also has one rule: never go anyplace without his gun. His image adorns a bottle of tequila called Diablo Tequila, and he can read and speak Chinese.

Paladin, a right-handed gunman, carries a Colt .45 revolver ("The balance is excellent; the trigger responds to the pressure of one ounce. It was handcrafted

Richard Boone as Paladin. © *CBS*

to my specifications." He rarely draws it—"But when I do I aim to use it"). He also carries a double-barrel derringer under his gun belt.

Paladin's work clothes are a black outfit with a silver chess knight—the Paladin—embossed on his black holster. Paladin is a graduate of West Point, and his experiences with the Union army have given him knowledge of war tactics that he uses to help people. He has a talent with a gun and a devotion to duty and relaxes in luxury at the hotel, genuinely enjoying life between assignments. (He reads the newspapers from various states and sometimes sends his calling card to people he believes may need his services; his fee is $1,000; in some episodes, he says, "$50 per hour, hard cash").

Part of the theme song exclaims, "There are campfire legends that the plainsmen spin, telling of the man with the gun, of the man called Paladin." Very little is known about the man behind the guise of Paladin. In the episode "Genesis," it is learned that an unnamed man (later to become Paladin) is from a distinguished and wealthy family but apparently has an addiction to gambling. In a room at the Hotel Carlton, the man has just lost at poker and owes $15,000 to a man named Norge (William Conrad), the owner of a town in the Delta Valley. The town, however, has been seized by a killer named Smoke (Richard Boone), who has forced Norge out, threatening to kill him if he ever returns. Norge, aware of the man's ability with a gun, had suckered him into the game and offers him a choice: disgrace to his family when he is arrested for gambling or force Smoke into a gun duel and kill him. With no other choice, the man elects to kill Smoke and erase the debt.

Smoke is a man who dresses in black and wears the symbol of a chess knight on his holster. He rules the town, but its citizens look on him as a hero, as he has forced Norge, who is apparently ruthless, out of town. The man's confrontation with Smoke is not what one would expect, as Smoke is quite willing to face the man in a gun duel. As Smoke gets to know a bit about his opponent, he calls him a Paladin—"a gentleman, a knight in shining armor; righteous"; a man who, in essence, hires out his gun for money. Believing he can outsmart his opponent, Smoke faces him with his back to the sun. Although blinded by the sun's glare, the man manages to defeat Smoke but is also wounded in the gun duel. Having just hired out his gun to wipe out a debt, the man feels regret but sees good in Smoke no matter how bad his reputation was (a killer and wanted in several states). Vowing to never kill unless it is absolutely necessary, the man becomes a hired gun (to help those who are unable to protect themselves), adopts Smoke's black outfit, and calls himself Paladin.

Kim Chang, called Hey Boy, and Kim Li, his sister (called Hey Girl), are Paladin's Chinese friends (and servants at the Hotel Carlton); Mr. McGuiness is the hotel manager. Beal Wong appeared as Hey Boy's uncle, Sing Wo, the owner of Sing Wo's Chinese Laundry.

Hawaiian Eye
(ABC, 1959–1963)

Cast: Anthony Eisley (Tracy Steele), Robert Conrad (Tom Lopaka), Grant Williams (Gregg MacKenzie), Connie Stevens (Cricket Blake), Troy Donahue (Phil Barton), Tina Cole (Sunny Day), Poncie Ponce (Kim Kasano).

Basis: Case investigations of Tracy Steele, Tom Lopaka, and Gregg MacKenzie, private detectives (called "The Eyes") based in Honolulu and operators of Hawaiian Eye-Investigation Protection (offices located in the lobby of the Hawaiian Village Hotel; the agency is also said to be a security firm).

TRACY STEELE

Character: Born in New York City and a graduate of New York Law School. Although he had become a third-generation lawyer (following in his father and grandfather's footsteps), he yearned for a life of danger and intrigue. He worked briefly in his chosen field but eventually gave it up to become a private investigator. He chose Hawaii to begin operations (a specific reason why is not given) and started Hawaiian Eye as a means of following that dream. He incorporates his knowledge of the law as a means to help solve crimes. His car license plate reads JK3 961.

GREGG MCKENZIE

Character: Gregg was born in Los Angeles and had originally planned to become a police officer. After graduating from UCLA, he became interested in private investigating and worked briefly in California before relocating to Hawaii and finding a position with Tracy. His car license plate reads LPQ 401.

TOM LOPAKA

Character: Tom, born in Hawaii, is the son of a fisherman but chose not to follow in his father's footsteps. He yearned for a more productive life and believed that becoming a law enforcer would give him that rush. He studied criminology at the University of Hawaii, but instead of becoming a police officer, he signed up with Tracy shortly after he established Hawaiian Eye. His car license plate reads 643 421.

CRICKET BLAKE

Character: Chrysies Blake, called Cricket, is a singer who runs Cricket's Corner, the hotel's gift shop. While not a detective, she assists "The Eyes" on cases when needed. Cricket is 20 years old and in love with life. She is 5 feet, 2 inches tall and measures 37-20-36. She was born in San Francisco and enjoys jazz. When she was a teenager, she would hang out at Fisherman's Wharf to hear a trumpet player named Joey Vito perform. She now frequents the Blue Grotto Club on Kalakalu Street in Honolulu to hear her idol perform. Cricket performs in the Hawaiian Village Hotel's Shell Bar (also seen as the Shell Lounge) and is an amateur photographer. She hopes to make it big one day by selling her pictures to newspapers. When Connie Stevens left the series for a short time in 1963, she was replaced by Tina Cole as Sunny Day, an aspiring singer who worked at the Hawaiian Village Hotel's information booth. Cricket drives a Jeep, license plate M31 071. Tom and Tracy call Cricket "Lover."

OTHER REGULARS
Phil Barton, the director of special events at the hotel. Phil was born in Florida and calls Cricket "the original do-gooder," as she will help people she believes are in trouble. Kim Kasano is a cab driver and owner of Kim's Cab, who does occasional work for Gregg (7T 403 is his license plate number). Danny Quon (Mel Prestidge) is the police lieutenant who assists "The Eyes."

The Honeymooners
(CBS, 1955–1956)

Cast: Jackie Gleason (Ralph Kramden), Audrey Meadows (Alice Kramden), Art Carney (Ed Norton), Joyce Randolph (Trixie Norton).
Basis: A good-natured New York City bus driver (Ralph Kramden) and his best friend, sewer worker Ed Norton, strive to rise above their meager living standards and provide a better life for their wives, Alice and Trixie, through harebrained schemes that always fail.
Series Setting: An apartment house at 728 Chauncey Street in Bensonhurst, Brooklyn, New York (the address is also given as 328 and 358 Chauncey Street).

RALPH KRAMDEN
Occupation: Bus driver for the Gotham Bus Company. He drives bus number 247 (also given as 2969) along Madison Avenue in Manhattan and earns $42.50 a week (he later says $60, then $62.50 a week). In 1949, when the bus company put on a play, Ralph starred in its production of "The 1949 Bus Drivers Follies."
Telephone Number: BEnsonhurst 0-7741.
Education: P.S. 73 grammar school.
Prior Jobs: At age 14, worked as a newspaper delivery boy.
Catchphrase: "Homina, homina, homina" is what Ralph says when he doesn't know what to say. When Ralph realizes he has said something he shouldn't have, he yells "I've got a big mouth!"

Character: Ralph had high hopes of playing the cornet in a band but couldn't afford the price of lessons. He took his future wife, Alice Gibson, dancing at the Hotel New Yorker on their first date, but three versions were given as to how he met her. It is first said that Ralph noticed Alice in a diner when she yelled to the waiter, "Hey Mac, a hot frank and a small orange drink." Next, it is a snowy winter day when Ralph, assigned by the WPA to shovel snow, meets Alice, a WPA employee who is handing out the shovels. Finally, Ralph mentions that he met Alice in a restaurant called Angie's when they both ordered spaghetti and meatballs. A marriage took place in 1941, and the newlywed Kramdens moved in with Alice's mother (whom Ralph calls "Blabbermouth"). They rented their first (and only) apartment when Ralph became a bus driver. Over the course of his 14 years with the company (at 225 River Street), Ralph has been robbed six times (five times the crooks got nothing; the sixth time they got $45).

Ralph's astrological sign is Taurus, and he owns two suits (one black, one blue). He has type A blood and is thought of as cheap (his electric bill is 39 cents a month, and he refuses to buy Alice a TV "until they invent 3-D TV").

Ralph has a dream of making it big. He ventured into a number of moneymaking schemes that all failed: low-cal pizza, a uranium mine in

Jackie Gleason, Audrey Meadows, Art Carney, and Joyce Randolph. © *CBS*

Asbury Park, glow-in-the-dark wallpaper, Kran-Mars Delicious Mystery Appetizer (Ralph mistook dog food for an appetizer Alice made and approached his boss, Mr. Marshall, with a plan to market it), and paying 10 cents each for 2,000 Handy Housewife Helpers (a combination peeler, can opener, and apple corer) that he and Norton tried to sell for one dollar each in a "Chef of the Future" TV commercial (during the third break in a Charlie Chan movie). Ralph suffered from stage fright and ruined the commercial. Ralph also started the Ralph Kramden Corporation (where, for $20, Ed got 35 percent of everything Ralph made above his salary). Ed also had an idea for making money—pabulum on pizza for babies.

Ralph appeared on the TV game shows *Beat the Clock* and *The $99,000 Answer* (his category was popular songs, but he failed to answer the first question correctly: "Who wrote Swanee River?" He answered "Ed Norton"; Stephen Foster is the correct answer). Ralph also did a commercial for Chewsey Chews Candy (for *The Chewsey Chews Musical Hour* on TV). Together, Ralph and Ed wrote a hit song called "Love on a Bus" (dedicated to Alice) that was later made into a movie, and won a radio contest with the song "Friendship."

ALICE KRAMDEN

Jobs: Said to have worked in a laundromat before meeting Ralph and held two part-time jobs to help pay the bills: jelly donut stuffer at Krausmeyer's Bakery (later promoted to donut taster) and secretary to a man named Tony Amico.

Character: Alice is a very tolerant woman and puts up with all of Ralph's nonsense because she truly loves him (even when he considers himself "The King of the Castle" and Alice a peasant—"I give the orders, I make the decisions"). Alice, whose birth sign is Aquarius (born February 8), was chosen "Cleaning Lady of the Month" by Glow Worm Cleanser. She and Ralph dine most often at the Hong Kong Gardens restaurant and attend dances at the Sons of Italy Hall. When they first married, Ralph called Alice "Bunny"; she called him "Old Buttercup." When Ralph realizes he made a bad decision and Alice was right to correct him, he utters, "Baby, you're the greatest," but when he gets upset with her, he waves his fist and says, "You're going to the moon Alice" or "Pow! Right in the kisser!"

EDWARD L. NORTON

Occupation: "Engineer in Subterranean Sanitation" (a sewer worker for the Department of Sanitation).

Telephone Number: BEnsonhurst 5-6698.

Education: P.S. 31 in Oyster Bay, Brooklyn (he also mentions he majored in arithmetic at a vocational school).

Character: Commonly called "Ed" and claims the "L" in his name stands for Lilywhite (his mother's maiden name). As a kid, Ed had a dog named Lulu (although in another episode he is allergic to dogs) and did a hitch in the navy (he later took up typing on the G.I. Bill). He found that he couldn't stand being cooped up in an office, so he took the job in the sewer (which he started in 1938). Ed's astrological sign was given as both Capricorn and Pisces. *Captain Video* is his favorite TV show (he is a ranger third class in the Captain Video Fan Club), and his hero is Pierre Francois de la Brioski (whom Ed thought designed the sewers of France; in reality, he condemned them). Ed can play the piano, but before he goes into the actual song, he warms up with "Swanee River." Ed shops with Trixie on Saturday afternoons, and Trixie claims, "Ed can't look into an empty refrigerator. It makes him cry" (as Ed loves to eat). Ed coaches the Cougars stickball team and calls Ralph "Ralphie Boy." It is mentioned that when Ed came down to invite Ralph and Alice to dinner, they became instant friends.

Lodge: Ralph and Ed are members of the Raccoon Lodge (also called the International Order of the Friendly Sons of Raccoons and the International Loyal Order of Friendly Raccoons. In some episodes, raccoon is spelled "Racoon"). Ralph is the treasurer; Alice and Trixie are members of the Ladies' Auxiliary of the lodge. A lodge uniform costs $35, and to become a member, one must comply with section 2 of the rules: "Applicants must have earned a public school diploma; applicants must have resided in the U.S. for at least six months; applicants must pay a $1.50 initiation fee." An executive meeting of the lodge means a poker game. Ralph and Norton also enjoy playing pool and bowling (they are members of the Hurricanes and use alley 3 at the Acme Bowling Alley on 8th and Montgomery).

How to Marry a Millionaire
(Syndicated, 1958–1960)

Cast: Merry Anders (Michele "Mike" McCall), Barbara Eden (Loco Jones), Lori Nelson (Greta Hanson), Lisa Gaye (Gwen Kirby).

Basis: Three beautiful young women (Mike, Loco, and Greta), seeking rich husbands, pool their resources to help each other marry a millionaire.

MICHELE "MIKE" MCCALL

Address: Penthouse G (22nd Floor) of the Tower Apartment House on Park Avenue in New York City (which she shares with Loco, Greta, and later Gwen).

Telephone Number: Plaza 3-5099.

Place of Birth: Manhattan.

Prior Address: An apartment house on Amsterdam Avenue (where Loco and Greta also lived).

Occupation: Analyst for the Wall Street firm of Hammersmith, Cavanaugh and Hammersmith.

Education: Lexington Avenue High School, University of Manhattan Business School.

Character: The schemer of the group and the most determined to find a million-aire husband. She talked Loco and Greta into pooling their resources and renting a luxury apartment they really can't afford ("We have something to sell—ourselves and we have to surround ourselves in the best possible surroundings"). She devised their credo, "Have money, will marry," and believes that "the only way for a girl to be smart is to be dumb." Mike, as she is always called, reads the *Wall Street Journal* and uses *Dunn and Bradstreet* for her "research material" (seeking out rich prospects). She feels that "we're gonna hit it big" and knows that women have to put on airs—"Men go for either the sophisticated Tallulah [Bankhead; actress of the 1940s] type or the slinky Marilyn Monroe type." In the 1957 unaired pilot version, Doe Avedon played Mike Page, a stockbroker.

LOCO JONES

Real Name: Rita Marlene Gloria Claudette Jones (Loco is her nickname, possibly based on the fact that she comes off as a bit confused about everything).

Place of Birth: North Platte, Nebraska.

Birth Date: February 25 ("That's all you need to know," she claims).

Education: North Platte High School (where she was voted "the one most likely to go further with less than anyone").

Occupation: Fashion model with the Travis Modeling Agency (later the Talbot Agency).

Measurements: 36-24-36.

Wardrobe: Sexy ("necklines that are a little too low; hems on her skirts that are too short; the back too low; the waist too tight").

Character: Loco, called "a fabulous blonde with an hour-glass figure," is a bit dense and naive when it comes to world affairs. She is an expert on use-less information (e.g., she has encyclopedic knowledge of the comic strips, which she keeps up to date with by reading *Super Comics* magazine) and is also a bit vain. She needs to wear eyeglasses to see clearly but refuses, fearing that a potential suitor will fail to be impressed if he sees her with glasses. She keeps up to date with the fashion scene by reading *Fashion Preview* maga-zine, and her stunning looks awarded her the title of "Queen of the Madison Square Garden" in 1958. She enjoys feeding the pigeons in Central Park, has a bad habit of falling for strays (nonrich men), and faints if she arises from a seated position too quickly. Charlotte Austin played Loco Jones, as a model, in the 1957 unaired pilot version of the series.

GRETA LINDQUIST

Occupation: Hostess on the television game show *Go for Broke.*
Place of Birth: Manhattan.
Education: Manhattan High School, State College (majored in psychology).
Character: Greta loves to take long, hot bubble baths and borrow Loco and Mike's clothes and is rather lazy at times and not the best housekeeper. As Mike puts it, "She borrows our nylons and gets runs in them; she doesn't make her bed and she hogs the bathroom." Greta has that Marilyn Monroe quality that lures men, but she is a bit too picky and can never seem to find one that meets her high standards (which are not mentioned but appear to be set higher than Mike and Loco). Her research material is *Who's Who in America* ("So I can see who has what"). At the end of the first season, Greta did find love and married (as Mike explained, "Greta wanted to marry an oil man, but she married a man who owns a gas station"). She was replaced by Gwen in second-season episodes. Lori Nelson played Greta Lindquist in the unaired 1957 pilot version (here as the hostess of a TV game show called *The Dunlap Quiz Show*).

GWEN KIRBY

Place of Birth: Illinois.
Education: Illinois State College (acquired a degree in journalism).
Occupation: Editor for *Manhattan* magazine ("Our Business is Publicity").
Character: Mike and Loco acquired Gwen as a roommate by placing an ad in the *Journal News.* Like Greta, Gwen also took Mike's pledge: "On my honor I promise to do my best to help one of us marry a millionaire. So help me, Fort Knox." Gwen was a Girl Scout and worked on a local paper in Illinois before coming to New York to make her mark on the world (although marrying a millionaire was not her original intention). In a way, Gwen is a combination of Loco (sexy and alluring) and Greta (a bit sloppy and a clothes borrower). Her philosophy soon becomes "Have money, will marry."

PROGRAM INFORMATION

The girls shop at Burke's Department Store and eat at Nate's Deli, and on occasions when they eat at home, they take turns cooking. The rent is due on the tenth of each month, and the girls have a perfect record—they haven't paid it on time yet. Joseph Kearns as Augustus P. Tobey and Dabbs Greer as Mr. Blandish were the apartment house managers; Jessie (Jimmy Cross) was the elevator operator. The program is based on the feature film of the same title.

Howdy Doody
(NBC, 1947–1960)

Cast: Bob Smith (Buffalo Bob Smith/voice of Howdy Doody), Bob Keeshan, Henry McLaughlin, Bob Nicholson, Lew Anderson (Clarabell Hornblow), Arlene Dalton (Story Princess), Bill Lecornec (Chief Thuderthud), Judy Tyler, Gina Ginardi, Linda Marsh (Princess Summerfall Winterspring), Allen Swift (voice of Phineas T. Bluster), Dayton Allen (voice of Flub-a-Dub).

Basis: With the town of Doodyville as the background, a small circus troupe attempts to entertain children over the objections of the town mayor, a 70-year-old mean man named Phineas T. Bluster.

History: On December 27, 1941, in the town of Doodyville, Texas, twin boys were born to the wife of a ranch hand named Doody. The boys, named Howdy and Double, grew quickly and enjoyed life on the ranch, where their parents earned a living by doing chores for the owner. At the age of six, the boys learn that their rich Uncle Doody has died and bequeathed them a small parcel of land in New York City. When NBC offered to purchase the land to construct a television studio, Mr. Doody arranged it so that Howdy, who yearned to run a circus, could have his dream. NBC built a circus grounds, surrounded it with cameras, and appointed Buffalo Bob Smith as Howdy's guardian. Howdy traveled alone by bus from Texas to New York. He met Buffalo Bob at the bus terminal, and the two became instant friends. Howdy's dream became a reality on his birthday in 1947, when NBC premiered a circus show they called *Puppet Playhouse* (first episode only, then *Howdy Doody*).

There is also another history regarding the formation of Doodyville: Chief Bungathud, the grandfather of Chief Thunderthud, is said to have founded the town. It somehow came into the possession of Phineas T. Bluster, and the Bluster National Bank holds the mortgage on the town. There was also a town law that stated that "anyone absent from Doodyville for more than ten days at a time would not be allowed back."

CHARACTERS

Howdy Doody is a red-haired freckle-faced boy with an enormous grin who dresses in dungarees, a plaid work shirt, and large bandana. He is honest, good-natured, and always eager to help people in trouble. He has 48 freckles, one for each state in the Union at the time (Alaska and Hawaii were not yet admitted). Howdy ran for president (of all kids) in 1948 and 1952 under the platform of two Christmas holidays, inexpensive banana splits, one school day a year, more pictures in history books, free circus tickets, and double sodas for 10 cents. In addition to Howdy and Double Doody, they also had a sister named Heidi Doody (voiced by Norma MacMillan and then Donna Miller). Heidi was actually a stranger who was adopted by Howdy's family after she saved Buffalo Bob's life in Africa.

Bob Smith, called "Buffalo Bob" for his adventurous past, dresses in a pioneer costume and oversees the circus for Howdy (he is also supposedly descended from Buffalo Bill).

Clarabell Hornblow is a skilled clown hired by Howdy when no other circus would stand for his habit of playing practical jokes. He assists Buffalo Bob but remains silent. He "speaks" by honking a "yes" or "no" bicycle horn.

The Flub-a-Dub is a strange animal that was discovered by Buffalo Bob while in South America in 1949. It was originally called "Flubdub" (but the writers felt it would be easier to pronounce with an "a" added. It had a duck's head, a giraffe's neck, a cat's whiskers, a cocker spaniel's ears, a raccoon's tail, a dachshund's body, a dolphin's fins, and an elephant's memory. It was given to Clarabell as a pet. The Flub-a-Dub's favorite food was flowers, but that was later changed to meatballs and spaghetti when children copied his habits and began eating flowers.

Chief Thunderthud, with the catchphrase "Kowabunga," is chief of the Ooragnak tribe ("kangaroo" spelled backwards). The Story Princess and Princess Summerfall Winterspring (of the Tinka Tonka tribe) provided additional entertainment for the Peanut Gallery. Princess Summerfall Winterspring was originally a puppet, but in 1951, when Buffalo Bob conducted a magic ceremony with the Tinka Tonka tribe, the little princess marionette became a real girl.

OTHER CHARACTERS

Dilly Dally, the carpenter; Dan Jose Bluster and Hector Hamhock Bluster, Phineas's brothers; J. Cornelius Cobb, the general store owner; Captain Scuttlebutt, the sea captain; Gumby, the green clay boy (who left to star in his own show, *Gumby*), John J. Fadoozle, the private eye; Lowell Thomas Jr., the world traveler.

I Love Lucy
(CBS, 1951–1957)

Cast: Lucille Ball (Lucy Ricardo), Desi Arnaz (Ricky Ricardo), William Frawley (Fred Mertz), Vivian Vance (Ethel Mertz), Richard Keith (Little Ricky).

Basis: A pretty but scatterbrained wife (Lucy) married to a Cuban bandleader (Ricky Ricardo) seeks fulfillment in her life by having a career in show business (something Ricky refuses to let happen, feeling a wife's duty is to her home and, in later episodes, caring for their son, Little Ricky Jr.).

Ricardos' Address: 623 East 68th Street in Manhattan (first Apartment 3B, then 3D) in a brownstone owned by their friends Fred and Ethel Mertz. Their rent is $125 a month, and they moved into the building on August 6, 1948 (at which time they lived on the fourth floor).

Telephone Number: Murray Hill 5-9975 (later Murray Hill 5-0099).

LUCILLE ESMERALDA McGILICUDDY

Birthday: August 6, 1921 (born in Jamestown, New York; another episode claims she was born in West Jamestown in May 1921). She has been juggling her age for so long "that I kinda lost track of how old I am."

Education: Jamestown High School (although another episode mentions Celeron High School). In grade school Lucy was called "Bird Legs" and played Juliet in the Jamestown High School production of *Romeo and Juliet*. Lucy also played the saxophone in the school band ("Glow Worm" was the only song she knew how to play).

Character: Lucy studied ballet for four years, gets the hiccups when she cries ("It's happened since I was a little girl"), and is famous for her "spider noise" ("Eeeuuuuu") when something doesn't go her way. She is a member of the Wednesday Afternoon Fine Arts League, has a hard time managing the family budget, appeared on the TV game show *Females Are Fabulous* ("Any woman is idiotic enough to win a prize"), and did the infamous Vitameatavegamin TV commercial on *Your Saturday Night Variety Show* (the vitamin product contained meat, vegetables, minerals, and 23 percent alcohol; Lucy became intoxicated during rehearsals). She loves to read murder-mystery novels and tried to market her Aunt Martha's salad dressing recipe as "Aunt Martha's Old-Fashioned Salad Dressing." She also wrote the article "What It Is Really Like to Be Married to Ricky Ricardo" for *Photoplay* magazine. In episodes set in Europe, Lucy was discovered by a producer and set to star in a movie called *The Bitter Grapes* (but the project fell through).

Lucy met Ricky in New York City in 1941 through a blind date arranged by her friend Marian Strong. They fell in love, and Ricky proposed to Lucy at the Byrum River Beagle Club in Connecticut on Christmas Eve (their song was "Jingle Bells," as it was the only song to which Ricky knew

Clockwise from upper left: Vivian Vance, Lucille Ball, Desi Arnaz, and William Frawley. *CBS/Photofest © CBS*

the words in English). Another episode claims that Lucy met Ricky while on vacation in Havana, Cuba. Lucy claims she married Ricky in 1942 (when she was 22 years old) and weighed 110 pounds at the time (she now weighs 132 pounds). In 1953, Lucy and Ricky become parents with the birth of Ricky Ricardo Jr., better known as Little Ricky (who later had several pets: Fred, a dog; Alice and Phil, parakeets; Tommy and Jimmy, turtles; and Mildred and Charles, fish).

RICKY RICARDO

Full Name: Ricardo Alberto Fernando Acha (aka Ricky Alberto Ricardo IV).

Occupation: A drummer (later leader of his own rumba band) who performs at the Tropicana Club in Manhattan. In 1956, Ricky buys a controlling interest in the Tropicana and renames it the Club Babalu after his favorite song (the club is also called the Ricky Ricardo Babalu Club and the Babalu Club).

Education: A graduate of Havana University.

Character: A kind and loving husband who is often plagued by Lucy's hare-brained antics, but he loves her very much and puts up with all her non-sense. He made a TV pilot for an unrealized musical series called *Tropical Rhythms* and traveled to Hollywood to star in a movie called *Don Juan.* The movie is shelved, and the film that Ricky eventually makes is never revealed. He and Lucy were interviewed on the TV program *Face to Face* and were the hosts of a morning show called *Breakfast with Ricky and Lucy* (sponsored by Phipps Drug Store). They also did a TV benefit for the Heart Fund. Lucy attempted to write a novel depicting her life with Ricky that she called "The Real Gone with the Wind."

FRED AND ETHEL MERTZ

Lucy and Ricky's best friends and landlords. Ethel was born in Albuquerque, New Mexico, and is the wife of cheapskate Fred Mertz. Ethel was called "Little Ethel" by her Aunt Martha and Uncle Elmo. She was also given the middle names of Louise, Mae, and Roberta. Ethel has become frugal over the years and is easily upset (Fred just slips her a tranquilizer to calm her down) and has failed numerous times to change Fred's cheap ways. Her and Fred's phone number is Plaza 5-6098 (later Circle 2-7099), and she and Fred ran a diner called A Big Hunk of America (right next to Lucy and Ricky's diner, A Little Bit of Cuba).

Fred, born in Steubenville, Ohio, met Ethel (both of them were perform-ers) in vaudeville. Fred worked in an act called "Mertz and Kertz" before he met Ethel (it is difficult to pinpoint when they married, as they gave up performing in 1925, and it is assumed they have been married for 18 years in 1951, making their marriage in 1933; another episode claims they have been married for 15 years in 1952, making 1937 their marriage year). Fred is seeking a way to make money by investing in something (he had an idea, Ethel says, "but he is mad at Edison for coming up with the idea of the lightbulb before him"). Ethel likes to eavesdrop, and Fred feels the only way Ethel can keep a secret is not to let her hear it. Fred sometimes works as Ricky's band manager when he goes on the road. Fred and Ethel have a dog (Butch) in one episode but not again.

Note: In the European-based episodes (December 1955 through June 1956), Fred becomes Ricky's band manager, and the quartet books passage on the ocean liner SS *Constitution*. While visiting friends in Connecticut, Lucy falls in love with an Early American–style house for sale. She convinces Ricky to move. When they find the cost of living higher than expected, they decide to raise chickens and take in boarders—Fred and Ethel Mertz. These particular episodes are also known as *Lucy in Connecticut*.

A TV pilot called *I Love Lucy* was produced in 1951 (it aired in 1990 after being lost for 39 years) that cast Lucille Ball and Desi Arnaz as Lucy and Ricky Ricardo (not Lucy and Larry Lopez as reported in *TV Guide*). Here, Lucy and Ricky live in a seventh-floor Manhattan apartment. Fred and Ethel are not a part of the concept (although Lucy's efforts to break into show business are).

I Married Joan
(NBC, 1952–1955)

Cast: Joan Davis (Joan Stevens), Jim Backus (Judge Bradley Stevens).
Basis: A levelheaded judge (Bradley Stevens) attempts to cope with the antics of a scatterbrained wife (Joan).

JOAN STEVENS
Address: 345 Laurel Drive (also given as 133 Stone Street, then 133 Stone Drive), Los Angeles, California.
Telephone Number: Dunbar 3-1232.
Age: "Let's not go there."
Weight: 112 pounds.
Occupation: Housewife.
Previous Job: Airline stewardess.
Nickname (called by Brad): Lover; Joanie.
Favorite TV Show: Two Hearts Against the Wind (mythical).
Favorite Orchestra Leader: Guy Lombardo.
Club Affiliations: The Women's Welfare League (also called the Women's Club).
Character: A pretty, well-meaning woman who has a natural ability to encounter mishaps in virtually everything she does. Joan doesn't mean to cause problems

for Brad, "it just happens." She is a good housekeeper (although Brad has to often bribe her with jewelry to make her work harder) and an excellent if not inventive cook (for example, "On certain days for dinner I take everything that's left over, put it all together and call it Hungarian Goulash"). Joan has a weakness for falling for harebrained schemes (although she also has a gift for creating her own) and is rather poor when it comes to handling financial matters (she often manipulates funds "to balance the books").

Relations: Beverly Wills as Beverly, Joan's 19-year-old sister (in real life too) who resides with her and Brad while she attends Southside Junior College.

BRADLEY J. STEVENS

Occupation: Domestic relations court judge, Los Angeles County.
Place of Birth: Los Angeles.
Favorite Music: Jazz
Recreation: Golf, hunting, and fishing.
Hobbies: Stamp collecting.
Favorite Foods: Pot roast (dinner); hot cakes with melted butter and coffee (breakfast).
Known For: Giving stiff sentences; showing a concern for the families of the felons he sentences.
Character: Bradley, called Brad, claims that, while he loves Joan, he had a miserable honeymoon and would have been better off without one (Brad spent most of his time locked in the room's [number 203] burglar-proof closet when the door closed and locked him in and Joan jammed the lock trying to open it with a paper clip). Brad first mentions he met Joan Davis (using her real name), a stewardess, on a flight he was taking; later it is revealed that they met in high school (and even later that they first met in college). Brad often gets upset becoming a part of Joan's antics but always forgives her in the end ("How else could I put up with all her shenanigans"). According to Joan, Brad likes to hear "Dinner is ready" the most. When Brad runs for reelection, his campaign posters read "Re-Elect Judge Bradley Stevens. Honest Brad. Always Keeps His Promises."

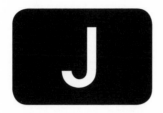

The Jack Benny Program
(CBS, 1950–1964; NBC, 1964–1965)

Cast: Jack Benny, Don Wilson, Dennis Day, Mary Livingston (Themselves), Eddie "Rochester" Anderson (Rochester Van Jones).

Basis: Incidents in the home and working life of television star Jack Benny.

JACK BENNY

Place of Birth: Waukegan, Illinois.

Age: 39 ("I've been 39 for so long I've forgotten how old I really am").

Weight: 158 pounds.

Height: 5 feet 11 inches.

Occupation: Entertainer.

Education: Waukegan High School.

Address: 366 North Camden Drive, Beverly Hills, California.

Office: Corner of Selmar and Vine on Sunset Boulevard.

Side Business: Christmas card salesman; laundry business operator; tuxedo rental business.

Outstanding Trait: Cheap ("My writers thought it would be funny to make me stingy with money").

Catchphrase: "Well!"

Pet Parrot: Polly (voice of Mel Blanc).

Bank: The California Bank.

Yellow Pages Telephone Book Listing: "Available for Parties."

Song Written by Jack: "When You Say I Beg Your Pardon, Then I'll Come Back to You."

Relations: Jack Benny as his father, Mabel Albertson as his mother, Barry Gordon as Jack as a young boy. Jack also mentions having a sister, Florence, who was born after him but is now older than him (as Jack is perpetually 39 years old).

First Girlfriend: Mildred Meyerhauser.

Character: Jack claims that he was born with show business in his blood. But before entering that world, he enlisted in the navy, and after his discharge in 1921, he broke into vaudeville. With his comical, off-key violin playing; inability to carry a tune; and lame jokes, audiences just seemed to despise him. Jack persevered and soon met another comedian, George Burns, who was having the same type of audience reaction to his off-key singing and comedy routines. Hoping for success, they teamed and formed the act "Benny and Burns." With George as the straight man and Jack as the foil, the act found little success and broke up after they played a club in Chicago (where George hooked up with a girl named Gracie Allen and found success in an act called "Burns and Allen"). Jack also hooked up with another performer, a crooner named Bing Crosby, before he became famous when he found his niche in radio.

While Jack does trust banks (as long as he can "visit" his money), he feels more secure "depositing" it in the secret underground vault he has beneath his home (which, to access, one must cross a minefield, overcome poison gas, avoid a man-eating alligator, and maneuver a rickety bridge to cross a moat). Once achieving that task, Jack opens his safe with the combination LSMFT (after his sponsor, Lucky Strike cigarettes—Lucky Strike Means Fine Tobacco). Jack drives an old 1920 blue Maxwell (license plate PU 8054) and takes music lessons from the long-suffering (having to put up with Jack's playing) violin teacher Professor Pierre LeBlanc (Mel Blanc). Jack mentioned buying his suits at the Fenchel and Gordon's Men's Shop. Jack claims that he became interested in playing the violin when he was six years old (his father played the violin in Sunday get-together musicales he held with friends).

OTHER REGULARS

Mary Livingston, a salesgirl at the May Company (the department store where Jack does his Christmas shopping) is Jack's girlfriend. She lives at 904 Santa Monica Road and hails from Plainfield, New Jersey. Jack is not as cheap with Mary as he is with others, although he considers a night at the movies going over to Mary's house ("because her TV screen is bigger than mine").

Rochester Van Jones, always called Rochester by Jack (and everyone else), is Jack's ever-faithful valet, butler, cook, maid, chauffeur—and whatever else Jack can think to make him do. Rochester has been with Jack since the early days of his radio career and rarely complains about the work but does comment about how cheap his boss is. Rochester lives with Jack and calls him "Mr. Benny" or "Boss."

Don Wilson is Jack's overweight announcer. He lives at 4946 West End Avenue in Beverly Hills with his wife, Lois (Lois Corbett), and their son Harlow (Dale White), whom Don is grooming to become an announcer. Don often assists Jack in sketches, and when Don first came to work for Jack, he was paid $5 a week plus meals. Don enjoys hunting, fishing, and horseback riding (at the J&M Stables). Jack mentions that Don came to work for him in 1933, when his radio program was under the sponsorship of the (mythical) Universal Corset Company. While he did work as Jack's announcer, Don also discovered a singing group, the Sportsmen Quartet (who appeared as regulars on Jack's early TV shows).

Dennis Day is Jack's vocalist, a "kid" (as Jack calls him) who can sing but also plagues Jack with his antics (always wanting more money). Jack required "a nice, clean-cut but cheap vocalist" fashioned after the style of then famous singer Morton Downey. When Jack heard Dennis sing but also saw that he had the ability to trade one-liners with him, he hired him at $35 a week. Dennis is a member of the Elks Club and often has to take outside jobs to pay the bills ("I can't survive on what Mr. Benny pays me"). Verna Felton appeared as Dennis's mother.

Jeff's Collie
(CBS, 1954–1957)

Cast: Tommy Rettig (Jeff Miller), Jan Clayton (Ellen Miller), George Cleveland (George "Gramps" Miller).
Basis: The adventures shared by a young boy (Jeff) and his collie, Lassie.

The Tommy Rettig era of the *Lassie* series. "To Jeff Miller I leave the best thing I've got, my dog . . . Lassie." With these words, read at the will of his neighbor, Homer Carey, 10-year-old Jeffrey "Jeff" Miller inherits a beautiful and intelligent collie named Lassie. Jeff lives with his widowed mother, Ellen, and his grandfather, George Miller, on a farm on Route 4 in Calverton, a small town about 30 miles from Capitol City.

George, affectionately called "Gramps," owns the farm—"I was born on the land, married on the land and raised a family on the land." Ellen was married to George's son, Johnny. (In episode 9, Gramps tells Jeff that he got Johnny a rifle when he was 12 years old and "put that gun away ten years ago when we heard about your father." In episode 81, it is mentioned that Johnny lost his life when he, a soldier, was killed attempting to save 20 men in his squadron, in 1944, during World War II.)

Ellen took French in college. She refers to herself as "George Miller's daughter" (although she is actually his daughter-in-law). She makes ice cream every Saturday, and the family has it with pie on Sunday. Ellen's sedan license plate reads 98916 (later 5J0773 and 559773).

Gramps was born on the 22nd (month not mentioned) and is a widower, volunteer fireman, and head of the school board. His pickup truck license plate is 9881 304 (then 3B 2675), and he calls anyone who irritates him a "pusillanimous polecat." Gramps has an unseen cousin named Alf, who ran away from the farm and retreated to Paris (where he married a French girl and became an artist). He also serves as head of the school board.

Jeff attends Calverton Elementary School and is hoping to become a veterinarian. He held his first job as an office assistant to the town veterinarian, Doc Weaver, at $10 a week. He was valedictorian at graduation (episode 113) and gave a speech on responsibility. Jeff's best friend is Sylvester "Porky" Brockway (Donald Keeler), who has a dog named Pokey (the dog is a basset hound and has the official name of Pokerman III). Jeff and Porky are blood brothers, and their signal to each other is "Eee-ock-eee." Jeff also had a horse (a yearling) named Domino, a cow (Daisy, later Bessie), and a burro (Lucky).

Florence Lake plays the rarely seen but often needed telephone operator, Jenny; Paul Maxey is Porky's father, Matt Brockway; and Marjorie Bennett is Porky's mother, Berdie Brockway. Dr. Peter Wilson (Frank Ferguson) was the original vet; he was replaced by Dr. Frank Weaver (Arthur Space), who is also the game warden. Clay Horton (Richard Garland) was the original sheriff; he was replaced by Sheriff Jim Billings (House Peters). Clay now runs a garage.

The spin-off series, *Timmy and Lassie* (CBS, 1957–1964), begins with episode 103. Lassie encounters a seven-year-old runaway orphan named Timmy Martin (Jon Provost) hiding in the barn. When Timmy's parents were killed in "the accident," he was sent to live with his elderly Uncle Jed (George Selk) and Aunt Abby Clawson (Hallene Hall) in Olive Ridge. Timmy ran away when he felt he wasn't wanted (Jed and Abby feel they are too old to care for Timmy, and they allow him to stay with the Millers). Timmy calls Ellen "Aunt Ellen."

Shortly after, Gramps dies (episode 114). When Ellen learns that a young couple named Paul and Ruth Martin are seeking to adopt Timmy and are looking for a place to live, she sells them the farm. Ellen and Jeff move to 311 Cedar Street in Capitol City (where Ellen will give music lessons and Jeff will attend high school). Before Ellen and Jeff depart, Jeff gives Lassie to Timmy (feeling she would be better off on the farm).

Cloris Leachman and Jon Sheppard first played Ruth and Paul Martin (to episode 141); they were replaced by June Lockhart and Hugh Riley. George Chandler plays Paul's brother, Petrie J. Martin; Todd Ferrell is Timmy's friend, Boomer Bates; and Andy Clyde is Timmy's elderly friend, Cully Wilson. Paul's truck license plate is 3B 2675; Boomer's dog is named Mike; and Silky, aka Sam, is Cully's dog. "Uncle Petrie," as Timmy calls him, previously lived in Millvale, Pennsylvania. Paul went on 22 missions during World War II.

Johnny Jupiter
(DuMont, 1953; ABC, 1953–1954)

Cast: Wayne King (Ernest P. Duckweather), Cliff Bole (Horatio Frisby), Patricia
Peardon (Katherine Frisby).
Basis: A look at life on the planet Jupiter when an amateur Earth inventor (Ernest) accidentally discovers intergalactic TV.

Ernest P. Duckweather is a likable young man who lives in the small, mythical
town of Clayville. He is a clerk at the Frisby General Store (owned by Horatio
Frisby; his daughter, Katherine, is Ernest's girlfriend).

Ernest is a jack-of-all trades and earns $15 a week. One day, while fooling
around with a TV set, he accidentally contacted the inhabitants of the planet
Jupiter. The planet is 600 million miles from Earth, and the Jupiterians are seen
as puppets Johnny Jupiter, Major Domo (the head robot), and Reject, "The factory rejected robot" (all voiced by Gilbert Mack).

Stories relate Ernest's mishaps as he seeks the Jupiterians' help in solving his
earthly problems. When Ernest contacts Johnny, he turns several dials on a large
television and says, "Duckweather on Earth, calling the planet Jupiter." Through
some primitive but effective special effects, Johnny comes into view. Ernest can
see and speak to Johnny and vice versa.

If Ernest requires help, Johnny sends Reject the Robot to Earth. To accomplish this, Johnny touches the puppet Reject and says, "Super Jelly Bean Power."
Reject is sent through time and space and appears to Ernest (the only person who
can see him). During the trip from Jupiter to Earth, the puppet becomes life-size
(the actor playing the role is not identified). Reject's favorite television show is *The
Robot Club* (all programs on Jupiter are educational and instructive). On Jupiter,
robots were built to service the humanoid population (for example, Johnny) and
are excellent repairmen. Johnny calls Ernest "Mr. Duckweather."

Reta Shaw (as Mrs. Cavendish, a townsperson) and Florenz Ames (as Mr.
Latham, Horatio's nemesis) were semiregulars during the ABC run of the series.

An earlier version aired on DuMont and found Ernest (Vaughn Taylor)
as a television station janitor who dreams of becoming a producer. One night
while cleaning the station's control room, he begins playing producer. While
fiddling with the various controls, he accidentally discovers interplanetary television when he contacts the people of Jupiter (Johnny, Major Domo, Reject,
and Johnny's pal, B-12). Due to the very limited material available on DuMont
programs, it is difficult to compare both versions. *TV Guide* first listed the series
as "Fantasy" but changed the genre to "Puppets" and later "Comedy." Its information for both versions is also extremely skimpy: "Mr. Duckweather tries to get
the Jupiterians on television. Vaughn Taylor" (June 6, 1953); "Vaughn Taylor

tunes his TV set to a far off spot and introduces another adventure" (June 13, 1953); "Adventures of Mr. Duckweather" (October 17, 1953); "Comedy starring Wright King with Pat Pearson and Cliff Hall" (November 7, 1953).

It appears that the DuMont version, which was broadcast live, had only two actors: Vaughn Taylor as Ernest and Gilbert Mack doubling as Ernest's boss and the puppet voices. Stories revolved around Johnny and Ernest assessing the values of their respective planets (which differed greatly; what was common on Earth was actually just the opposite on Jupiter).

Judge Roy Bean
(Syndicated, 1955–1956)

Cast: Edgar Buchanan (Judge Roy Bean), Jackie Loughery (Letty Bean), Jack Beutel (Jeff Taggard).

Basis: Self-proclaimed judge and lawman Roy Bean attempts to maintain the peace during the 1870s.

During the 1870s, as the railroads pushed their way west, they attracted the most vicious characters in the country. Soon, the desolate region west of the Pecos River built a reputation as "the wildest spot in the United States." It was said that civilization and law stopped at the east bank of the Pecos. "It took the courage of one man, a lone storekeeper who was sick of the lawlessness to change all this. His name was Judge Roy Bean."

Roy Bean, the self-appointed judge of Langtry, Texas, is also the town's sheriff and owner of Roy Bean's General Store. He is a bit on the heavy side, nearsighted without his glasses, older than the typical Wild West lawman, and fond of apple pie. He is not quick on the draw, does not carry a fancy gun, but does possess a genius for figuring out the criminal mind and conning the con man. The judge does take an active part in apprehending lawbreakers; the rough work, however, falls on the shoulders of his deputy, Jeff Taggard, a young man who is fast with his guns and quick with his fists.

Assisting Roy in the store is his niece, Letty Bean, who came to live with him after the death of her parents. She is beautiful, extremely feminine, and dynamite with a gun (her dress conceals a gun strapped to her ankle). While Jeff does court her, he calls her "a big tomboy" and admires her ability to handle a gun—"You shoot just like a man." Letty is forever getting angry when Jeff thinks of her as a man and remarks, "Can't you think of me as a woman just once?" He tries—at least for the remainder of that particular episode.

Carson City is the neighboring town, Salt Lake City is the community north of Langtry, and the Southern Pacific Railroad services the area. When Roy established the first signs of law and order in the town he founded, he named it Langtry after his favorite saloon entertainer, Lily Langtry.

Lawman

(ABC, 1958–1962)

Cast: John Russell (Marshal Dan Troop), Peter Brown (Deputy Johnny McKay), Peggie Castle (Lily Merrill), Bek Nelson (Dru Lemp), Barbara Lang (Julie Tate).

Basis: A dedicated Marshal (Dan Troop) and his deputy (Johnny McKay) maintain the law in Laramie, Wyoming, during the 1880s.

When a girl ("someone special to Dan Troop") is killed by a stray bullet in a pointless gunfight, Dan is overcome with grief and chooses to devote his life to upholding the law. As the years pass, Dan becomes a legend—"The Famous Gun from Texas." It is 1879 when Dan, the marshal of Abilene, receives a telegram from the town council in Laramie, Wyoming, asking him to help rid their town of three outlaw brothers, one of whom killed the previous marshal ("The town is tough on lawmen and horse thieves").

Dan is fast with his guns and tough with his fists. He is also high priced and likes his gratitude once a month waiting for him at the bank. The town council members want a city where their wives and children can walk down the street without being afraid. Dan realizes that he can't do the job alone and advertises for a deputy (a job that pays $50 a month). A young man named Johnny McKay applies for the position but is turned down by Dan for being too young and inexperienced. However, when Dan arrests one of the three murdering brothers and the other two trap him in a cross fire, Johnny comes to his defense—and is hired by Dan.

As a kid, Dan worked in a hash house. He believes that a man has to wear a gun because of the way things are now; he also believes that there will be a time when it is not necessary.

Lily Merrill owns the town's watering hole, the Birdcage Saloon; Dru Lemp runs the Blue Bonnet Café (where Johnny worked prior to becoming a deputy; it was then called Good Eats); and Julie Tate is the editor of the town newspaper, the *Laramie Weekly* (originally called the *Laramie Free Press*). The Hotel Laramie, the Bank of Laramie, and the Laramie Trading Post are other businesses in town.

Leave It to Beaver
(CBS, ABC, 1957–1963)

Cast: Hugh Beaumont (Ward Cleaver), Barbara Billingsley (June Cleaver), Tony Dow (Wally Cleaver), Jerry Mathers (Theodore "Beaver" Cleaver), Ken Osmond (Eddie Haskell).

Basis: Brothers Wally and Beaver, the children of Ward and June Cleaver, experience the ups and downs of life in the small town of Mayfield.

Address: 211 Pine Street (also given as 211 Maple Street and 211 Pine Avenue), then 211 Lakewood Avenue. Madison is the neighboring town, and Wally and Theodore play ball at Metzger's Field.

Telephone Number: KL5-4763.

WARD CLEAVER

Birth Year: 1918 (in Shaker Heights, Ohio). He has four siblings (two brothers and two sisters) and was said to have been raised on a farm. At some point, presumably when he was a teenager, his family moved to Mayfield and purchased a house on Shannon Avenue. In another episode, it is mentioned that Ward was born and raised in Mayfield.

Occupation: Never revealed.

Car License Plate: WJG 865 (later KHG 865).

Character: As a child, Ward earned money by washing neighbors' windows and was good at baseball. He fished for eels (with liver as bait) "near the old drain pipe" and shot rats at the local dump. *Weird Tales* magazine was his favorite reading matter, and he had seen the 1931 Bela Lugosi movie *Dracula* four times. He was a member of the 4-H Club and won a prize for his hog at the state fair (this incident referring to his being raised on a farm). Ward was a second-string halfback on his high school football team and was also a member of the shot-put team. In college, he was a member of the school's basketball team and was said to be both an engineering and a philosophy major. He served with the Seabees during World War II. Ward reads the *Mayfield Press*, enjoys fishing at Crystal Lake, and takes his coffee cream with no sugar.

JUNE CLEAVER

Birth Year: 1920 as June Evelyn Bronson.

Education: The Grant Avenue Elementary School, an unnamed boarding school (she was captain of the girls basketball team and told her classmates that her mother was a famous actress [LaVerne Laverne] who gave up a show business career to marry her father), then State College.

Character: June's early background varies by dialogue in various episodes. As a child, when she did something wrong, she would wish it were tomorrow. She has an uncle who served as a judge and a grandfather who was considered a genius. At one point, it was said that June and her family moved to Mayfield when she was a child. June was said to have had her first job in the book section of a department store and first met Ward when he was in the service and she performed as an entertainer with the USO (United Serviceman's Organization) during World War II. June later mentions she was a teenager when she moved to Mayfield (thus, she never attended the Grant Avenue School), that she met Ward in high school, and, finally, that she met Ward in college and that they married after graduating. June is an excellent cook and loves to wear jewelry (during filming, it was noticed that Barbara Billingsley photographed with a brown spot on her neck. This was due to her muscle tone, and she wore pearls to hide it.)

From top to bottom: Tony Dow, Barbara Billingsley, Hugh Beaumont, and Jerry Mathers. *ABC/Photofest © ABC*

Ward and June are strict but not stern parents. They never spank their sons, but when it comes to punishing or disciplining them, Wally and Theodore know what to face: a lecture by their father in the study (Ward often asks his sons what their punishment should be). June rarely disagrees with Ward's decisions.

WALLACE "WALLY" CLEAVER

Education: Eighth grade at the Grant Avenue School (when the series begins); later Mayfield High School, then State College. In high school, Wally is a three-letter man and captain of the varsity football team, and 53.2 seconds is his best time on the Mayfield High swim team. He has locker number 221 at Mayfield High (10-30-11 is the combination lock number), and homeroom is held in room 211.

Jobs: Soda jerk at Gibson's Soda Fountain; soda jerk as the Mayfield Drug Store; candy and ice cream vendor at Friends Lake; loading dockworker at the Mayfield Dairy.

Character: The elder son of June and Ward, Wally is athletic and good-looking (although he never uses his looks to achieve a goal). He uses Arabian Knights aftershave lotion and drives a run-down convertible with the plate JHJ 335. While Wally did date different girls, he was most associated with classmate Julie Foster (Cheryl Holdridge) and had their first date at the White Fox Restaurant. Wally first mentions that he wants to be an engineer, then a tree surgeon, and, finally, an electrical engineer (to work on missiles for the space program).

THEODORE "BEAVER" CLEAVER

Education: The Grant Avenue School, then Mayfield High School.

Pets: A monkey (Stanley), a rat (Peter Gunn; named after his favorite TV show of the same name), racing pigeons (Miss Canfield and Miss Landers, after his teachers), and a frog (Herbie).

Jobs: Caddy at the local golf course, selling water and lemonade, and delivering newspapers.

Character: Named after June's Aunt Martha's brother. He acquired the nickname of "Beaver" when Wally couldn't pronounce Theodore and said "Tweeder." Ward and June thought "Beaver" sounded better; he is also called the "Beave." He wears a green baseball cap, hates "mushy stuff," and likes "to mess around with junk." He would "rather smell a skunk than see a girl," and Miller's Pond is his favorite "fishin' hole." The most challenging thing Beaver does is walk half on the curb and half in the street on his way home from school. He played a tree in a kindergarten play and Hans in his fifth-grade production of "The Little Dutch Boy." Beaver had a teddy bear named Billy and tried playing the clarinet for the second grade school orchestra. Mary Margaret Matthews (Lori Martin) was the first girl Beaver found attractive (she called him "Teddy"). The first mishap Wally and Beaver encountered was buying an alligator for $2.50 from an ad in the comic book *Robot Man of Mars*. Math is his poorest subject in school. As a baby, Beaver would fall asleep in his bowl of cereal, and when he gets upset, he locks himself in the bathroom; when he does something wrong, he hides in the branches of a tree near the railroad tracks or in the cave near Miller's Pond. He also appeared on the TV show *Teenage Forum*.

EDWARD W. HASKELL

Address: 175 Grant Avenue.

Education: Same as Wally.

Jobs: Gas station attendant (at his father's garage), Mayfield Dairy dockworker (with Wally), pickup truck driver for the Mayfield Diaper Service.

Pet: "A genuine police dog" named Wolf.

Character: Better known as Eddie, Wally's wisecracking friend (he and Wally met in the second grade). Although Eddie has the middle initial of "W" and his father's name is George, Eddie claims his full name is Edward Clark Haskell Jr. Eddie is extremely polite to adults (he fears their authority) but mean to everyone else, especially Beaver (whom he calls "Squirt"; he calls Wally "Sam," "Gertrude," and "Ellwood"). *Woody Woodpecker* is his favorite TV show, he is allergic to mayonnaise, and chocolate pudding is his favorite dessert. Eddie was the first to get a credit card (number 06212312) from the Universal Gas and Oil Company and will go out of his way to stay after school and watch cheerleading practice. He is poor at sports but talked his way onto the Mayfield High track team.

OTHER REGULARS

Clarence Rutherford (Frank Bank), the overweight friend of Wally and Eddie, is nicknamed "Lumpy." He takes tuba lessons and drives "a sickly green car" with the plate PZR 342; his phone number is 433-6733, and his father, Fred (Richard Deacon), works with Ward. Fred calls Ward "Lord of the Manor." He is married to Geraldine (Helen Parrish); his wife in later episodes is named Gwen and is played by Majel Barrett, then Margaret Stewart. Fred originally talked about having three children: a girl, Violet (Wendy Winkelman), and two boys who were offered football scholarships. Later, he has only two children: Lumpy and Violet (Veronica Cartwright).

Beaver's friends were Larry Mondello (Rusty Stevens), Gilbert Grover (Stephen Talbot), and Hubert "Whitey" Whitney (Stanley Fafara). Larry was first credited as Robert Stevens; Gilbert was first introduced as Gilbert Harrison, then

Gilbert Gates, and, finally, Gilbert Bates. Judy Hessler (Jeri Weil) is the obnoxious girl who kisses up to teachers and annoys Beaver and his friends with her smug attitude. She was replaced by Penny Woods (Karen Sue Trent), a similar character, in last-season episodes. Cornelia Raeburn (Doris Packer) is the principal of the Grant Avenue School, Alice Landers (Sue Randall) is Beaver's caring teacher, and Gus (Burt Mustin) is the old fire chief Beaver visits at Fire Station Number 5 (in some episodes, he is with Auxiliary Station Number 7).

The Life of Riley
(DuMont, 1949–1950; NBC, 1953–1958)

Cast (1949–1950): Jackie Gleason (Chester A. Riley), Rosemary DeCamp (Margaret "Peg" Riley), Gloria Winters (Barbara "Babs" Riley), Lanny Rees (Chester A. Riley Jr.), Sid Tomack (Jim Gillis), Maxine Semon (Olive "Honeybee" Gillis), George McDonald (Egbert Gillis).

Cast (1953–1958): William Bendix (Chester A. Riley), Marjorie Reynolds (Margaret "Peg" Riley), Lugene Sanders (Barbara "Babs" Riley), Wesley Morgan (Chester A. Riley Jr.).

Basis: A lovable but bumbling family man (Chester A. Riley) and the complications that arise as he tries simply to be himself.

On April 3, 1932, Chester A. Riley married Margaret "Peg" Barker in a small chapel on East Bradford Drive in Brooklyn, New York. The marriage was, perhaps, a bit premature, as Chester was broke and with no other choice they moved in with Peg's mother and father. Shortly after, when Riley (as Chester is always called) learned that Peg was pregnant (with Babs), he told her to quit her job ("I want you to be with the baby when it's born") and found employment as a milkman for the Sunbeam Dairy (he had a horse-drawn wagon, a route "with mostly the beer-drinking crowd," and a basic pay of $4 a day. His horse was named Daisy; the milk sold for 13 cents a quart, and he made a commission on every quart he sold).

With their newfound prosperity, Riley and Peg moved into their own apartment—a $15-a-month "walk down" (basement) apartment located under a bowling alley near the East River and next to the subway. Peg was, as Riley wanted, with the baby when she (Babs) was born. With enough money saved, Riley and Peg decided that better opportunities awaited them on the West Coast and moved to Los Angeles (their best friends, Jim and Honeybee Gillis, moved along with them).

Riley and Peg found a home of their own at 1313 Blue View Terrace (Jim and Honeybee at 1311 Blue View Terrace), and both men acquired jobs as riveters for Stephenson Aircraft and Associates (1949–1950; at Cunningham Aircraft, 1953–1958). Exactly how Riley acquired riveting skills (having been a milkman) is not stated. As Riley and Peg had a second child (Junior), Honeybee and Jim became the parents of a son (Egbert). When the 1949 series begins, Babs attends North Hollywood High School; Junior and Egbert attend John J. Boskowitz Junior High School. Other regulars at this time are Digby "Digger" O'Dell (John Brown), "The Friendly Undertaker," who always manages to help Riley overcome his worries (Digger's catchphrase: "It is I, Digby O'Dell, the friendly undertaker"); Carl Stevenson (Bill Green, then Emory Parnell), Riley's boss; and Waldo Binny (Bob Jellison), Riley's girl-shy friend.

The second series found the Rileys moving from 1313 Blue View Terrace to 5412 Grove Street (address also given as 3412 Del Mar Vista). Babs also married Don Marshall (Martin Milner) and set up housekeeping at 1451 Blue View Terrace, Apartment 3. Riley's catchphrase (when he gets into trouble) is "What a revoltin' development this is."

Tom D'Andrea played James "Jim" Madison Gillis, Riley's friend and co-worker; Veda Ann Borg (then Marie Brown and Gloria Blondell) as Jim's wife, Honeybee; Gregory Mitchell as their son, Egbert Gillis; Sterling Holloway as Waldo Binny, Riley's friend; and Henry Kulky as Otto Schmidlap, Riley's and Jim's friend.

RELATIONS
James Gleason, then James Gavin, as Chester's father, Pa Riley; Sarah Padden as Chester's mother, Ma Riley; Larraine Bendix as Chester's niece, Annie Riley; Mary Jane Croft as Chester's sister, Cissy Riley; Bea Benaderet as Peg's mother; Jack Kirkwood as Peg's Uncle Bixby.

Note: On April 13, 1948, NBC presented *The Life of Riley*, a pilot for a TV version of the radio series of the same title. Herb Vigran was Chester A. Riley, a riveter for Cunningham Aircraft in Los Angeles; Alice Drake was his wife, Peg; and Lou Krugman and Jo Gilbert were their neighbors, Jim and Honeybee Gillis. When the program failed to sell, NBC attempted a second pilot with Lon Chaney Jr. as Chester A. Riley.

The Lone Ranger
(ABC, 1949–1957)

Cast: Clayton Moore, John Hart (the Lone Ranger), Jay Silverheels (Tonto).
Basis: A masked man, known only as the Lone Ranger, and his Indian companion, Tonto, battle injustice in the early days of the Old West.

JOHN REID (THE LONE RANGER)

Place of Birth: Texas.

Original Occupation: Texas Ranger.

Relations: Younger brother of Dan Reid, a Texas Ranger captain.

Trademark: The silver bullet.

Horse: Silver.

Character: Brave and fearless as a Ranger; equally brave, fearless, and cunning as the Lone Ranger. Reid uses silver bullets not only for his trademark but also as a reminder to shoot sparingly and remember the high cost of human life (although he never shoots to kill). He wears a black mask to conceal his true identity—"Keeping my identity a secret makes the pursuit of outlaws easier." To help others in a capacity other than the Lone Ranger, Reid has several well-disguised aliases: Professor Horatio Tucker, the smooth-talking medicine man; Don Pedro O'Sullivan, the Swede; Juan Ringo, the Mexican bandit; and the old-timer). Reid has a distinctive voice, and it sometimes becomes a threat to the Ranger's true identity when he goes undercover ("There's something about that voice," an outlaw would say, "but I can't place my finger on it"). Silver is a white horse that the Ranger also calls "Big Fella" and who will let only Reid or Tonto ride. Reid never accepts a reward of money for his services—"Seeing justice is done is our reward."

TONTO

Tribe: Pottawatomie Indian.

Horse: Scout.

Catchphrase: "Kemo Sabe" (translated as both "faithful friend" and "trusted scout"), which he calls Reid.

Character: Quick with his gun and an expert with a knife, Tonto has joined with Reid in his quest to end injustice (while not clearly stated, perhaps to avenge the death of his family who were killed by renegade Indians). Tonto does experience the prejudice the white man held toward Indians and is often shot and beaten. Although he does not wear a disguise, Tonto will go undercover to help the Ranger achieve a goal as Red Dog, an outlaw Indian.

PROGRAM INFORMATION

It began with an assignment to track down the notorious Butch Cavendish Hole-in-the-Wall Gang. Dan Reid, a Texas Ranger captain, formed a squad of five other men: John Reid, Jim Bates, Jack Stacey, Joe Brent, and Ben Cooper. As the unit neared Bryant's Gap, a canyon about 50 yards wide and bound by cliffs, Butch Cavendish attacked and left after all the Rangers were killed. Tonto, hunting for food, finds that one Ranger had not been killed—John Reid. Tonto brings Reid to the shelter of a small cave and begins nursing him back to health. As Reid recovers, he recalls Tonto as the Indian he befriended as a child. Years earlier, when Tonto's village was raided by renegade Indians and Tonto was left for dead, a young John Reid found him and helped him recover from his wounds.

To conceal the fact that one Ranger lived, Tonto digs six graves, each marked with a crudely constructed cross. The sixth grave bears the name of John Reid, dug by Tonto to convince Cavendish that all the Rangers had been killed and conceal the fact that the one Texas Ranger had lived to avenge the others—the Lone Ranger. To conceal his true identity, Reid fashions a mask from his brother's black vest. At first, he and Tonto posed as outlaws to enable them to capture the Cavendish gang. Once their goal was accomplished, they became a force for good—"Wherever you find a wrong to be righted that's where you'll find the Lone Ranger."

OTHER CHARACTERS

Dan Reid (Chuck Courtney), John's nephew (who rides a horse named Victor); Jim Blaine (Ralph Littlefield), the old-timer who works the Reid family's silver mine; George Wilson (Lyle Talbot), Reid's secret banker in Border City (who exchanges the silver for the money he needs); Father Paul (David Leonard), the padre at the San Brado Mission.

Love That Bob
(NBC, 1955, 1957–1959; CBS, 1955–1957)

Cast: Bob Cummings (Bob Collins), Rosemary DeCamp (Margaret MacDonald), Dwayne Hickman (Chuck MacDonald), Ann B. Davis (Charmaine "Schultzy" Schultz).

Basis: The life of a handsome and suave photographer (Bob Collins) as he dates beautiful models but seeks to avoid one thing—marriage.

ROBERT "BOB" COLLINS

Occupation: Owner of "Bob Collins—Photography" (in downtown Hollywood, California).

Address: 804 Grummond Road.

Place of Birth: Joplin, Missouri (descended from Scottish ancestors).

Education: Joplin High School, Drury College.

Hobbies: Girls, flying (he has a rarely seen twin-engine Beechcraft plane), girls, anything that interests girls.

Favorite Cologne: Moustache ("It drives girls crazy").

Military Service: U.S. Air Force pilot during World War II. He became a colonel before his discharge.

Worst Month of the Year: June ("When girls are the most marriage-minded" and Bob finds it difficult to remain a bachelor).

Bob's Favorite Models: Shirley Swanson (Joi Lansing), a gorgeous blonde (measures 38-26-36) who lives opposite Bob's studio "in a large white building with a red roof." Besides being beautiful, she has a talent in the kitchen: "I can cook ham and eggs." She also wears a perfume called Bachelor's Doom. Maria DiPaolo (Donna Martel), the Italian bombshell (36-23-34) Bob called "My Little Venetian Ambassador of Loveliness" (she calls him "Roberto," and her kitchen specialty is meatballs and spaghetti); and Colette DuBois (Lisa Gaye), the French girl, measuring 36-22-34, Bob calls "My Sly Little Thief" (her culinary expertise is pancakes).

Favorite Activity: Judging beauty contests (for example, "Queen of the Air" [choosing one of 53 women representing U.S. Air Force bases as their queen], Miss Hollywood—and "Miss" anything else).

Bob Collins (Bob Cummings) is surrounded by Schultzy (Ann B. Davis), Chuck MacDonald (Dwayne Hickman), and Margaret MacDonald (Rosemary DeCamp). *NBC/Photofest © NBC*

Character: Bob's interest in girls began at an early age—at four, "when he learned to play "Post Office" (in another episode, Bob states that he became interested since he was 12 years old and realized they weren't "soft boys"). Bob, called "The Casanova of the Camera" by his sister, Margaret, claims that "I'm a confirmed bachelor, but I'm married to my camera. Any other type of marriage is a serious commitment and I need time before settling down. I need time to find the right girl—no matter how many girls I have to date to find her." Margaret adds, "All the Collins men are confirmed bachelors until something snaps and they suddenly get married."

Bob photographs some of the world's most beautiful models and considers them "lumps of clay" ("I mold them into bright, shimmering butterflies. I give them grace, style and charm"). For a girl to model for Bob (especially in swimsuits), Bob insists that they cannot have a waist larger than 23 inches and a bust no larger than 36 (Shirley, listed above, is an exception; as Bob says, "I may be strict but I'm not crazy"). He is especially fond of "Bikini Time" shoots and will pretend to be interested in anything a girl is (from bird watching to taking pottery classes) to impress her. He has also characterized his models: "Girls come in many different models like automobiles. Some are flashy, some are convertibles, some are expensive, some are economical." His views have also tagged him by some women as "the biggest wolf in Hollywood."

MARGARET MACDONALD
Place of Birth: Joplin, Missouri.
Education: Joplin High School.
Status: Widow and the mother of Chuck.
Character: Bob's younger sister. She lives with Bob, cooks, and keeps house. Bob feels Margaret is young and attractive and should settle down again— "I keep telling her she should get married again, but does she listen to me? No." (Margret feels she is not ready for that step. She did have a brief romance with Paul Fonda [Lyle Talbot], Bob's air force buddy. Paul, an airline pilot, and Margaret later broke up, and Paul found romance with and married another woman, Betty Havilland [Dorothy Johnson].)
Relations: Tammy Johnson (Tammy Marihugh), Margaret's and Bob's niece.

CHUCK MACDONALD
Place of Birth: California.
Age: 16 (when the series begins).
Education: Hollywood High School (where he was on the ROTC drill team), Gridley College (majoring in premed).
Military: The National Guard (joined after graduating high school).

High School Girlfriend: Francine Williams (Diane Jergens).

College Girlfriend: Carole Henning (Olive Sturgess), a student at Beaumont College.

Hobbies: Girls. Girls. Girls.

Character: A teenage ladies' man (although he has a girlfriend) who wishes that whatever his Uncle Bob has (when it comes to women) can be inherited by a nephew. Although Margaret considers Bob a father to Chuck ("He lets us share his house and is putting Chuck through school"), she also worries about his upbringing, as "Chuck has been raised in an atmosphere of girls, girls, girls." Chuck plays the bongo drums and was undecided about his future until completing his service with the National Guard when he became interested in becoming a doctor.

JOSHUA "JOSH" COLLINS

Place of Birth: Joplin, Missouri.

Occupation: Retired (formally a photographer, owner of Josh Collins—Photography in Joplin).

Character: Grandpa, as he is called (Bob Cummings in a dual role), lives in a drafty old house his father built (and died in from pneumonia). He has an eye for the ladies, just like his grandson, Bob, and like Bob he can accurately guess their measurements. Although his age is not revealed (assumed to be in his late 70s), he is young at heart. He is a member of the Joplin Globetrotters basketball team, and although he has a roving eye for the ladies, he is romantically involved with the elderly Dixie Yates (Lurene Tuttle). Josh calls Bob "Young Rooster," Margaret "Mag Pie," and Chuck "Chuckie Boy."

CHARMAINE "SCHULTZY" SCHULTZ

Occupation: Bob's girl Friday.

Character: Little is revealed about Schultzy. She is plain-looking but determined to be the girl who marries Bob (whom she calls "Boss"). As she says, "I can't compete with the models on the sofa, but give me the kitchen and food and I'll land him." Schultzy will do whatever job Bob assigns her, no matter how unpleasant, to impress him, but it never dawns on Bob that she has romantic feelings for him—"I feel comfortable with her. Before Schultzy I would train girls only to lose them to marriage."

Relations: Bonita Granville as Bertha, Schultzy's cousin.

OTHER CHARACTERS

Harvey Helm (King Donovan), Bob's friend, the henpecked wholesale furniture salesman for the Gravener Furniture Company. He is married to Ruthie (Mary Lawrence), a former swimsuit model of Bob's (Carol, Chuck's girlfriend, is

Ruthie's niece). Harvey was Bob's copilot during World War II and calls Bob "Bobby Boy." Charlie Herbert plays their son, Tommy Helm. Pamela Livingston (Nancy Kulp) is Schultzy's friend, a dedicated member of the Bird Watchers' Society with eyes on Bob. Frank Crenshaw (Dick Wesson) is the military man (sailor) with a crush on Schultzy, Martha Randolph (Rose Marie) is Schultzy's husband-hunting friend, and Kay Michael (Lola Albright) is the actress Bob dated who threatened to end his bachelor ways.

Note: The series was originally broadcast as *The Bob Cummings Show* but has since become known by its syndicated title, *Love That Bob*. Some episodes in the syndicated package reflect the show's original title but with the original sponsor's tag deleted.

Make Room for Daddy/
The Danny Thomas Show
(ABC, 1953–1957; CBS, 1957–1964)

Cast: Danny Thomas (Danny Williams), Jean Hagen (Margaret Williams), Marjorie Lord (Kathy Williams), Sherry Jackson, Penny Parker (Terry Williams), Rusty Hamer (Rusty Williams), Angela Cartwright (Linda Williams).

Basis: The mostly home life of a nightclub entertainer (Danny Williams) whose work often leaves him little time to spend with his wife (Margaret, then Kathy) and children (Terry, Rusty, and Linda).

DANIEL "DANNY" WILLIAMS

Address: The Parkside Apartments (Apartment 1204, later 573) in Manhattan (ABC episodes), 505 East 56th Street, Apartment 542 (CBS episodes; also seen as 543, 642, and 781).

Telephone Number: Plaza 3-0198 (CBS episodes).

Occupation: Nightclub entertainer at the Copa Club in Manhattan (although in a 1957 episode, he calls the nightclub Club Rio). He also mentions that he worked at the 5100 Club in Chicago before the Copa Club and before that selling popcorn at Havermeyer's Carnival when he was 10 years old.

Place of Birth: Toledo, Ohio (Danny also says he was born in Deerfield, Michigan, but raised in Toledo).

Ancestry: Lebanese.

Education: Ursuline Academy (a Catholic school run by the nuns of the Ursuline Order). He later says he attended Woodward High School.

Favorite Reading Matter: The *Saturday Evening Post.*

Catchphrase: "Holy Toledo."

Activity: Playing golf.

Pet Dog (ABC episodes): Laddie.

Relations: Tonoose (Hans Conried), Danny's uncle; Steven (Tony Bennett), Danny's cousin.

Character: Enjoys smoking a cigar and spending time with his family (as he often works nights when the children are asleep and sleeps during the day). Danny is most often associated with the Manhattan-based Copa Club (owned by Charlie Halper [Sid Melton]) and gets a paycheck every Tuesday. Danny mentions that he was the first star produced by the Copa Club (he began his career there on the club's opening night). Although he is not seen enjoying the sport of fishing, he is seen reading a magazine called *Fisherman*; he is also said to enjoy golf and is also seen reading *Variety*. Danny dines at Lindy's restaurant (where a sandwich has been named after him—the Danny Williams—consisting of Swiss cheese and chicken on an onion roll). Kathy calls Danny "a meat and potatoes man," he dislikes spices on his food, and never eats a heavy meal before an opening show. Show business is in Danny's blood (having been in the business since he was a teenager), and when he is not working, he becomes impatient and restless (as Kathy says, "When Danny isn't working he is worse than a restless child"). He also likes "a little starch" in his shirts ("I like them soft"). Danny mentioned that he dropped

Standing: Sherry Jackson; seated (from left to right): Rusty Hamer, Angela Cartright, Danny Thomas, and Marjorie Lord. *CBS/Photofest © CBS*

out of high school (Woodward) "to rush into show business" and held jobs as a kid shining shoes, washing windows, and "hustling newspapers on cold, windy streets." He proposed to Kathy after 14 dates and claims he was raised in a family of 10 children.

MARGARET WILLIAMS
Occupation: Housewife.
Place of Birth: Baraboo, Wisconsin.
Maiden Name: Margaret Summers.
Former Job: Part-time waitress and piano player in a nightclub.
Relations: Julie Summers (Nana Bryant), Margaret's mother; her father was mentioned as being named Harry; Faye (Louise Lorimar), Margaret's aunt; Uncle Carl (Hans Conried), Margaret's uncle "who drank a lot and traveled with jugs of wine."
Character: The daughter of show business parents (Julie and Harry) who was often left in the care of her parents' friends, Mom and Pop Finch, while they toured the vaudeville circuit. Margaret married Danny when she was 17 years old, and they became the parents of Terry and Rusty. Margaret mentions that she met Danny, a struggling young comedian, when she was a waitress and he had come to Wisconsin to perform at her club. In another episode, however, Margaret mentions that she and Danny have known each other since they were children.

Note: After playing the role of Margaret for two years, actress Jean Hagen wanted to leave the series, and the concluding episode of the 1955 season ended with Danny's emotional talk with Terry and Rusty that their "mother had gone to Heaven." The following season found Danny as a widower struggling to raise two children with the help of his maid, Louise (Amanda Randolph). It was also during this time that the series became known as *The Danny Thomas Show.* Various actresses were brought on to date Danny and win over the affections of the children. Before the switch to CBS in the fall of 1957, Marjorie Lord, a widow with a young daughter named Linda (Lani Sorenson), was added to the cast as Kathy, a nurse Danny hires to care for Terry and Rusty when they are affected with measles. Marjorie Lord then became a regular as Danny's second wife.

KATHLEEN "KATHY" WILLIAMS
Occupation: Housewife.
Former Occupation: Receptionist, secretary, and nurse (a bachelor's degree from Columbia University; a nursing degree from Johns Hopkins). She was in charge of 500 soldiers during the Korean War.
Place of Birth: Peoria, Illinois (she later says Albany, New York).

Late Husband: Tom O'Hara (with whom she had Linda).

Maiden Name: Kathy Daly.

Education: Peoria High School, Illinois State College.

Activity: Playing tennis.

Nicknames: Kathy, Irish, Lover, and Clancy (as Danny calls her).

Relations: William Demarest as Kathy's father, John Daly; Tom Tully as Sean O'Hara, Kathy's uncle (on her late husband Tom's side); Charles Coburn, Kathy's grandpa; Madge Blake, Kathy's aunt; Noel Purcell as Francis Daly; J. G. Devlin as Shamus Daly (both Kathy's uncles); and Barbara Mullen as Kathy's aunt, Molly Daly.

Character: Although Kathy can make "a great pot roast" and is an excellent housekeeper and mother to her own daughter and stepchildren, she often yearns to spread her wings and experiment with something exciting (like singing with a band, which reflects her high school days when she and her girlfriends started their own band). To prove to Danny that she was capable of holding down a job, she took a position as an assistant editor at *Silhouette,* a fashion magazine. When Danny felt she was spending too much money, he got her a job with his agent, Phil Brokaw (played by Sheldon Leonard). She also did a TV commercial for Clean-O (arranged by Danny to dissuade Kathy from going into show business). Kathy can play the piano, is an excellent dancer, is always fashionably dressed, but is not always the easiest person to live with (as her father says, "You inherited your mother's Irish temper—and my good looks") when she becomes upset. In high school, Kathy was editor of her school newspaper.

Kathy and Danny married in 1957 and (along with their children) honeymooned in Las Vegas (where they occupied room 504 at the Sands Hotel). Kathy's introduction into the family was the most challenging part of her new life. Danny hails from a long line of Lebanese traditions, one of which involves new family members (such as wives and babies) being accepted into the family. In the United States, Danny's Uncle Tonoose (Hans Conried) is the unofficial (as Danny says) family "inspector." It is his job to either approve or disapprove them—being handed a cigar indicates that a male has been accepted, while "a pinch" on the rear is acceptance for women.

TERESA "TERRY" WILLIAMS

Character: The oldest of Danny's children (by Margaret). Before Kathy's arrival, Terry took over the responsibility of caring for the house. She is always fashionably dressed and well behaved and has her first job as a salesgirl at Miss Alman's Shop, a neighborhood clothing store. She was a Girl Scout (sold the most cookies in her troop—116 boxes) and had the Social Security number 540-29-2993. She first attended West Side High School (also given as Hamilton High School), then an unnamed college (where she was a member of the Alpha Beta Chi sorority). Annette Funicello was brought on to temporarily replace her as an exchange student (from Palermo, Italy) who came to live with the Williams family. At this point, Terry was written out but returned to marry Pat Hannigan (Pat Harrington Jr.), an up-and-coming comedian. Incidents in Terry's life changed on the CBS pilot *Make Room for Granddaddy* (September 14, 1969) when Terry is married to Bill Johnson (not seen), a serviceman stationed in Japan, and the mother of a six-year-old son (Michael). No explanation is given as to what happened to her original husband, Pat Hannigan. The pilot led to the 1970–1971 ABC series of the same title and found Danny and Kathy not only as grandparents but also caring for Michael when Terry joins Bill in Japan. Her first crush was on actor-singer Dean Martin.

RUSSELL "RUSTY" WILLIAMS

Character: Danny's son by Margaret. Born on February 15, 1947, he first attended P.S. 54 (later said to be P.S. 52) Elementary School, then Clairmont Junior High School, and finally West Side High School (he later marries Susan MacAdams [Jana Taylor]), the daughter of an army colonel he met during his enlistment in the army (seen on the NBC TV special *Make More Room for Daddy* on November 6, 1967). He was a Cub Scout (Den 3) and Boy Scout (Troop 44), and in 1956 he called himself "Elvis Earp," combining his fascination with singer Elvis Presley and the TV series *The Life and Legend of Wyatt Earp*. Rusty also experienced the "I don't love you" blues and ran away from home to begin a new life as an orphan at Miss Martin's Children's Home. While Rusty tolerated school, he felt its best parts were "recess, lunch and holidays." Rusty is somewhat of a wise guy, always responding to something with a smart remark, and had his first crush on a girl named Sylvia Watkins, played by Pamela Beaird (although in 1957 ABC episodes, Rusty had a girlfriend named Ruthie Mattson, played by Anna Maria Nanasi). Rusty is a member of the Little League (wherein Kathy is the official scorekeeper) and discovered four talented child singers: the Four Angels (and even arranged an appearance for them on *The Ed Sullivan Show*). He mentioned that in 1961, his allowance was 50 cents a week and in 1963 mentions that he would like to become a doctor.

LINDA WILLIAMS

Character: Kathy's daughter by her late husband Tom O'Hara. Linda was made younger (born in 1952) when she replaced Kathy's original daughter (who was seven years old in 1957 on ABC episodes). Linda shows promise as being a talented dancer (loves ballet) and attends P.S. 54 Elementary School.

She believes in Santa Claus and the Tooth Fairy and idolizes Rusty (to whom she has attached herself and does what he asks of her). She is a member of the Brownies Blue Birds Troop (of which Kathy is a den mother), is a cheerleader for Rusty's unnamed football team, and became "The Darling of Television" after she performed a song at the Copa Club and was signed to appear with Danny on a TV special. Linda receives an allowance of 50 cents a week and is learning from Rusty that money is everything. She is also picking up his bad habit of what Danny calls being "a blabbermouth." "Oh, you just make me so mad!" is her catchphrase. When Linda is first seen on ABC episodes, she is very mischievous and would put the blame on Rusty for everything she did wrong. Linda later attends West Side High School and a boarding school (college) in Connecticut (which was seen in the NBC TV special *Make More Room for Daddy* on February 14, 1965).

OTHER CHARACTERS
Gina Minnelli (Annette Funicello), the Italian exchange student Danny took in when Terry left to attend college (arranged by American Field Services, which arranges for foreign students to live with American families); Louise (Amanda Randolph), the Williamses' maid; Buforidina "Bunny" Halper (Pat Carroll), Charlie's wife. Uncle Tonoose has the nickname "Hashush-al-Kabaar" (Lebanese for "The Man Who Made a Monkey Out of a Camel") and claims the family history dates back to King Achmed the Unwashed. Tonoose is a very fussy eater and prefers goat cheese in a grape leaf. "Tonoose," he says, is Lebanese for "Anthony."

The Many Loves of Dobie Gillis
(CBS, 1959–1963)

Cast: Dwayne Hickman (Dobie Gillis), Bob Denver (Maynard G. Krebs), Sheila James (Zelda Gilroy), Tuesday Weld (Thalia Menninger), Steve Franken (Chatsworth Osborne Jr.), Frank Faylen (Herbert T. Gillis), Florida Friebus (Winnie Gillis), Yvonne Craig (Linda Sue Faversham), Annette Gorman (Amanda Jean Faversham).

Basis: High school "ladies' man" Dobie Gillis seeks that one special girl—although finding her means dating beauty after beauty and never realizing that his one true love is the girl he constantly avoids—Zelda Gilroy.

DOBIE GILLIS
Parents: Herbert T. and Winifred (Winnie) Gillis.
Address: 285 Norwood Street in the mythical Central City. Address also given as 285 Elm Street, 9th and Main, and 3rd and Elm.

Education: Central High School (one-half mile from his home), S. Peter Pryor
   Junior College (where he was second assistant editor of the school news-
   paper, the *Pryor Crier*). He also served a hitch in the army before college
   (platoon given as Company A, Company C, and finally Company Q).
Pet: Although never seen, Dobie mentions he has a dog named Spot.
After-School Hangout: Charlie Wong's Ice Cream Parlor (serving "31 Celestial
   Flavors").
Character: An average student (teachers say that if he applied himself, he could
   be brilliant). Girls are constantly on Dobie's mind, and he considers himself
   a thinker (devising ways to impress girls; he loves "beautiful, soft, round
   creamy girls" and "wants just one girl for his very own"). Unfortunately,
   Dobie always picks girls with "caviar tastes for his peanut butter wallet" and
   claims there is "a powerful force" standing between him and money—his
   stingy father.
Infatuation: Thalia Menninger, then Linda Sue Faversham (see below).
Relations to Dobie: Darryl Hickman as Davy Gillis, his older brother, and Roy
   Hemphill as Virgil T. Gillis, his cousin.

MAYNARD G. KREBS
Relationship: Dobie's best friend.
Address: 1343 South Elm Street.
Weekly Allowance: 35 cents.
Catchphrase: "You rang?"
Character: A beatnik who has poor school grades, avoids work, loves playing the
   bongo drums and jazz music, and hanging out at Riff Ryan's Music Store.
   He claims the "G" in his name stands for Walter and was turned down 46
   times in six years for his driver's license. He professes to have the world's
   largest collection of tinfoil and has a stuffed armadillo named Herman.
   "Delicatessen" is the largest word that Maynard knows, and his idea of great
   Americans includes General MacArthur, Admiral Dewey, and Captain Kangaroo (from the TV series of the same name). Watching the old Endicott
   Building being dismantled and watching workmen paint a new white line in
   the center of Elm Street appear to be his favorite activities. *The Monster That
   Devoured Cleveland* is his favorite horror movie (apparently the only film
   that plays at the Bijou Theater). He responds with "You Rang?" when his
   name is mentioned and has a panic attack when he hears the word "work."
   For Maynard, the commercials are the best part of a TV show (he thinks
   they are educational). Maynard can play the piano and always sits in the first
   row in a movie theater "because I always sit in the first row." Maynard calls
   Dobie "Good Buddy" and is not really attracted to girls like Dobie—"Not

me Big Daddy. I tried girls and it's nowhere. They spend my money, they won't kiss me good night and they giggle about me in the powder room. You [Dobie] try girls if you want to; I'm sticking to jazz" (Dizzy Gillespie is his favorite jazz musician). Every morning, while walking to school, Maynard trips over the trolley car tracks at 9th and Main Street.

Relations to Maynard: Kay Stewart as Maynard's mother, Alice Krebs (also called Ethel Krebs); Willis Bouchey as Maynard's father (first name not given); and Michael Pollard as Jerome Krebs, his cousin. Mentioned but not seen were Maynard's cousins Mopsy, Flopsy, and Cottontail.

THALIA MENNINGER

Character: A beautiful blonde who dated what appeared to be only the sons of wealthy families but became attracted to Dobie despite the fact "that he is the son of a cheap father." Thalia had high hopes that Dobie could make "oodles and oodles of money" to help support her family—"a mother who isn't getting any younger, a sister who married a loafer and a brother who is becoming a public charge." She attributes her father's condition to the money he spent on her braces and sending her to dancing school—"So I could be beautiful and graceful and charming and the way I am" (she considers Dobie "the fine, sweet sensitive boy who will never make a dime"). Although Dobie was unable to afford even one ounce of her favorite perfume ("MMMM" at $18 an ounce), Thalia kept returning to Dobie, hoping to one day improve him (one such way was trying to turn him into a pop singer). Dobie met Thalia for the first time at the Bijou Theater on Jackpot Night (for a drawing of $100). Later (second episode), Dobie and Thalia had already known each other, as they are classmates (in still a later episode, Thalia mentions that "Dobie has longed for me since he was in knee pants"). Though he loves Thalia, Dobie describes her as "the most hard hearted, greedy, grasping selfish conniving girl in the world." Thalia continually dumps Dobie but also continually comes back to him because she thinks he is something special (what that "special" is she has yet to figure out). Her favorite ice cream is Strawberry Won Ton Sundae (which she orders at the ice cream parlor).

Their relationship ended when the rich Milton Armitage (Warren Beatty) stole her heart and Thalia realized Dobie could never be the man of her dreams. The wealthy Milton considers himself "handsome, attractive, manly and cultured." When Warren Beatty left the series, aspects of his character were incorporated into his replacement, Chatsworth Osborne Jr. Doris Packer played both of their mothers. Milton was called "You Nasty Boy" by his mother and used the term "mice and rats" when something went wrong. Milton prided himself as being captain of the school's football team.

LINDA SUE FAVERSHAM

Character: Like Thalia, seeks to only marry money and, like Thalia, not for herself but to support her unemployable family. Linda Sue considers herself blessed with a "stunning body, perfect teeth, beautiful hair and a fabulous face"—her "equipment," as she calls it, is for only one purpose: "marry money and support her dismal relatives." Linda Sue also has an equally gorgeous younger sister, Amanda Jean, who has the same "fabulous features" and is being groomed by Linda Sue to marry money.

ZELDA GILROY

Character: A brilliant girl of modest means, not as sexy or pretty as the girls Dobie falls for but the girl who has a never-ending crush on him. It appears that Zelda is the only girl Dobie can get but doesn't want. Dobie sees Zelda as a nuisance, constantly tries to avoid her, and is forever saying, "Zelda, get off my back." Zelda doesn't see herself as a bother. She and Dobie grew up together (she even taught Dobie how to tie his shoelaces and play the guitar) and believes fate intended them to be man and wife. Dobie doesn't see this—but Zelda is determined to make him see things her way. She also believes Dobie loves her because when she wrinkles her nose, Dobie wrinkles his back at her (he insists it is only a reflex, not a sign of love). Zelda is the daughter of Walter and Edna Gilroy and has six siblings—all sisters. She believes because she is so smart is the reason Dobie is not attracted to her. She calls Dobie "Poopsie" (to which Dobie replies, "Now cut that out").

Relations to Zelda: Dabbs Greer as Walter Gilroy, her father, and Joan Banks as her mother, Edna Gilroy.

Zelda's Sisters (character names not given): Sherry Alberoni, Jeri Lou James, Larraine Gillespie, Judy Hackett, Marlene Willis, and Anna Maria Nanassi.

CHATSWORTH OSBORNE JR.

Relationship: Friend of Dobie and Maynard.

Residence: The 47-room Louis XIV home on the top of the hill with the broken glass embedded in the wall that surrounds it.

Catchphrase: "Mice and rats."

Character: The spoiled-rotten son of Clarissa Osborne and heir to the "fabulous Osborne National Bank empire." He is a friend of Dobie and Maynard's, but, strangely, neither Thalia nor Linda Sue found him the man of their dreams. He has type "R" blood (for royal) and is a member of the Down Shifters Club and president of the Silver Spoons Club (for snobs) at S. Peter Pryor Junior College. He dreams of attending Yale University, and his mother, constantly fed up with his antics, calls him "you nasty boy." He calls Dobie "Dobie Do" and his mother "Moms" and "Mumsey." When he needs his mother's help to get him out of a jam and she refuses to help him, Chatsworth throws a fit by lying down on the floor and holding his breath until he turns purple.

Relations to Chatsworth: Doris Packer as Clarissa Osborne, his mother; Lynn Loring as Edwina Kagel, his cousin, twice removed; Iris Mann as Sabrina Osborne, his cousin; and Barbara Babcock as Pamela Osborne, his cousin.

HERBERT AND WINNIE GILLIS

Dobie's parents, the owners of the Gillis Grocery Store (also seen as Gillis's Groceries). Dobie's antics, especially his refusal to work in the family store and his constant need for money, have Herbert utter, "I gotta kill that boy, I just gotta." Herbert is known as a cheapskate, and his refusal to most often give Dobie money for dates has Dobie saying, "I'm not only penniless, but dime-less, quarter-less and dollar-less."

During World War II, Herbert was a first sergeant "with the Good Conduct Medal" and is a member of Chapter 47 of the Benevolent Order of the Bison. He makes deliveries every afternoon at 4:00 p.m. Herbert first fell in love with Winnie in high school when she entered a beauty pageant (she finished 27th out of 29 contestants).

Relations to Winnie: Gordon Jones as Wilfred, her brother; Jeane Wood as Gladys, her sister; and Esther Dale as Winnie's mother (name not given). Mentioned but not seen were Herbert's brother (Duncan's father), Tim, and Winnie's sister, Margaret (who lives in Cleveland).

Note: The series is also known as *Dobie Gillis* (its 1960–1963 title). In the CBS pilot, *Whatever Happened to Dobie Gillis?* (May 10, 1977), Dobie is married to Zelda and the father of a teenage son, Georgie (Stephen Paul). Maynard is now an entrepreneur, and Dobie and his father, Herbert, have an expanded Gillis Grocery Store.

Martin Kane, Private Eye
(NBC, 1949–1954)

Cast: William Gargan (Martin Kane, 1949–1951), Lloyd Nolan (Martin Kane, 1951–1952), Lee Tracy (Martin Kane, 1952–1953), Mark Stevens (Martin Kane, 1953–1954).

Basis: A private investigator's relentless pursuit of justice in New York City.

MARTIN KANE

Business: Martin Kane—private investigator.

Office: In the Wood Building in zone 20 (ZIP codes had not yet come into being).

Fees: Based on the case; up to $500.

Vice: Pipe smoker.

Tobacco Brand: Old Briar Pipe Tobacco.

Hangout: McMann's Tobacco Shop (15 cents a pouch for tobacco).

Shop Phone Number: El Dorado 5-4098.

Character: Rugged, two-fisted, and not afraid to use a gun. He incorporates determination and force of character to achieve results. While he does have an eye for the ladies, he often refers to them as "Doll Face" or "Sweetheart" (as opposed to just calling them by their given names). While he does work with the police, especially Captain Burke (Frank M. Thomas) and Lieutenant Grey Redford (King Calder) of the Homicide Squad, it is basically to help his case along as opposed to helping the police collar a suspect first. Kane appears to be somewhat of a loner and often discusses cases with Tucker McMann, the tobacco shop owner he calls "Hap" (Walter Kinsella). Hap does double duty—providing information to Kane and pitching the sponsor's (the United States Tobacco Company) products—Old Briar and Dill's Best Pipe Tobacco, Encore Filter Tip Cigarettes, and Sano Cigarettes (no filter tip). In 1953–1954 episodes, Hap was replaced by the new shop owner, Don Morrow, who played himself.

Maverick
(ABC, 1957–1963)

Cast: James Garner (Bret Maverick), Jack Kelly (Bart Maverick), Roger Moore (Beau Maverick), Robert Colbert (Brent Maverick).

Basis: Western saga of the Maverick brothers (Bret and Bart) and their cousin (Beau).

Bret and Bart Maverick are not only brothers and gentlemen gamblers who roam the Old West in search of rich prey but they are also cowards, and although it against the nature of a Maverick to involve themselves in the plight of others, they often find that when a beautiful woman is involved, tradition takes a backseat. Bret and Bart (as well as Beau) are self-centered, unconventional, and untrustworthy—but they do have a knack for outsmarting con men (and women) and the law (when necessary).

Bret and Bart were born in Texas and served as Confederates during the Civil War. However, a Maverick is not one to really get into fighting (as the theme states—"smooth as a handle on a gun"), and when they were captured by the enemy, they switched sides and joined the Union (to them, anything was better than spending time in jail, here meaning a Union prison camp). But joining the Union was no free ticket. As "Galvanized Yankees" (as Bart puts it), they were assigned duty away from the battlefields to keep the peace between Indians and settlers out west. Meanwhile, at this same time, Cousin Beau brought extreme disgrace to the name of Maverick when he became a hero. The Mavericks were raised by a stern father (Beauregard "Pappy" Maverick), and he instilled in his sons not only a con-artist genius but cowardice as well. When Pappy learned of Beau's (his nephew's) "disgrace," he branded him "the white sheep of the family" and banished him to England until he could once again tarnish the Maverick name (which also accounts for Beau's English accent).

But in all honesty, Beau claims, he became a hero by accident. Beau also served with the Confederacy and was also captured. But unlike his brothers, Beau used his genius to befriend a Union general and avoid harsh treatment. While Beau and the general engaged in a game of poker, Confederate troops attacked the camp. After losing the hand to Beau, the general exclaimed, "Son, I give up." Confederates mistook what was said and credited Beau with the capture—a hero to the Confederacy, a disgrace to Pappy, and five years of suffering until he was able to tarnish his "good name" and come back into Pappy's good graces.

A Maverick's serious vice is curiosity—it could get them killed. Once something intrigues them, they will not let it rest until they figure out what is going on. Little Bent, Texas, is home to Bret and Bart, and it is against a Maverick's principles to drink alone—or lose at a game of poker (as the theme states, "Natchez to New Orleans, livin' on Jacks and Queens"). A town sheriff or marshal (or even a deputy) is not a Maverick's best friend. A Maverick is not fast on the draw, and if there is a way to get out of a situation without a gunfight, a Maverick will find a way to do it. While marriage is the furthest thing from a Maverick's mind, Bret promised Pappy that on his 38th birthday he would find a wife and raise 12 Mavericks. Not working for money but winning it at cards keeps a Maverick going. While Bart whistles to think and Bret enjoys a good cigar, Bart also states, "Sometimes it frightens me what I'll do for money." Bret calls Bart "Brother Bart."

Each Maverick carries a $1,000 bill (which they pin to their shirt pocket) given to them by Pappy—money to be used for emergencies only and numerous "words of wisdom" from Pappy (for example, "Never hold a kicker and never draw to an inside straight"; "As my Pappy would say, no use crying over spilled

James Garner and Jack Kelly as brothers Bret and Bart Maverick.
ABC/Photofest © ABC

milk; it could have been whiskey"; "As my Pappy would say, there are worse things in life than being broke—but he don't know of any"; "As my Pappy would say, stay clear of weddings as one of them is liable to be yours").

While poker is their livelihood and money is their hobby, money is not always counted in the winnings. Bret had won a half-share in a saloon and Bart the most unusual pet—a camel named Fatima. To trip up a card shark, Bret likes to deal the cards (which is not always pleasing to the shark).

In addition to outlaws, Indians, and the law, another threat to Bret and Bart was Samantha "Sam" Crawford (Diane Brewster), a beautiful con artist who was also as clever and cunning as the Mavericks. A northern girl at heart, Sam faked a southern accent and used, besides her genius at the con, her feminine wiles to acquire money. Richard Long as Gentleman Jack Darby and Efrem Zimbalist Jr. as Dandy Jim Buckley had recurring roles as gamblers who also sought easy money. On-screen, Pappy is credited as "Pappy . . . ?" (actually James Garner in a dual role); Jack Kelly also played Pappy's brother, Bentley Maverick (in the episode "Pappy").

Meet Corliss Archer
(CBS, 1951–1952; Syndicated, 1954–1955)

Cast (1951–1952): Lugene Sanders (Corliss Archer), Fred Shields (Harry Archer), Frieda Inescort (Janet Archer), Bobby Ellis (Dexter Franklin).

Cast (1954–1955): Ann Baker (Corliss Archer), John Eldredge (Harry Archer), Mary Brian (Janet Archer), Bobby Ellis (Dexter Franklin).

Basis: Life's everyday mishaps as encountered by a pretty teenage girl named Corliss Archer.

CORLISS ARCHER

Address: 1214 Sycamore Road; later 32 Oak Street.

Age: 16 (then 17 years old).

Date of Birth: June 9, 1935.

Height: 5 feet, 2½ inches.

Weight: 105 pounds.

Parents: Harry and Janet Archer.

Occupation: High school student.

School: City High School (where she is a sophomore); also called Central High School and Jefferson High School.

Allowance: $1.00 a week.

Favorite Breakfast: Two eggs, toast, orange juice.

Favorite Dinner: Lasagna.

Catchphrase: "Golly."

Favorite Section of the Newspaper: The funnies.

Favorite Place to Shop for Clothes: Benson's Department Store.

Favorite Doll: A Betsy doll.

Pet: Veronica (a dog).

Jobs: Selling lemonade, collecting empty bottles for their deposits, newspaper delivery girl.

Boyfriend: Dexter Franklin (whom she hopes to mold in the image of her father).

Nemesis: Betty Campbell, the girl she fears is out to steal Dexter away from her ("I just know that scatterbrain is putting on acts to woo the boys").

Favorite Movie Star: Gregory Peck ("He's so dreamy").

Nickname for Her Father: "Daddy Angel" (when she wants something); "Daddy Dear" (when Corliss is just being herself).

Character: Corliss lives in a small suburban town (called only "City" or "Our Town") and has a knack not only for finding trouble but also for creating it. As times change, Corliss wishes her father would increase her allowance but he won't ("A dollar doesn't go far these days"). Corliss would like to join school clubs but finds she is ill equipped to do so (for example, she tried joining the Glee Club but was told "that if I sang with the Glee Club there would be no glee in the Glee Club"). Her singing has also been described as "who's beating that poor horse to death?"

Corliss realizes that she is prone to encounter mishaps but can't for the life of her figure out why, as she thinks she is "cursed." She believes it may have begun when she was three years old and decided to wear her bowl of oatmeal as a hat, causing her mother to scold her and then make her clean up the mess. Like a female Dennis the Menace, Corliss doesn't mean to cause trouble, but her good intentions always backfire. While life seems to be against Corliss, she also has a knack for dropping the toothpaste tube cap down the drain.

DEXTER FRANKLIN

Age: 16.

School: City High School (where he is a sophomore).

Address: 131 Maple Street.

Catchphrase: "Holy cow."

Favorite Movie Star: Marilyn Monroe.

Character: Money-wise, Dexter shares Corliss's woes ("I have an allowance that rattles. I wish I could get one that rustles"). Dexter is, as Corliss calls him, "a meat and potatoes man," and his one talent appears to be drinking a bottle of soda with one breath through a straw. Dexter owns a hot rod with a sign posted on it: "Taxi Lady? Ride in Style. Rates Are Low—A Kiss a Mile."

Relations: In 1954–1955 episodes, Ken Christy and Vera Marshe played Dexter's father and mother.

HARRY AND JANET ARCHER

Character: Harold, called Harry, is a private practice lawyer ("Harold Archer, Attorney-at-Law") and has been married to Janet for 18 years. Janet worked for Harry as his secretary for two years before they tied the knot. Harry is a very patient man and does manage to resolve the situations created by Corliss. He often wishes he had the same patience when it comes to some of his clients (who appear to be eccentrics, for example, Luella Grummond [Doris Packer], a wealthy client who will not invest in a stock until she consults a fortune-teller). Janet is described by Harry as "a remarkable woman. She is not only attractive and intelligent, but she is also a wonderful housekeeper and an extremely talented cook." As for Dexter, he is trying to get on Harry's good side because "If I and Corliss marry, we may want to live here one day."

Meet Millie
(CBS, 1952–1956)

Cast: Elena Verdugo (Millie Bronson), Florence Halop (Bertha Bronson), Marvin Kaplan (Alvin Prinzmetal), Ross Ford (Johnny Boone Jr.), Earle Ross, Roland Winters (John Boone Sr.).

Basis: A Manhattan secretary (Millie) seeks the man of her dreams—with a little help from her matchmaking mother (Bertha).

MILLIE BRONSON

Address: 137 West 41st Street (Apt. 3-B), a brownstone in Manhattan.

Rent: $55 (1952), then $65 (1953), a month.

Place of Birth: Brooklyn, New York.

Age: 21.

Occupation: Secretary (to investment broker Johnny Boone Jr. in Boone Investments, a company owned by his father, John Boone Sr. [Earle Ross, then Roland Winters]). The company is also called J. R. Boone and Son.

Education: P.S. 58, Central High School, Manhattan Junior College.

Character: Millie is a very pretty young woman who lives with her widowed mother, Bertha, in a two-bedroom apartment. She was born in 1931 and raised during the Great Depression. Her childhood was difficult, as money was tight, and for her and other children her own age, luxuries (like a candy bar) were most often not possible. Her father struggled to earn just enough money to get by, and by 1939 the family saw better times when her mother was able to acquire a part-time day job (as a seamstress) while Millie attended school. Two years later, shortly after the start of the U.S. involvement in World War II, Millie's life would again change, this time for the worse when her father, a soldier stationed in Europe, was killed in action. Bertha managed to provide for herself and Millie, and Millie again found a stable life. While Millie had dreams of pursuing a glamorous career, she felt the need to help with finances and acquired a job after school (college) as a part-time secretary at Boone Investments. When the secretary to Johnny Boone resigned to get married, a full-time position opened, and Millie was promoted to fill the position. It was also a life-changing promotion for Millie, as she had become infatuated with her boss and now found herself working full-time with him. But Millie felt she was a common girl (below his social scale) and had little chance of marrying him. Fate intervened when her mother learned about her crush and set her goal to bring the two together (which eventually occurred, somewhat due to Bertha's meddling, as the series progressed).

OTHER CHARACTERS

Bertha, Millie's mother, is often called "Mama." She is 48 years old (when the series begins), but she tells people she is 37; in some episodes, she claims she is "48 minus 10 minus 5." While Millie is an only child, Mama says that if she had had a second daughter, she would have named her Gwendolyn. Mama cares for the house while Millie works, and she and Millie vacation each year at a resort called Live Right Lodge (although in 1956, Millie and Mama were seen vacationing in Texas at the Weems Cattle Ranch). Mama believes there are two types of men: "the type that want to settle down with a wife and the type that wants to enjoy life." She also compares relationships to baseball: "My daughter goes steady with a foul ball" (because Johnny will not propose to Millie). Millie states simply, "I love him and that's the only thing that counts." In a dream sequence, Millie and Johnny did marry—but it was only a dream.

Alfred Prinzmetal, Millie and Mama's friend, claims that "it all started the day I was born. My father said he wanted a girl and my mother said she wanted a boy. I was born and they were both disappointed." He lives with his parents but claims he can't get along with them, especially his father. Alfred, who also claims his life is depressing, seems unemployable, and his current "occupation" is standing in line at the unemployment office. Although he considers himself "a painter, sculptor and poet," he has tried everything—from stock clerk to salesman to soda jerk—but failure is the only thing he says he can accomplish. He has a pet parrot (Irving) that won't talk for him, and he likes girls but doesn't understand them ("I'll never understand women. They're too complicated. I'll wait until there is something else to marry"). Alfred's biggest hope is to one day build up enough courage to leave home and find his own apartment. Despite the fact that he and his parents apparently do not get along, his mother does cater to his peculiar wants—like starched socks ("So they can stand up in my dresser drawer") and strange eating habits (like breakfast at lunchtime or dinner for breakfast).

Johnny Boone's father, John Boone (called "Pop"), believes in the old saying, "There is a sucker born every minute." While Pop is a shrewd businessman, he redirects the phrase (said by P. T. Barnun and referring to people and a way to relieve them of their money) to refer to women and how they hook men into marrying them (as Pop is henpecked and at his wife's beck and call). Isabel Randolph played his wife.

Note: The series is based on the radio program of the same title that starred Audrey Totter as Millie.

The Mickey Mouse Club
(ABC, 1955–1959)

Cast: The Original Mouseketeers (1955–1956): Nancy Abbatte, Sharon Baird, Billie Jean Beanblossom, Bobby Burgess, Lonnie Burr, Tommy Cole, Johnny Crawford, Dennis Day, Dickie Dodd, Mary Espinosa, Annette Funicello, Darlene Gillespie, Judy Harriett, Dallas Johann, John Lee Johann, Bonnie Lou Kern, Carl "Cubby" O'Brien, Karen Pendleton, Paul Petersen, Mickey Rooney Jr., Tim Rooney, Mary Lynn Satori, Bronson Scott, Michael Smith, Ronnie Steiner, Mark Sutherland, Doreen Tracy, Don Underhill.

Cast: Second-Season Mouseketeers (1956–1957): The above plus Sherry Allen, Eileen Diamond, Cheryl Holdridge, Charley Laney, Larry Larsen, Jay Jay Solari, Margene Storey.

Cast: Third-Season Mouseketeers (1957–1958): Don Agrati, Sharon Baird, Bobby Burgess, Lonnie Burr, Tommy Cole, Bonnie Lynn Fields, Annette Funicello, Darlene Gillespie, Cheryl Holdridge, Linda Hughes, Carl "Cubby" O'Brien, Karen Pendleton, Lynn Ready, Doreen Tracy.

Cast: Fourth-Season Mouseketeers (1958–1959): Annette Funicello, Tim Considine, and Tommy Kirk (but in repeat segments, as the Mouseketeers had been disbanded and the program consisted of edited material from the prior seasons).

Basis: A group of talented children (the Mouseketeers) entertain through songs, dances, and skits.

"Who's the leader of the club that's made for you and me?" signaled the start of *The Mickey Mouse Club*, a daily hour-long (later half-hour) program of music, songs, serials, educational features, and cartoons—but most of all, a group of talented children called the Mouseketeers. While the animated Mickey Mouse (voice of Jim MacDonald) served as the official host, it was the live-action host, Jimmie Dodd, and his cohost, Roy Williams, who actually conducted the daily festivities. A third adult, appearing mostly in bit parts with the Mouseketeers in sketches, was Bob Amsberry from 1955 to 1957.

The sight of Mickey Mouse seated at a piano meant it was Monday and "Fun with Music Day." Tuesday found Mickey in a tuxedo and preparing for "Guest Star Day." A flying carpet carrying Mickey (attired in a sorcerer's outfit) meant Wednesday's "Anything Can Happen Day." Thursday's "Circus Day" found Mickey attired as a ringmaster. And "Talent Round-Up Day" was the Friday theme with Mickey dressed as a cowboy.

Each program was geared to a specific theme, and each had its own song (for example, "Today is Tuesday, you know what that means, we're gonna have a special guest, so get out the brooms, sweep the place clean . . . 'cause Tuesday is Guest Star Day"). Wednesday, first called "Stunt Day," had the song "To-day is the day that is full of surprises; nobody knows what is going to happen, 'cause Wednesday is Anything Can Happen Day." Anything Can Happen Day featured several Mouseketeers in specific outfits during the lengthy day song: Bobby (riding a unicycle), Sharon (Indian maiden), Dennis (pneumatic street drill operator), Cheryl (bird in a gilded cage), Lonny (cowboy), Doreen (bal-lerina), Tommy (fireman), Darlene (dancer), Jay Jay (Keystone Cop), Annette (1920s flapper), Cubby (a rabbit who pulls a magician out of his hat), Karen (marionette), Roy (marionette master), and Jimmie (astronaut).

Guest-star day featured up-and-coming performers (like Carol Lynley), musical groups (like the Firehouse Five Plus Two), and established performers (for example, Judy Canova).

"Time to twist our Mousekedial to the right and left with a great big smile; this is the way we get to see a mouse cartoon for you and me. Meeska, Mooseka, Mouseketeer, Mouse Cartoon Time now is here" (a door to the Mickey Mouse Treasure Mine would open, and a Disney cartoon would be seen).

"From the four corners of the Earth; from across the seven seas, the stories of today for the leaders of tomorrow" signaled the start of "The Mickey Mouse Club Newsreel" (reported by Hal Gibney). "Fun with a Camera" was a segment with photographer Earl Kyser teaching the Mouseketeers various aspects of photography. Other segments included the animated Jiminy Cricket (voice of Cliff Edwards) in safety segments for children and "Sooty and His Friend Harry Corbett" (Harry is the straight man for his nonspeaking puppet Sooty, who plays songs on his electric organ).

Jimmie Dodd, who played the Mouseguitar, especially made by the Mattel Toy Company, concluded each show with "Words of Wisdom" (a short speech telling children what is right from what is wrong) followed by the Mouseketeers singing, "Now it's time to say goodbye to all our company. M-I-C . . . K-E-Y . . . M-O-U-S.Eeeeeeee."

Perhaps the best-remembered parts of the program were the various serials that were an integral part of the program. These were the following:

Adventure in Dairyland. Annette Funicello and Sammy Ogg as themselves and representing *The Mickey Mouse Club*, learn about the operation of a dairy farm by visiting the Sunny Acres Dairy Farm in Wisconsin. It included the antics of Moochie McCandless (Kevin Corcoran), the mischievous young son of the farm owners, Jim and Linda MacCandless (Herb Newcombe and Mary Lu Delmonte).

The Adventures of Clint and Mac. A mystery in which Clint Rogers (Neil Wolfe), an American boy living in England, and his friend, Alistair MacIntosh (Jonathan Bailey), attempt to solve a crime—the theft of the original manuscript of *Treasure Island*.

Animal Autobiography. Edited segments from Disney's true life adventure films that explore the animal kingdom.

Annette. Annette Funicello as a teenager attempting to make friends in a new town after she moves in with her aunt and uncle (Sylvia Field and Richard Deacon).

Border Collie. Hamilton County, a small southern Illinois town, provides the backdrop for a story about Rod Brown (Bobby Evans) and his efforts to train a Scottish Border Collie named Scamp for competition in a local dog show.

The Boys of the Western Sea. A Russian-produced film (edited into a serial) about a teenage boy named Per (Kield Benzen) and his struggles to support his family (as a fisherman) after his father's death.

Children of the World. Two-part serial that explores in the first part life in the Arctic as seen through the eyes of an Eskimo boy (Makaluk), and in the second life in Siam through the eyes of a young boy named Pok (appearing as himself).

Christmas 'Round the World. Seasonal program wherein various Mouseketeers narrate scenes of how Christmas is celebrated around the world. Annette Funicello narrates the 1956–1957 episodes.

Corky and White Shadow. Darlene Gillespie as a small-town girl who, with her dog White Shadow, attempts to help her sheriff father (Buddy Ebsen) apprehend an escaped outlaw.

Danish Correspondent. Life in Denmark is explored by correspondent Lotte Waver.

The Eagle Hunters. Two boys (Kent Durden and Gary Hoffman) are seen in a narrated program (by Tommy Kirk) as they hunt for Jupiter, a golden eagle.

English Correspondent. A look at England with Dick Metzger as the guide-correspondent.

The First Americans. Iron Eyes Cody narrates and Tony Nakina hosts a program that explores Indian lifestyles and history.

The Hardy Boys and the Mystery of the Applegate Treasure. Adaptation of the "Hardy Boys" stories with Tim Considine and Tommy Kirk as Frank and Joe Hardy, the sons of world-famous detective Fenton Hardy (Russ Conway). Frank and Joe attempt to solve the mysterious disappearance of pirate treasure from the estate of old man Silas Applegate (Florenz Ames). *Additional Cast:* Carole Ann Campbell (Iola Morton), Sarah Selby (Gertrude Hardy), Donald MacDonald (Perry Robinson), Robert Foulk (Jackley), Arthur Shields (Boles).

The Hardy Boys and the Mystery of Ghost Farm. A second serial that relates the efforts of Joe and Frank Hardy to solve the mystery of a farm supposedly haunted by a ghost. *Cast:* Tim Considine (Frank Hardy), Tommy Kirk (Joe Hardy), Carole Ann Campbell (Iola Morton), Russ Conway (Fenton Hardy), Sarah Selby (Gertrude Hardy), John Baer (Eric Pierson), Hugh Sanders (Mr. Binks), Yvonne Lime (Gloria Binks), Bob Amsberry (Sam).

Italian Correspondent. Annette Funicello hosts a tour of Italy, the home of her ancestors.

Japanese Correspondent. Japan is viewed through the eyes of a young Japanese American boy (George Nagata).

Junior Safari to Africa. Annette Funicello and Tommy Kirk host screenings of life in the Kruger Game Park in Africa.

Let's Go. Alvy Moore reports on the unusual occupations some people have.

Mexican Correspondent. A tour of Mexico is seen by correspondents Gabriel Lopez and Andy Velasquez.

A Mousekatour of Samoa. Annette Funicello and Tommy Kirk team up again to explore the South Pacific island of Samoa.

San Juan River Expedition. Alvy Moore narrates a serial about a trip down the San Juan River by a group of explorers.

The Secret of Mystery Lake. Naturalist Bill Richards (George Fenneman) and his guide, Lanie Thorne (Gloria Marshall), explore the wonders of Real Foot Lake in Tennessee.

Sierra Pack Trip. A tour of Yosemite National Park with Chris Brown. Alvy Moore narrates.

Spin and Marty. Two teens, Spin Evans (Tim Considine) and Marty Markham (David Stollery), share mishaps together as campers at the Triple R Ranch, a summer boys' camp. Jim Logan (Roy Barcroft) is the ranch head; Bill Burnett (Harry Carey Jr.) is the counselor. Other campers are Ambitious (B. G. Norman), Joe (Sammy Ogg), George (Joe Wong), and Speckle (Tim Hartnagel). J. Pat O'Malley played Perkins, the rich Marty's guardian, and Lennie Geer was Ollie, the camp cook.

The Further Adventures of Spin and Marty. Events in the lives of Spin and Marty are continued in a story that finds them competing for the affections of two very pretty Circle H Girls Ranch campers: Annette (Annette Funicello) and Darlene (Darlene Gillespie). Joyce Holden plays Helen Adams, the head of the girls' camp (which is across the lake from the Triple R).

The New Adventures of Spin and Marty. Spin and Marty attempt to stage a variety show to pay for damages caused by Marty's jalopy when it ran into the ranch house. The cast from the prior two serials reprise their roles.

What I Want to Be. Two 10-year-old children, Pat Morrow and Duncan Richardson, join *Mickey Mouse Club* reporter Alvy Moore for a look at the airline industry.

Mike Hammer

(Syndicated, 1957–1959)

Cast: Darren McGavin (Mike Hammer).
Basis: A hard-boiled private detective tackles cases for clients in New York City. Based on the character created by Mickey Spillane.

MICHAEL "MIKE" HAMMER

Business: Mike Hammer, private detective.
Business Address: Undisclosed (he rents room 812 of a building located in Manhattan).
Home Address: A hotel on West 47th Street.
Main Source of Research: The newspaper morgue of the *Chronicle* at 220 East 42nd Street (the actual address of the New York *Daily News*, which was used for the series).
Character: A loner out to battle injustice to make a buck. He has an eye for the ladies (as people say, "Watch it Mike, your fangs are showing"). Mike is tough (even with women). He calls the fairer sex "Doll" or "Dish" and will go out of his way to help a beautiful damsel in distress (even if it means dispensing with his fee). Mike uses force (his fists) to get results and considers roughing up a suspect a social call. He dishes out his own brand of justice—violence—and gets away with it. Although his friend, Patrick "Pat" Chambers (Bart Burns), a captain with the Homicide Division of the New York Police Department, should arrest him for all the laws he breaks, he doesn't, as working with Mike often nets him the criminal he is seeking.

Note: Brian Keith was originally cast as Mike Hammer but was dropped when it was felt he was not right for the role.

The Millionaire

(CBS, 1955–1960)

Cast: Marvin Miller (Michael Anthony), Paul Frees (voice of John Beresford Tipton).
Basis: What happens to people who receive an anonymous gift of $1 million tax-free dollars.

A man, seated behind a large desk in a moderately furnished office, speaks: "My name is Michael Anthony. For many years I was the executive secretary to the late John Beresford Tipton. He was one of the very few men who ever earned, by the use of his phenomenal brain, a fortune that ran into the billions of dollars. Among my duties was the unique job of delivering one million dollars which Mr. Tipton frequently gave away tax free to a total stranger."

Of the 2.5 billion people populating the world in 1955, only 19 were worth $500 million or more. One such man was John Beresford Tipton. Tipton (never fully seen) lived a life of treasured seclusion and conducted his business activities from Silverstone, his 60,000-acre estate. Here, he indulged in many hobbies, the most unusual of which began when his doctor ordered him to rest and find a means of relaxation.

Mr. Tipton, seated in his study, is toying with one of his ivory chess figures when he sends for his executive secretary, Michael Anthony. "You sent for me sir?" "You know Mike," Tipton says, "these chessmen were the first luxury I ever allowed myself. . . . I decided to make my hobby a chess game with human beings. . . . I'm going to choose a number of people for my chessmen and give them each a million dollars. The bank will issue the check. . . . No one is to ever know that I am the donor, I want a complete report on what happens to each person's life in writing."

After Mr. Tipton's death, the will instructed Michael Anthony to reveal the files of people, selected by a means known only to Mr. Tipton, who were mysteriously presented with a tax-free cashier's check for $1 million.

John Beresford Tipton issued 206 checks for $1 million each (drawn on the Gotham City Trust and Savings Bank). His unique hobby was related to the subject of human nature. "Every subject in his vast store of knowledge was a close analysis and was always related to the behavior and destiny of man." Each check recipient must sign a document agreeing never to reveal the exact nature of the gift or its amount. Spouses can be told, but telling anyone else results in forfeiture of any remaining monies. The program's catchphrases were "You sent for me, Sir" (Mike) and "Mike, our next millionaire" (Tipton, handing Mike a check).

On December 19, 1978, CBS presented an unsold pilot film called *The New Millionaire*. Robert Quarry played Michael Anthony in a revised version of the series. Prior to this, NBC aired an unsold pilot film called *If I Had a Million* on December 31, 1973. It was based on the 1932 feature film of the same title (wherein an elderly man, not wanting his greedy relatives to have his money, chose to give it away to total strangers by selecting names from a phone book). For TV, Peter Kastner played a wealthy man who decides to give million-dollar checks to people he has never met (at the local library, he would randomly choose a name from a phone book and deliver to that person a check for $1 million).

Mister Peepers
(NBC, 1952–1955)

Cast: Wally Cox (Robinson Peepers), Marion Lorne (Bernice Gurney), Tony Randall (Harvey Weskit), Patricia Benoit (Nancy Remington), Georgann Johnson (Marjorie "Marge" Bellows), Joseph Foley (Gabriel Gurney), Ruth McDevitt (Ma Peepers), Jenny Egan (Agnes Peepers).

Basis: A gentle, shy, and kind schoolteacher and his experiences as the General Science teacher at Jefferson Junior High School in Jefferson City.

ROBINSON PEEPERS

Place of Birth: Williamsport, a town outside of Jefferson City (it is a seven-hour bus ride from Williamsport to Jefferson City; five hours by car).

Address: 312 B Street, Williamsport (according to Robinson, "B Street is between A and C Streets"). His family moved to Williamsport in 1918.

Age: 26 (born in 1926).

Nickname: Sonny (as called by his mother). Ma Peepers calls Agnes "Sister."

Mother: Called only Ma Peepers. Mrs. F. R. Peepers is the name seen on the mailbox. His father, presumed to be deceased, owned a hardware store. Ma Peepers constantly worries that if Robinson doesn't wear his hat during the winter months, he will get an ear infection (something he had as a child).

Sister: Agnes Peepers, a teacher at the Jefferson Observatory; later a science instructor in Chicago. Robinson also mentions that his sister was married and moved to Ohio, where she and her husband own a restaurant. When a very small planetoid was discovered at the observatory, it was named after Agnes and called "Agnitoid."

Education: Williamsport Grammar and High Schools; Upstate Teaching College (Class of 1948; the college was founded in 1896; Robinson shared a dorm room with Rock Burns).

Current Teaching Assignment: Jefferson Junior High School in Jefferson City (the address of which is given as Jefferson Junior High, Jefferson City). Blue and chartreuse are the school colors, and Jefferson High, located in Lincoln County, houses 478 students. It is mentioned that Lincoln County supports 433 high schools.

Classroom: 2A.

Number of Students: 18.

Childhood Activity: Member of the Boy Foresters (a Boy Scout–like organization).

Current Residence: Mrs. Murchison's Rooming and Boarding House.

Rent: $13 a week.

Salary: $43 a week ($6.10 of which is taken out for federal withholding tax).

Social Security Number: 118-20-5961.

Hobbies: Bird watching, botany, rocks, butterflies. As a child, he collected bottle caps.

Favorite Game: Chess.

Award: A bronze bird for an article ("The Sparrow Speaks His Mind") for *Bird* magazine (located at 4350 Lexington Avenue in New York City). He also writes articles for *Petal and Stem* magazine (where he was offered a $20,000-a-year job but rejected it, figuring that in the long run his current salary was sufficient).

Jefferson High School Activity: Organized "The Fungus Watchers" (involves his class in exploring the world of fungus because "Fungus is fun") and "The Fall Guys" (a class project that explores nature in the outdoors in October, November, and December).

Current Affiliation: The International Society for Root Nourishment.

Phobia: A fear of high places.

Favorite Eatery: The Drug Store (across the street from the school, where Robinson enjoys breakfast and lunch).

Favorite Sandwich: Peanut butter and butter.

Military Career: Varies by episodes. He is first said to be an army private who received an honorable discharge for having poor eyesight. Next, he was said to be an army corporal and finally a PFC (private first class).

Army Serial Number (as a PFC): 1313658.

Army Camps: He served two years. He did his basic training at Camp Cullesters and was then assigned to Camp Corder, then Camp Kilmer. At one point, he was the camp's "Greenish Supervisor" (in charge of vegetables).

Girlfriend: Nancy Remington, the county nurse (who later has an office, the Dispensary, at Jefferson Junior High). They became engaged in the episode of April 25, 1954, and married in the episode of May 23, 1954. Following their honeymoon at the Concord Hotel and Resort in Indian country, Robinson and Nancy rented the top floor of Mrs. Gurney's large home. The series concluded with Robinson hoping for a raise in salary and prepared to teach at the Angola Military Academy if the school board refused to raise his pay (as he and Nancy were now expecting a baby). Prior to Nancy, Robinson's love interest was Royala Deen (played by Norma Crane), the school's music appreciation teacher. Ernest Truex and Sylvia Field played Nancy's parents, called Pa and Ma Remington (Pa was a real estate agent, a member of the Lancers of the Southern Star Lodge, and eager to catch an elusive trout called "Old Colonel").

Locker Door Ritual: To open his locker at school, Robinson goes through the following ritual: he first bangs on the radiator on top of the lockers three times with a hammer, then pushes up and down on the handle of the locker next to his. At the end of the lockers (left side), he measures thirty-one inches up from the floor and kicks the first locker door. His locker door (second from the right) then opens.

Relations: Robert Emmett as Uncle Luther; Reta Shaw as Aunt Lillian (called Aunt Lil); Paula Trueman as Aunt Borghild; and Earl George as Uncle Lyman.

OTHER CHARACTERS

Bernice Gurney (maiden name Bernice Hester) is the English teacher (married to the school principal, Gabriel Gurney [first season only; later a widow]). She fusses, mutters to herself, sentimentalizes, and forgets what she is about to say. Each year for the past 30 years, she recites a poem she wrote to welcome her new students: "Welcome, Welcome on Your First Day of School." The problem: she can never remember it. She also makes her own homemade marmalade (from lemon peels) she calls "Gurnelade."

Harvey Erskine Weskit, called Wes, is Robinson's best friend, the history teacher. He called Robinson "Sport," "Rob," and "Ace." He became engaged to Marjorie "Marge" Bellows (whom he later married). They honeymooned in Sun Valley and moved into an apartment (at $60 a month) at 4031 Camorilla Street (which is managed by Nancy's father). Wes and Marge became the parents of a boy they named Harrison Brookfield Weskit. Marge was born in Chicago and calls Robinson "Robbie."

A narrator opens the show: "NBC television presents *Mister Peepers*. Created by David Swift. And now, here's Jefferson City's most popular general science teacher, Robinson J. Peepers."

Mr. and Mrs. North
(CBS, 1952–1953; NBC, 1954)

Cast: Richard Denning (Jerry North), Barbara Britton (Pamela North), Francis DeSales (Lieutenant Bill Weigand).

Basis: A beautiful wife (Pamela North) with an affinity for finding trouble, especially murders, seeks the help of her husband, Jerry, a former private detective, to help her solve the crimes. Based on the characters created by Frances and Richard Lockridge.

Address: 24 Sainte Anne's Place, Apartment 6A, in New York's Greenwich Village. Also given as 23 Sainte Ann's Place, Apartment 408 (even though Apartment 6A is seen in the opening theme).

Telephone Number: Gramercy 3-4098 (also given as Gramercy 3-8099 and Gramercy 3-4370).

Car License Plate: NN 1139.

GERALD "JERRY" NORTH

Occupation: Former private detective turned mystery book editor for a publishing house (not named). It is also said that Jerry is a publisher.

Character: Understanding and loving man who adores his wife despite the chaos she causes in their marriage. He was a navy lieutenant during World War II and began his career as a detective following his discharge. It was shortly after that he met Pamela during a case investigation. She sort of attached herself to Jerry, and the two fell in love and married in 1947 (on a Friday afternoon; they honeymooned in Paris); three years later, Jerry opted to live a quieter life (or so he thought) as an editor of mystery books. When on a case again, Jerry and Pam are helped by (and assist) their friend (best man at their wedding), Lieutenant Bill Weigand with the Homicide Division of the New York Police Department (PE 6-0599 is his office phone number).

PAMELA "PAM" NORTH

Occupation: Housewife.

Character: A former secretary who believes that, after meeting Jerry, she too has the ability to solve crimes (although she causes more trouble than solutions, and Jerry finds himself turning detective again because "it is easier to give in to Pam than to argue with her when she has her mind set on something"). Pamela has a suspicious mind, and her curiosity always gets her into trouble (Jerry fears for Pam's safety and always accommodates her—"Since I married Pam, disrupted plans are the only thing in life that I can positively depend on"). Changing jobs, Pam feels, has made Jerry lazy, while she claims she is always full of energy: "I used to go to parties and dance and stay up all night and work the next day and go to another party that evening. I'm just as young as I ever was." Unfortunately, she can't convince Jerry to relive his youth.

Pamela does solve crimes on her own. She is so unassuming that criminals are unaware of her brilliance and are caught by surprise. She is very proud of herself when she solves a crime and tells Jerry, "If I hadn't used my brains, I'd be dead. You'd have a corpse for a wife" (of course, she always says things like this to Jerry when he is trying to sleep or deeply involved with a manuscript, and her words fall on deaf ears).

My Friend Irma
(CBS, 1952–1954)

Cast: Marie Wilson (Irma Peterson), Cathy Lewis (Jane Stacey), Mary Shipp (Kay Foster), Sid Tomack (Al), Brooks West (Richard Rhinelander III).

Basis: Life with Irma Peterson, a gorgeous dumb blonde, as she struggles to navigate life in New York City.

IRMA PETERSON

Address: Mrs. O'Reilly's Boardinghouse (Apartment 3-B; later 2-C) at 185 West 73rd Street in Manhattan (which she first shared with Jane Stacey then Kay Foster). Mrs. O'Reilly's is located next to Al's Delicatessen. The boardinghouse was originally located at 8224 West 73rd Street, and Irma and Jane lived in Apartment 3B.

Place of Birth: Minnesota (also said to be Montana), where she grew up on a farm.

Date of Birth: May 5, 1916.

Age: Irma is not quite sure but believes she is 34 years old (in 1952 episodes).

Weight: 115 pounds (any higher than that will cause her to cry and go on a diet).

Occupation: Secretary for Milton J. Clyde (also called Irving Clyde), owner of the Clyde Real Estate Company (also seen as I. Clyde Real Estate and Insurance) at 631 East 41st Street.

Nickname (by Jane): Sweetie.

Nicknames (by Al): Chicken; Beautiful.

Relations: Bobby Peterson (Richard Eyer), Irma's nephew.

Character: Although she was raised on a farm, Irma wanted more than "just chickens, cows and crops" to make her mark on the world. Like all people, Irma too had a mother and father—"They were just like parents to me." After graduating from high school, where she learned her secretarial skills, Irma ventured on to New York City, where she found a job with Clyde Real Estate.

The shapely Irma Peterson is the personification of what a dim-witted blonde of the era would have been called—"a dizzy dame" or "a dumb blonde." Irma finds life in the big city exciting, but she is sensitive and realizes she is not like other people (as Jane says, "If she thinks it could be dangerous"). Irma talks to walls—"So I can clear the cobwebs of my mind"—and reads "Flash Gordon" comics to learn about the future. "When I don't want people to know I know something, I pretend I'm dumb," she says. Irma is always fashionably dressed (if she is not good at anything else, she is an expert at looking beautiful). If the phone should ring when Jane is home, Irma will not answer it "because I'm not sure it's for me." When it is Irma's turn to keep house (she and Jane rotate weeks), Jane is driven to the point of hysteria because she can't find anything and "has to figure out where an idiot would put things" (like the coffeepot in the refrigerator). Irma also has a bit of trouble figuring out fruit (for example, she peels a banana, tosses away the fruit, and nibbles on the inside of the peel).

Irma is so sweet and so innocent that people just can't help but love her. She has a tendency to cry and whine when she doesn't get her way, and she rarely ever realizes that she said or did something dumb. Jane best describes Irma's predicament: "Mother Nature gave some girls brains, intelligence and cleverness. But with Irma, Mother Nature slipped her a Mickey."

Irma is rather secure in her job due to her crazy filing system (Clyde can't dismiss her because it would take another secretary two years to figure out where Irma put things). To avoid the hassle of always having to do her nails, Marie Wilson wears white gloves in virtually every episode. And, as Jane says about Irma's antics, "Anything can happen when you live with My Friend Irma."

JANE STACEY

Place of Birth: Connecticut (where she lived with her parents at 1362 Post Valley Road).

Age: As Jane says, "Let's just leave that a question mark."

Occupation: Private secretary to Richard Rhinelander (Brooks West), the wealthy owner of the Rhinelander Investment Company at 113 Park Avenue (also seen as Rhinelander Investments).

Education: Willow High School, Connecticut State University.

Character: Irma's levelheaded roommate (1952–1953) who moved to New York City to fulfill a dream: marry a rich man. She believes only money can buy happiness (although she is slowly learning that, living with Irma, money isn't everything). Jane and Irma met in a most unusual way. Irma seldom looks where she is going when walking on the street. She didn't see Jane, who was looking for an apartment, and bumped into her, knocking her to the ground. When helping Jane to stand up and discovering that Jane was seeking an apartment, Irma offered to let Jane move in with her ("A one-room furnished basement," as Jane calls Irma's home).

Jane secretly loves Richard and desperately tries to impress him but feels her chances will be ruined by Irma, who is well below his social scale. Jane, the daughter of a druggist, feels she is an average girl and hates it. "I come from an average family. Now that I'm grown up I don't wear the cheapest clothes but I can't afford an original. I don't starve but I don't drink champagne. I'm just someplace hanging in the middle, Oh sure, it's an average life but I'm sick and tired of being average" (and the reason why she wants to marry Richard and live the good life). Jane can't function without her morning cup of coffee and mentioned that, to acquire the job as Richard's private secretary, she befriended Richard's prior secretary (Alice) hoping that when Alice left, she would recommend her for the job (Jane invested $65 taking Alice to lunch each day).

KAY FOSTER

Place of Birth: Ohio.

Occupation: Newspaper reporter for the *New York Globe*.

Education: Ohio State College (where she majored in journalism).

Nickname (for Irma): Honey.

Character: Irma's second roommate (1953–1954) and the recipient of Irma's misguided but well-meaning intentions to help others. Kay was introduced to viewers in an opening-curtain speech wherein Irma explained that Jane had been transferred to Panama and that she acquired a new roommate, Kay Foster, through an ad she placed in a newspaper. Kay is bright, pretty, and charming, and like Jane, talks directly to the audience to comment on the situations that arise and develop due to Irma's unpredictable antics. Kay is a bit more tolerant of Irma's antics, and although she does get upset with Irma, she quickly forgives her. Kay is dating Brad Jackson (played by Gerald Mohr), a fellow reporter for the *Globe*, who also becomes a victim of Irma's misguided attempts to do the right thing. Kay often felt the urge "to kill Irma" for the problems she causes, but "they have capital punishment in New York and I don't think I'll beat the rap." Irma's crying always calms Kay and fosters forgiveness.

RICHARD RHINELANDER III

Character: Richard is a graduate of Harvard Business School and, despite his encounters with Irma, finds her delightful. He inherited the business from his father and is fond of Jane but not yet set on marrying her. Richard handles stocks and bonds, is shy when he dictates notes, and smokes a pipe after having lunch. He is also very predictable in what he does. As Jane puts it, "On Monday you go to the Plaza [Hotel]; on Tuesday you go to the 21 Club for lunch; on Wednesday you have dinner with your mother on Long Island; on Thursday you play poker in your penthouse on Park Avenue; on Friday you go to the Athletic Club and the Stork Club; on Saturday you play golf; on Sunday you go horseback riding in the early morning if you don't have a hangover from Saturday night. If you do, you go to Jim's Steam Room for a massage."

Relations: Margaret DuMont as his mother.

AL

Character: Irma's con-artist boyfriend (known only as Al and the owner of Al Enterprises). He has been unemployed for four years (he claims to be "technically retired") and bets on the horses, and the most "work" he does is stand in the unemployment line. He and Irma have been engaged for five years, and Irma fears that if they do not marry soon, the unthinkable will happen: "I'm not getting any younger and when I get married and have children I don't want them to be older than me." While money is important to Al, it is not to Irma: "I have nothing, you have nothing. We both have nothing." Al considers himself "a live wire" (Jane says, "And it's only a matter of time before they hook him up and put a chair under him") and hopes to one day hit on a scheme to make a fortune. He claims that Irma has a tendency to drive him crazy: "The way that dame swings back and forth between the fine line that separates genius from insanity has made me a nervous wreck." When Jane left, Al was also replaced with Joe Vance (played by Hal March), a much more respectable boyfriend for Irma. Joe worked at the Spic and Span Cleaners, and he and Irma planned to marry, but the series ended before this occurred (there were plans to continue the program as *My Wife Irma*). Irma had hoped that Kay would be her "best man" at her wedding.

OTHER REGULARS

Kathleen O'Reilly (Gloria Gordon), the owner of the boardinghouse; Professor Kropotkin (Sid Arno), Irma's neighbor, who plays violin at the Paradise Burlesque Theater (later the Gypsy Tea Room). He calls Jane and Irma "My Little Pigeons. One with her head in the air (Jane) the other with air in her head (Irma)."

Note: Based on the radio series of the same title.

My Little Margie
(CBS, 1952–1953; NBC, 1953–1955)

Cast: Gale Storm (Margie Albright), Charles Farrell (Vernon Albright), Don Hayden (Freddy Wilson), Hillary Brooke (Roberta Townsend), Gertrude Hoffman (Clarissa Odetts).

Basis: A meddlesome daughter (Margie), a conservative father (Vernon), and their efforts to live a normal life without continually meddling in each other's affairs.

MARJORIE "MARGIE" ALBRIGHT

Age: 21 (when the series begins).

Date of Birth: October 12, 1930.

Ancestry: Irish.

Address: Apartment 10-A of the Carlton Arms Hotel in Manhattan.

Telephone Number: Carlton 3-8966.

Education: Gorman Elementary School, Lexington Avenue High School, Manhattan College.

Talents: Singing, dancing, meddling.

Relations: Sally Albright (Gale Storm), Margie's younger sister.

Character: Described as "Pretty, shapely and attractive," Margie took dancing lessons while in grammar school and has ever since dreamed of attending the International Ball (but was never allowed, as it is a prestigious dance allotted only for blue bloods). Margie's mother passed away shortly after giving birth to her, and she has been raised solely by her father.

Margie lives off the allowance her father gives her, although she is seen tackling several jobs (but only for the duration of that particular episode). Margie claims that her first job was a department store beauty consultant (in actuality, she handed out cosmetics samples at Stacy's Department Store). She also worked as a secretary, model (where the photographer could never remember her name and called her "Miss Whoozis"), dance instructor, waitress, and salesclerk. She is never seen on unemployment lines, is always fashionably dressed, and is easily angered when she gets upset or something bothers her. Margie also has a bad habit—smoking (she is seen reaching for, lighting up, and smoking a cigarette). In one episode, "Margie's Millionth Member," it appeared that Margie and Vern were to have their own unnamed TV series as the hosts of a science fiction show for adults on WBCA-TV in New York (they play "the first father-daughter space team"). The show is never mentioned or seen again.

VERNON "VERN" ALBRIGHT

Age: 50 (when the series begins).

Date of Birth: August 11, 1902.

Place of Birth: Boston.

Education: Boston University (possesses a bachelor's degree in business). He also starred in several plays.

Occupation: Investment counselor at Honeywell and Todd Investments in Manhattan.

Military Service: Army captain during World War II.

Favorite Movie Actor: Charlie Farrell (Vern mentions enjoying "Old Charlie Farrell movies on TV. I wouldn't miss them for anything," which refers to actor Charlie Farrell's real-life career before TV).

Character: A handsome ladies' man who has tried to raise Marjorie as best he could. While Vern seems capable of taking care of himself, Margie constantly worries about him, feeling that at his age he needs to settle down and become "a nice old comfortable father," not the playboy he has become (at least in Margie's eyes, as he dates, stays out all night, dances, and exhausts himself). Vern sees it as fun and believes age has nothing to do with age—"I have the constitution of a 17-year-old boy" (which Margie wishes he'd give back).

Vern has his shoes polished at Joe's Shoe Stand and eats Boomies, "The Atomic Energy Cereal," for breakfast (Margie donates the box tops to the Junior League Toy Drive). It is usually Vern's actions that set up each episode's story line when he meddles into Margie's affairs or vice versa. It begins with "I've got to teach that girl a lesson." However, when Margie discovers what Vern is doing, she turns the tables and plots to teach him a lesson (then it's Vern plotting to teach Margie a lesson for trying to teach him a lesson—and Margie again turning the tables). After all is resolved, Vern ends episodes with "Well, that's My Little Margie."

FREDERICK WILSON

Character: Frederick "Freddy" Wilson is Margie's impoverished boyfriend. Although Vern despises him (calls him a "Droop" and a "Goofball"), Margie loves him and sticks by him (Vern knows Margie can do so much better than Freddy and wishes she would show a little more taste in boyfriends. Margie insists, "There is nothing wrong with Freddy"). It was Freddy who made Margie realize there were men—"When Freddy pointed one out to me." Freddy seems to be permanently unemployed (as Vern says, "Freddy is the only person who got fired from five different jobs in one week. He is too lazy to work. One night he dreamed he was working and he was pooped for the next two days"). Margie also knows Freddy is smart ("He won several contests working crossword puzzles"), and despite what Vern claims, Freddy did hold two jobs for more than one day: night watchman ("Not one night was stolen when I was watching them") and window mattress demonstrator (sleeping) at Farley's Furniture Store. Even attempting to become a military man has failed (the army recruitment office sent him home with a note pinned to his chest: "If this is dead we don't want it; if this is alive, we don't believe it"). Freddy's one accomplishment (other than having Margie for a girlfriend) is the play he wrote, "Girl Against the World," which told "the story of a typical American girl with the odds stacked up against her."

Freddy enjoys the TV program *Captain Stratosphere* and when he visits Margie at home, "eats all the leftovers."

Relations: Lila Bliss Hayden and Harry Hayden as Freddy's parents, Mrs. and Mr. Wilson.

CLARISSA ODETTS

Character: Clarissa Odetts, called Mrs. Odetts, is Margie's 82-year-old, young-at-heart neighbor (Apartment 10-C) who thoroughly enjoys becoming a part of Margie's plans to turn the tables on Vern. Mrs. Odetts is of British ancestry and has ancestors who date back to Valley Forge. She dreamed of becoming an actress and looks in on the Albrights (which Vern says she does all the time—"through the keyhole"). Margie sometimes acquires a job babysitting Mrs. Odetts's 10-year-old granddaughter, Norma Jean Odetts (played by Sheila James).

Relations: Gloria Talbott as Amy McKenna, Clarissa's granddaughter; Crystal Reeves as Clarissa's sister; Fess Parker as Lonny Crunchmeyer, Clarissa's nephew.

ROBERTA TOWNSEND

Character: Roberta is Vern's romantic interest. She is a very pretty older woman (closer to Vern's age) and lives across the hall in Apartment 10-B. She appears to be a receptionist-secretary (although not specifically stated).

OTHER REGULARS

George Honeywell (Clarence Kolb) is Vern's employer at Honeywell and Todd; Charlie (Willie Best) is the building's elevator operator.

Our Miss Brooks

(CBS, 1952–1956)

Cast: Eve Arden (Connie Brooks), Robert Rockwell (Philip Boyington), Gale Gordon (Osgood Conklin), Richard Crenna (Walter Denton), Jane Morgan (Margaret Davis), Gloria McMillan (Harriet Conklin), Leonard Smith (Stretch Snodgrass).

Basis: A small-town schoolteacher's (Connie Brooks) life at home, at school, and with friends.

CONSTANCE "CONNIE" BROOKS

Occupation: English teacher at Madison High School (in the town of Madison, 1952–1955); Mrs. Nestor's Elementary School (in the San Fernando Valley, 1955–1956).

Education: The Pace Avenue Grammar School, Madison High School, State College.

Age: 42 (although she would like to keep that a secret. She also says, to cover her age, "I was a leap year baby").

Faculty Adviser: Oversees publication of the school newspaper, the *Madison Monitor.*

Place of Birth: Town of Madison.

Prior Address (as a child): 239 Pace Avenue.

Current Address: Mrs. Davis's Boarding House at 295 Carroll Avenue (1952–1955). When the series switched locales (1955–1956), Mrs. Davis relocated and opened a boardinghouse on Maple Street. Connie became her first tenant.

Favorite Breakfast: Pancakes and tomato juice.

Favorite Dinner: Lasagna.

Musical Ability: Plays the piano.

Character: As a child, Connie became impressed by her schoolteachers and made a promise to herself: to become a teacher. Although she was not the most popular girl in school, she did have friends who were boys and a steady boy-friend (Efrem Lintz) during her high school years. Right before graduating, Efrem proposed to Connie, but marrying would shatter Connie's childhood dream, and she chose instead to pursue her education. After acquiring her teaching degree and returning to her alma mater to begin her career, she met Philip Boyington, a shy biology teacher she has made it her goal to win over and marry (see Philip Boyington, below).

Connie loves her job, hoping to educate the youth of America, but she often finds that her days are filled with aggravation and frustration trying to educate that youth. She has created what she calls "Schoolteacher's B&B" (bath and bed)—a relaxing bath followed by a good night's sleep. Connie doesn't like to talk about her age (she has a tendency to forget her birth-day) and considers herself a softhearted person (as she will go out of her way to help others). While Connie appears to make a decent salary, she is often in need of money (as she frequents Fisher's Pawn Shop) when things become tight. She shops at Sherry's Department Store, becomes a friend to her students, and, now that she is growing older, hopes to marry and start

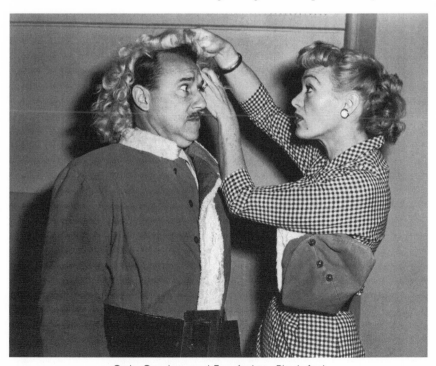

Gale Gordon and Eve Arden. *Photofest*

a family. But her choice for a husband (Philip Boyington) may not be the right choice. Connie's life became the subject of the TV show *Here Is Your Past* (a *This Is Your Life* type of program), wherein an exaggerated history of Connie was presented (what could have been a background story turned out to be worthless, as Connie blew a horn to avoid letting viewers hear personal details of her life; it was also interwoven with exaggerated facts [like Connie supported dozens of orphans] as supplied by Mrs. Davis [who wanted to make Connie interesting]).

PHILIP BOYINGTON

Occupation: Biology teacher at Madison High School (1952–1955). He mentions that he previously taught chemistry. When the series switched locales, Philip was dropped and was said to have become a biology teacher at Arizona High School.

Place of Birth: Seattle, Washington.

Education: Cavendish High School, Seattle State University.

After-School Activity: School track team coach.

Address: 981 Evergreen Road ("My Bachelor Pad").

Pet Lab Frog: McDougall.

Lodge: The Elk's Club.

Musical Ability: Plays the ukulele.

Character: Philip has become the man Connie hopes to marry, but first, as she says, "I must make a man of him." Philip and Connie met in 1948 when he acquired the job at Madison High. He is shy, introverted, and totally dedicated to his job. He realizes that there is an opposite sex, but his shyness makes him uncomfortable around women. Connie wishes "he would take brave shots" and believes Philip needs to realize that there is "a big difference between teaching biology and learning it." Philip is just not romantic and treats her with respect ("Too much," she says). But Philip has his own point of view: "I know I haven't been the most aggressive chap in the world and I do think of other things than my biological experiments. Things that are more personal, things like a man thinking about a woman whether she is a teacher or not." As Connie hopes to hear more, Philip either becomes distracted by an ongoing experiment, changes the subject matter, loses confidence, or is interrupted by someone before he can go any further. Connie sometimes thinks Philip has more interest in his lab frogs, rabbits, and guinea pigs than he does in her.

Connie recalls that she had a similar problem with boys when she was younger, and if she could overcome them, she is determined to see that Philip overcomes his problem with females. Philip believes that jellybeans are one of the best sources of quick energy (for the dextrose they contain) and in 1952 became excited—not for Connie but over a confidential research project dealing with the fertilization of the long-stem lily. All Connie wants is a little affection—and a kiss—but with Philip, it is only a dream. As the series progressed, Philip did muster up some courage, as he would take Connie to Outpost Road (the local teen make-out spot). Kissing, however, was another story; if Connie "tried to steal a kiss," Philip considered it "Petting Larceny" and would just rather enjoy the moonlit night conversing about school.

When Madison High School is demolished to make way for a highway in 1955, Connie relocates to San Fernando while Philip relocates to Arizona. Although their romance has ended, Connie finds a new romance when she meets Gene Talbot (Gene Barry), the athletic director at Mrs. Nestor's Elementary School. By coincidence, Gene and Philip were born in Seattle, and both attended Cavendish High School. In 1956, Philip paid Connie a visit, giving her not flowers or candy but a box of Arizona desert lizards. Gene wasn't the only teacher at Mrs. Netsor's with an eye for Connie, as Gene found competition from Clint Albright, the gym teacher.

OTHER REGULARS

Osgood Conklin, the stern, easily upset principal of Madison High School, frowns on teachers becoming romantically involved with each other and runs the school as if it were a military camp, reflecting on his career in the army during World War II (where he attained the rank of major and spent four years as the commander of Camp Fabrick in Ohio). He is married to Martha (Virginia Gordon, then Paula Winslow) and the father of Harriet, a student at Madison High (who, in some episodes, acts as her father's student assistant). Osgood, who is allergic to dogs, considers Connie his "Faculty Comrade," while Harriet feels her father is also a principal at home. When the series switched locals, Osgood became the principal of Mrs. Nestor's, a school owned by the widowed Mrs. Nestor (Nana Bryant).

Walter Denton, a student at Madison High, is considered "a lame-brain dunce" by Osgood. Walter, who calls Mr. Conklin "Old Marblehead," is mishap prone, manages the track team for Philip, and is "crazy in love" with Harriet, much to Osgood's objections. Walter considers Harriet "A wonderful girl." Harriet considers Walter "My life, my future, my all." But if someone else should catch her fancy—"Who needs Walter," she says. Walter is also friends with Connie and often drops by her home not only to drive her to work (in a jalopy that cost him $30) but also to have a second breakfast. Walter, whose catchphrase is "Holy Cow," appears to be the school newspaper's most frequent author, as he constantly writes articles about Miss Brooks. When Connie left Madison, Walter gave Connie an apple and the right door of his car to remember him by.

Fabian "Stretch" Snodgrass is Madison High's star basketball player and the only hope the school has of winning the state championship. Unfortunately, for Connie, Stretch is also her worst student—and flunking him could mean defeat. As Stretch says, "I know I ain't no good in English, Miss Brooks. Ever since the first test you give me, I know I was gonna improve and get the kind of marks in English that I've stroven for." Stretch has an unseen sister named Rapunzel and a brother, Winston "Bones" Snodgrass (Eddie Ryder). In the revised version of the series, Benny Romero (Ricky Vera) became the new student who presented Connie with numerous problems.

Margaret Davis, always called Mrs. Davis, has run her rooming house since the early 1930s (at which time she did so with her late husband). Mrs. Davis has a pet cat named Minerva and is basically seen only in rooming house scenes, where she converses with Connie. She attended school with Osgood and recalls that as a student he was called "Stone Face" because he never laughed (although she did admit she saw him laugh once—when she fell down and broke her leg).

The People's Choice
(NBC, 1955–1958)

Cast: Jackie Cooper (Sock Miller), Patricia Breslin (Mandy Peoples), Margaret Irving (Gus Bennett), Paul Maxey (John Peoples), Dick Wesson (Rollo), Leonid Kinskey (Pierre), Mary Jane Croft (voice of Cleo).

Basis: Life with Sock Miller, first as an ornithologist, then district councilmen, and finally sales manager for a housing project.

SOCRATES "SOCK" MILLER

Address: Paradise Park Trailer Camp (where he lives with his Aunt Gus).

Occupation: Ornithologist for the Bureau of Fish and Wildlife; 5th District city councilman; sales manager for the Barkerville Housing Project.

Education: Cornell University (member of the Phi Beta Kappa fraternity).

Military Service: Marine sergeant during the Korean War (stationed at Fort Baxter, where he was the platoon bayonet champion).

Pet Dog: Cleo.

Nickname: Nature Boy (as called by the mayor)

Character: Sock was raised by his aunt, Augusta Bennett (always called Aunt Gus), after his parents were killed in a car accident (when he was three years old). Sock had always been interested in wildlife and chose to become an ornithologist for the government (his job is described as "Following the birds." He files reports on migratory birds, as their flights foretell climatic conditions and aid farmers when planting crops). Aunt Gus accompanies Sock on his assignments and found a permanent home in New City, California. New City was a city built in a hurry. While it is famous for its lettuce crops, it is also noted for its misappropriated funding, which left some areas with paved streets and sewers and other areas with bad roads, no sewers, and no streetlights. It was meeting Mandy Peoples, the mayor's (John Peoples) daughter, that changed Sock's life. He helped her fix a flat tire that had left her stranded, and when she learned that Sock was going to be transferred to Ohio (to discover why the rose-breasted grosbeak was laying smaller eggs that season), she convinced him to run for public office not only because he was the best man for the job but also because she has experienced a love at first sight.

Sock ran on a platform that he would improve the neglected areas of New City and not be in the mayor's back pocket just because he is romantically involved with his daughter. Sock was elected and received special permission from the Department of Fish and Wildlife, Western Division, to remain in New City until his term of office is completed. Sock and Mandy married in 1957, at which time Sock applied for a position as a lawyer for Barker Amalgamated in New York City. He is hired—but he is to remain in New City and manage Barkerville, a housing development with 294 homes "for sale 20 miles from nowhere" (homes sell for $15, 995, and Sock and Mandy reside in Model Home 119).

AMANDA "MANDY" PEOPLES

Address: 39 Birch Road.

Place of Birth: Los Angeles.

Education: Valley High School, California State College.

Occupation: Secretary to her father, Mayor John Peoples (also acts as his campaign manager).

Nickname: My Ruby Throated Hummingbird (as called by Sock. It is "a dainty little atom possessing exquisite beauty").

Beauty Contest Title: Runner-up in the Miss New City Pageant.

Character: Mandy is a young woman who has taken up her father's political cause of improving the conditions that exist in New City. Mandy and her father were the earliest residents of the community, and John found that the only way to improve the city was to govern it (although his actions were somewhat ineffectual—until Sock came along and became the actual figure to see that things happen). Mandy appeared to be a behind-the-scenes person until Sock came into her life. Her father apparently controlled things, and she had little involvement in what actually happened (because she was a woman?). When she knew a change had to be made and tricked Sock into becoming a councilman, Mandy's political future also seemed brighter, as she was "the woman behind the man."

When Sock became a councilman and Mandy wanted to work for him as his secretary, Sock refused to hire her, fearing bad publicity, as she is the mayor's daughter. Mandy understood—until Sock hired Vickie Summers (Joi Lansing), a gorgeous girl (38-24-34), as his secretary (at $250 a month). Sock insisted he hired Vickie because she can take shorthand and type 110 words a minute. Mandy became jealous and convinced her father to find Vickie another job (which he did in sanitation at $255 a month), and Mandy convinced Sock to let her become his secretary. Prior to Sock, Mandy dated a lawyer named Roger Crutcher (John Stephenson); Sock's prior girlfriend was Valerie Delmar (Jean Porter).

CLEO

Character: A basset hound that comments on the situations that occur (heard only by the viewing audience). Cleo was six months old when Sock, a marine, won her in a poker game. As a puppy, Cleo liked to roam around the base and make her sleeping quarters the camp's dynamite shed. Cleo mentions that she is glad Sock can't talk for her—"If he could, I'd be off the show."

OTHER CHARACTERS

Mayor John Peoples runs the city from the Municipal Building (phone extension 40). He also found romance with Aunt Gus and married her shortly after Sock and Mandy wed. He also owns part interest in a whaling ship in Seattle. He calls Aunt Gus "Mousey."

Hexley "Hex" Rollo is Sock's childhood friend who now resides in New City. They served in the marines together and Hex is considered a jinx, as he is cursed with bad luck (in the service, for example, he lost a 20-ton amphibious tank).

Pierre Quincy is another friend of Sock's, an eccentric painter called "The Michelangelo of the Paradise Trailer Park." He calls Cleo "Funny Face" and is a member of the local Artist's Club.

Perry Mason
(CBS, 1957–1966)

Cast: Raymond Burr (Perry Mason), Barbara Hale (Della Street).
Basis: A brilliant attorney (Perry Mason) and the step-by-step process he uses to
   solve a criminal case and bring the guilty party to justice.

Suite 904 of the Brent Building in Los Angeles is the office of Perry Mason, a brilliant criminal attorney known for the unexpected (especially during courtroom proceedings) in his defense of clients. Madison 5-1190 is his office phone number, and his retainer fees range from $1,000 to $5,000. Perry works strictly by the book and performs best when the odds are stacked up against him. Although he does not like to admit it, Perry uses whatever legal tactics he can find to win his case—but always within that fine line that separates legal from illegal. Plea bargaining is something Perry will not consider; the risk of losing a case is much better to him than winning a case under suspicious cir-cumstances or with a reduced sentence.

While Perry seems stern and one to fear, he is not without compassion. If he sees a client cannot afford his services but honestly believes the client is innocent, he will either reduce his fees or defend the case for free. While most lawyers would just sit back and let their investigators do the legwork (here by Paul Drake), Perry feels he needs to get into the thick of things and, with Della's help, will investigate his own cases. While Perry is competent as a detective, it is in the courtroom where his abilities shine. He is shrewd and cunning and never lets it be known that he does not have sufficient evidence to defend a client (he became famous for waiting for that vital piece of evidence at the last possible

Raymond Burr as Perry Mason and Barbara Hale as Della Street.
© CBS Photofest

minute during a trial). Perry delivers his opening and closing statements with such eloquence that he can mesmerize jurors. He is also famous for doing the unordinary—bringing in last-minute witnesses who would ultimately clear his client. Perry's constant devotion to work often left him little time for home-cooked meals. He ate regularly at McQuade's Bar and Grill or at Clay's Grille.

Perry is, without a doubt, tough, persistent, and an unrelenting force for right when it comes to his clients. Della Street, his proficient, pretty, dedicated secretary (and investigative assistant), is the only woman who can tame his roughness. Della has as much passion as (or even more than) Perry and gives of herself to help her friends or clients she feels are in deep trouble. Della assisted Perry in various ways but most often appeared in various disguises and always uses her feminine intuition to best serve Perry. She is always elegantly dressed and loves to wear perfume (she is sort of an expert on it). Hollywood 2-1799 is her home phone number.

In a series of 1980s TV movies, Raymond Burr and Barbara Hale reunited to continue playing the roles of Perry Mason and Della Street. In the interim, Perry had become a judge and Della a secretary to Arthur Gordon of Arthur Gordon Industries. When Della is framed and arrested for Arthur's murder, she calls on an old friend, Perry, for help. Perry, eager to get away from what he considers a boring job, accepts the case. He clears Della, resigns from the Appeals Court ("Let's say, I just got tired of writing opinions"), and reestablishes his practice with Della again by his side.

The series update, *The New Perry Mason* (CBS, 1973–1974), features Monte Markham as Perry Mason, with Sharon Acker as Della Street, Harry Guardino as Hamilton Burger, Dane Clark as Arthur Tragg, and Brett Somers as Gerdie Lade.

Paul Drake (William Hopper) is Perry's investigator; Hamilton Burger (William Talman) is the prosecuting attorney; Gertie Lade (Connie Cezon) is Perry's receptionist; Margo (Paula Courtland) is Drake's secretary; David Gideon (Karl Held) is Perry's associate (later episodes) and Perry works with the following L.A.P.D. police officials: Lt. Arthur Tragg (Ray Collins), Lt. Steve Drumm (Richard Anderson), Sergeant Brice (Lee Miller), and Lt. Andy Anderson (Wesley Lau). Based on characters created by Erle Stanley Gardner; only the last of 245 episodes was filmed in color.

Pete Kelly's Blues
(NBC, 1959)

Cast: William Reynolds (Pete Kelly), Connee Boswell (Savannah Brown), Phil Gordon (George Lupo), Anthony Eisley (Johnny Cassiano).

Basis: The life of a jazz musician (Pete Kelly) in Kansas City, Missouri, in 1927 (as Pete says, "This one's about Pete Kelly. It's about the world he goes around in; it's about the big music, the big trouble and the big Twenties").

PETER "PETE" KELLY

Place of Birth: Chicago.

Parents: Paul and Doreen Kelly.

Address (Chicago): 18th Street and Halstead Avenue.

Address (Kansas City): Grand Avenue near Washington Square.

Occupation: Jazz musician (plays the cornet); leader of a band called the Big Seven.

Employment: Lupo's, a speakeasy (formally a brownstone turned funeral parlor).

Address (Lupo's): 17 Cherry Street.

Work Hours: 10:00 p.m. to 4:00 a.m.

Character: As a kid, Pete became fascinated with music, especially the cornet, and set his goal on becoming a jazz musician. Pete first mentions that a musician named Gus Trudeaux taught him how to play the cornet. They became friends, but when Gus became involved with the Chicago mob, Pete left him and chose to make it on his own, heading for Kansas City. He next relates his origins as a struggling musician who befriended Gus at a musician's union meeting. At this same time, he also met a piano player named Angie and teamed with him, playing small clubs until they drifted to Kansas City, where Pete later formed his jazz band. Although Pete lives to play music, he often finds himself turning unofficial private detective to aid people looking to him for help.

OTHER REGULARS

George Lupo, the owner of the speakeasy. He was born in Kansas City (Linback County) and, as Pete says, "was a tough kid who got turned down for reform school." He served with the 102nd Infantry during World War I and pays Pete's band scale—"with a five dollar kickback." Savannah Brown is Pete's friend, a jazz and blues singer at Fat Annie's, a speakeasy on the Kansas side (Kansas City, Kansas). Savannah was born in Georgia and, like Pete, drifted to Missouri (they met each other playing small clubs). Savannah discovered her ability to sing when she was a youngster and was pushed by her parents to pursue a musical career (as Annie says, "It's easy to sing the blues—all you need to do is be born when there is rain on the roof"). Fat Annie's is a speakeasy a bit higher in class than Lupo's (which is plagued by trouble and, as Pete says, "which you can get by the yard, the pound, wholesale and retail"). Johnny Cassiano is the police officer with the Kansas City Police Department, which becomes part of the troubles Pete encounters. Musician Dick Cathcart is the off-screen cornet player for Pete; the Matty Matlock Combo provide the music for the club scenes.

Peter Gunn

(NBC, 1958–1960; ABC, 1960–1961)

Cast: Craig Stevens (Peter Gunn), Lola Albright (Edie Hart), Herschel Bernardi (Lieutenant Jacoby), Hope Emerson, Minerva Urecal (Mother).

Basis: Case investigations of Peter Gunn, a suave and sophisticated detective based in Los Angeles, California.

PETER GUNN

Occupation: Private detective (owner of Gunn Investigations; also seen as The Peter Gunn Private Detective Agency and Peter Gunn's Private Detective Agency, which he established on July 7, 1957).

Business Address: 731 Ocean Park Drive.

Mobile Telephone Number: JL1-7211.

Home Address: 351 Park Road.

Home Phone Number: KR2-7056.

Character: Peter Gunn is the first actual private detective created for TV (as opposed to adapting radio and movie characters). He is sophisticated, always well dressed, and more respectful than his predecessors. He frequents a classy hangout (Mother's), although he can also be seen entering such dives as Nate's Hot Dogs, the Green Café, and Cooky's, a beatnik coffeehouse. Although Peter Gunn is a TV original, he inherited a flare for violence—whether it is by fists or gunplay. While Peter most often works alone, he does have snitches that supply information (the most notable being "Babby" [Billy Barty], a diminutive pool player whom Gunn pays $10 and who often tells him to "Think tall." When Babby sees that Gunn is troubled, he says, "You've got that eight-ball look"). Lieutenant (no first name) Jacoby of the Los Angeles Police Department is the homicide detective Gunn assists (and vice versa). His office desk phone number is 366-2561.

EDITH "EDIE" HART

Occupation: Singer at Mother's, a waterfront nightclub.

Address: The Bartell Hotel, Apartment 15, at 1709 Verbanna Street.

Phone Number: KL6-0699.

Character: Glamorous, always fashionably dressed, and the one steady influence in Peter's life (could be considered his romantic interest). Edie later purchases the club from Mother and renames it Edie's. She is not the typical private detective's sidekick and rarely becomes involved in Gunn's actual case investigations. Her role is to add a touch of glamour and elegance to the program, and she accomplishes that in an era when such crime series did not focus on that aspect (Connie Stevens, in her role of Cricket Blake on *Hawaiian Eye*, could be considered the second such woman to inherit Edie's accomplishment).

Craig Stevens as Peter Gunn and Lola Albright as Edie Hart. © *NBC*

The Phil Silvers Show
(CBS, 1955–1959)

Cast: Phil Silvers (Ernest Bilko), Paul Ford (Colonel Hall), Maurice Gosfield (Duane Doberman), Billy Sands (Dino Paparelli), Herbie Faye (Sam Fender), Mickey Freeman (Fielding Zimmerman), Allan Melvin (Corporal Henshaw), Joe E. Ross (Rupert Ritzik).

Basis: Life in a fantasized U.S. military camp as seen through the eyes of Ernest Bilko, a man who sees the army as a means to become rich through elaborate cons (that almost always fail).

Master Sergeant Ernest Bilko, serial number 10542699, is stationed at the Fort Baxter army base in Roseville, Kansas. There he is in charge of the 3rd Platoon of the Company B Motor Pool (24th Division) and is totally dedicated to acquiring money by manipulating the U.S. Army for his own personal benefit.

When Bilko buys an old army trunk at an auction, he discovers it contains a map indicting gold in California's Grove City. Through an elaborate scheme to get the army to declare a closed and decrepit army base (Camp Fremont) to be a historic military site (and allow him to dig for gold), he literally manipulates the top military brass to reopen the camp and have his Fort Baxter crew transferred to Grove City. The camp is, at first, anything but inviting; Bilko's dreams of finding gold and becoming rich are shattered (as the land contains only fool's gold), and the final-season episodes (1958–1959) are set at Camp Fremont, where Bilko continues his conniving ways.

Bilko, a master con artist, does not get up before noon and began his "career" during World War II. At that time, he was with the 38th Division and stationed in New Guinea; he supplied the USO (United Serviceman's Organization) girls with something they desperately needed but were unable to get—nylons at $5 a pair. After the war, Bilko, a master at pool and cards, was transferred to Fort Baxter, where he now oversees the 3rd Platoon of Company B, which includes Privates Duane Doberman, Dino Paparelli, Sam Fender, Fielding Zimmerman, and Corporal Henshaw. The base cook, Rupert Ritzik, is Bilko's main patsy. Ritzik eats Crispy Crunchies breakfast cereal, reads comic books, and believes in flying saucers (he keeps a nightly watch in the hope of spotting one). His favorite television show is *Captain Dan, Space Man*, and he claims to have, although he is very forgetful, a photographic memory. Bilko serves as the chairman of the Camp Base Shows and finds bedtime both a pleasure (when he dreams about money) and a nightmare (when he can't count it or acquire it).

OTHER CHARACTERS

John T. ("Jack") Hall is Bilko's commanding officer. He spent four years at West Point, three years at War College, and two years at Field Officer's School, and, as he says, "I still can't outmaneuver a greedy sergeant" (referring to Bilko, whom he knows is a con artist but can't prove it). Elisabeth Fraser is WAC Master Joan Hogan, Bilko's girlfriend; Julie Newmar is "Stacked" Stacey, the waitress at the local diner, the Paradise Bar and Grill (Fort Baxter episodes); and George Kennedy plays various military police roles.

OTHER SOLDIERS

Corporal Rocco Barbella (Harvey Lembeck), Sergeant Francis Grover (Jimmy Little), Private Mullin (Jack Healy), Private Lester Mendelsohn (Gerald Hiken), Private Greg Chickeriny (Bruce Kirby), and Sergeant Stanley Sowicki (Harry Clark).

RELATIONS

Beatrice Pons (Rupert's nagging wife, Emma Ritzik), Hope Sansbury (John's wife, Nell Hall), Sal Dano (Rocco's brother, Angelo Barbella), Betty Walker (Sam's wife, Hattie Fender), Toni Romer (Stanley's wife, Agnes Sowicki), George Richards (Stanley's son, Stanley Jr.), Doreen McLean (Joan's mother), Harry Adams (Joan's father). Not seen were Sam's kids: Raoul, Olivier, Benji, Claude, Cindy, and Tab.

Note: The series was originally titled *You'll Never Get Rich* and is also known as *Sergeant Bilko.*

Private Secretary
(CBS, 1953–1957)

Cast: Ann Sothern (Susie McNamara), Don Porter (Peter Sands), Ann Tyrrell (Vi Praskins), Jesse White (Cagey Calhoun).

Basis: The life of a glamorous New York secretary (Susie McNamara). Now known by its syndicated title *Susie* (copies of the program under its original title have been withdrawn due to copyright issues).

SUSAN CAMILLE "SUSIE" MCNAMARA

Employment Company: International Artists.
Business Address: Suite 2201 at 10 East 56th Street in Manhattan.
Place of Birth: Mumford (mentioned as being in Iowa).

Education: Mumford High School.

Ancestry: Scottish.

Birth Sign: Libra.

Military Service: Three years as a WAVE (1942–1945) during World War II.

Date of Employment: June 1945.

Work Skills: Types 65 words a minute; takes 125 words a minute in shorthand.

Home Address: The Brockhurst Apartments (Apartment H) on East 92nd Street in Manhattan.

Character: A beautiful middle-aged, incurably romantic woman with a penchant for always being in style. Susie, as she is called, enjoys the excitement of the big city and recalled that a big Saturday night in Mumford "was to get all dressed up, go to City Hall and watch them polish the cannon." She is most famous for writing an article called "How to Handle the Boss" for *New Feature* magazine (for which she received $500). Although not mentioned in the article, Susie often uses flattery to handle Peter.

Relations: Gloria Winters as Patty, Susie's niece.

PETER SANDS

Occupation: Theatrical agent.

Business: Owner of International Artists, Inc. (which he established in 1945).

Phone Number: Plaza 5-1955.

First Notable Talent Discovery: Harriet Lake (Ann Sothern's real name).

Education: University of New York (where he was voted "Most Likely to Succeed").

Birth Sign: Aries.

Military Service: Air force captain during World War II (1941–1945).

Character: A charming ladies' man who enjoys looking at women's legs ("I enjoy exercising that privilege"). Peter calls Susie "the most faithful and loyal secretary I ever had" and enjoys being babied, at times by Susie (who, for example, prepares Peter's coffee with only an eyedropper of milk and makes two copies of every letter she types). When Susie first came to work for Peter, he took her to lunch at the Penguin Club. Susie defines Peter as "alluring, popular and intelligent."

Relations: Alma Sands as Peter's mother, Mrs. Sands.

OTHER REGULARS

Violet "Vi" Praskins is the office receptionist and began working for Peter on October 23, 1949. Vi, whom Susie says is "the first line of defense in the office," is not as aggressive as Susie when it comes to men ("I'm still looking for Mr.

Right"). She is a Scorpio and believes in fortune-tellers and horoscopes (she can be seen reading *Advanced Astrology* magazine).

Michael "Mickey" Calhoun, called "Cagey," runs the rival (although far less prestigious) theatrical agency (M. C. Calhoun & Co., Ltd-Inc.). Cagey, as he is always called, calls Susie "Foxy" and "Foxy McNamara" and acquires clients (virtually all unknowns) through schemes.

Rawhide

(CBS, 1959–1966)

Cast: Eric Fleming (Gil Favor), Clint Eastwood (Rowdy Yates), Sheb Wooley (Pete Nolan), Paul Brinegar (G. W. Wishbone), James Murdock (Harkness "Mushy" Mushgrove).

Basis: Saga of a cattle drive from Texas to Missouri and of the men who brave the hardships of the trail to get cattle to market.

It is 1861, and Gil Favor, a widower with two children, Gillian (Candy Moore) and Margaret (Barbara Beaird), leaves his home in Philadelphia to join the Confederacy. Gil's sister-in-law, Eleanor Bradley (Dorothy Green), cares for the children. Gil, a courageous soldier, earns the rank of lieutenant when the war ends in 1865. For reasons that are not explained, Gil heads to Texas to establish himself as a trail boss. He begins by trailing cattle for "an old trail boss" and eventually establishes the Gil Favor Herd (transporting up to 3,000 cattle to market from San Antonio, Texas, to Sedalia, Missouri). Gil is paid $25 a head and must endure the treacherous 1,000 miles of the Sedalia Trail and likes to take things at a normal pace and not lose any cattle; he feels a sigh of relief when the job is done—"When I got the money in hand and those beef are out of my sight."

Rowdy Yates, the ramrod, is the son of Dan Yates (Tom Tully) and was born in South Texas. Although he was always in trouble for doing something, his mother wanted him to be a preacher or a doctor. But that was not what Rowdy wanted. He joined the Confederacy at the age of 16 and made the rank of corporal when he was captured by Union soldiers and sentenced to prison. He was freed when the Civil War ended and apparently headed to Texas to begin a new life. It is not explained how, but Rowdy met Gil and was hired by Gil to serve as the cattle drive's ramrod when he saw potential in him.

Gil is not the easiest boss for whom to work. He is tough (especially on Rowdy, whom he is grooming to become the trail boss when the time comes; it happened in the last season, when Eric Fleming left the series).

G.W. (George Washington) Wishbone, called Wishbone, is the cook; he also tends to "the doctoring" and is assisted by Harkness Mushgrove (called Mushy). Pete Nolan is the trail scout and Indian expert (in the episode "Deserters Patrol," Pete left the cattle drive to become an Indian scout at Fort Brace). Also facing hardships along the trail are Jim Quince (handles flank; played by Steve Raines), Hey Soos Petinas (horse wrangler; played by Robert Cabal) and Joe Scarlet (handles swing; played by Rocky Shahan). Frankie Laine sings the theme, "Rawhide."

The Real McCoys
(ABC, 1957–1962; CBS, 1962–1963)

Cast: Walter Brennan (Amos McCoy), Richard Crenna (Luke McCoy), Kathleen Nolan (Kate McCoy), Lydia Reed (Hassie McCoy), Michael Winkelman (Little Luke McCoy), Tony Martinez (Pepino Garcia).

Basis: A poor but proud farming family (the McCoys) struggle to begin a new life in the San Fernando Valley as farmers: Amos, the head of the family; his son, Luke; Luke's wife, Kate; and Luke's sister and brother, Hassie and Little Luke.

THE McCOYS

Farm Address: Located on "The Back Road 4½ miles outside of town."

Acreage: 20 acres ("15 acres of land fit for growing crops; the east five acres covered with rocks").

Mortgage: Held by the Sun Mortgage and Loan Company.

Telephone Number: Valley 4276.

Crops: Tomatoes, lettuce, potatoes, strawberries, apples (sold to Mother Norman's Frozen Apple Pie Company), peaches, beans, alfalfa (sold to the Tilford Stables).

Livestock: 56 chickens (laying hens Marie, Loretta, Ethel, Harriet, Lazy Susan, and Henrietta are their favorites); a bull (Old Abe); a horse (Rick); milk cows (Bessie, Jenny, Agnes, and Rosemary). They also have hogs, Dirty Jack being Amos's favorite.

Side Business: Roadside Egg and Fresh Milk Stand (eggs are 60 cents a dozen; milk is 25 cents a quart).

Car: 1930 Ford Model A Touring Car (license plate LBV 179; 260,511 miles on the engine in 1958); called both Gertrude and Emily by Grandpa.

Pet Dog: Mac.

Family Ancestors: Two moonshiners, a horse thief, and a riverboat gambler.

Family Tradition: No McCoy ever backs out of a problem.

Family TV Set: A 1947 Philco with a seven-inch screen.

Family Weakness: "The McCoys have a weakness for flattery" (as Grandpa claims).

Family Bank: The Cookie Jar in the kitchen (also said to be "The Sugar Bowl in the dish cabinet").

Tony Martinez, Walter Brennan, and Richard Crenna. © ABC ABC/Photofest

AMOS McCOY

Year of Birth: July 23, 1894, in Smokey Corners, West Virginia ("The year the still blew up"). He is 64 years old when the series begins and has been a widower for 17 years. He previously lived in Smokey Corners and inherited the ranch from his late brother, Ben.

Late Wife: Julie.

Expertise: Birdcalls.

Musical Ability: Plays "The Jug" (that usually holds moonshine).

Prized Family Recipe: The McCoy Tonic (an alcoholic beverage that can cure a variety of aliments; it has been handed down from generation to generation for over 100 years).

Affiliations: A member of the Royal Order of the Mystic Nile Lodge (where he is Grand Imperial Mummy) and president of the West Valley Grange Association.

Most Treasured Item: Henrietta, a Revolutionary War musket (a Baker Flint Lock) that he says "Zachary McCoy used to whip the Red Coats."

Favorite Meal: Fried chicken, apple pie.

Favorite Movie Star: Clara Bow.

Favorite Activities: Whittle on the front porch, playing checkers, pitching horseshoes.

Catchphrase: "Tar-nation," "Gall-darn-it."

Secondary Job: Salesman at the McGinnis Hardware Store; salesman at the Feed Store.

Character: Fondly called Grandpa, he is the second oldest living McCoy. His great great "grandpappy," Ezekiel Phineas McCoy, fought with George Washington during the American Revolution. When it comes to planting crops, Grandpa knows what goes where by tasting the dirt—"I got a taste for dirt." He balks at women wearing lipstick and perfume because "McCoy women are born good looking and smooth-skinned and with strong muscles." He enjoys pitching horseshoes, fishing, playing checkers, and relaxing in his rocking chair on the front porch. Amos is also most embarrassed by the fact that he can't read or write (he signs with an "X." If it is important, it is done with a capital "X"; if not, he uses a lowercase "x"). He also believes mothers-in-law were born to be mean—"It's the nature of the beast." He can play the jug (that once held moonshine) and is the oldest of 13 children. In Smokey Corners, Grandpa was known as "Twinkle Toes" for his dancing expertise and was a volunteer fireman (wore helmet 1); in California, he is a member of the Valley Volunteers Fire Brigade. "Rest Thy Head" appears on the back of Grandpa's rocking chair; Henry is his skeet-shooting rifle; Iron Mule is his stubborn (never starts) tractor, and he can tell what the weather will be by the feel in his knuckles. Amos considers himself "charming and delightful," and a pair of Buster Baker shoes were the first he could call his own (that he didn't have to share with his brother Ben when they were kids).

Relations: Tina Louise as his niece, Tildy; Torin Thatcher as his uncle, Fergus; Virginia Gregg as his niece, Sara; Edward Arnold as Sara's husband, Harry Burns; Sterling Holloway as Orville McCoy (the family jinx); Jane Darwell as Great Grandma McCoy, the oldest living McCoy (100 years old).

LUCIUS "LUKE" McCOY

Age: 23 years old when the series begins.

Affiliations: The Grange Association and the Mystic Nile Lodge (which raises money for charity, promotes brotherhood in the community, and helps people in need). In Smokey Corners, Luke was a member of the State Militia Marching Band.

Honor: Arm wrestling champion (Virginia State).

Secondary Job: County dog catcher (Badge 7014; Car Code AR-3); salesman at Russell's Shoe Store (at $12 a week); deputy game warden.

Character: Luke and Kate married shortly before leaving West Virginia (they honeymooned at the Colonial Palms Motel and stayed in room 24). "Margie" was the song they first danced to when they met at the June Social (another episode claims they first met at Sunday school), and Luke courted Kate by letting her ride on the handlebars of his bicycle. Luke wrote a song called "In the Name of Rotten Love" and entered an amateur radio contest and attempted to win prizes by singing the song "In Old West Virginny." He struggles to do what is best for the farm and sometime encounters resistance from Grandpa, who is sometimes reluctant to accept the new methods of farming; they are also members of the Valley Co-op Poultry Association. In Smokey Corners, Amos and Luke were known as expert marksmen and "took the shootin' prizes in contests." Amos was displeased with the fact that Luke had married Kate (a female he thought was too soft for farming). He wanted Luke to marry 16-year-old Elviry Goody (the daughter of his friend Frank Goody), who "could lick two men in the morning and plow a field in the afternoon." Amos considered Kate to be a woman who was brought up "in a house of curtains" (elegance) and not fit for farm living ("a skinny woman in her twenties who didn't even know how to shoe a mare"). However, when Amos realizes that Luke truly loves Kate (Luke says "she's mighty pleasant company"), he refrains from calling her "Ma'am" and starts calling her Kate (Kate wishes Luke were a bit more romantic at times).

Relations: Hal Baylor as Charlie McCoy, Luke's cousin; Doris Singleton as Charlie's wife; Pat Buttram as Gill McCoy, his uncle; Henry James as Jed McCoy, Luke's uncle; Eve McVeagh as Myra McCoy, Jed's wife.

KATHERINE "KATE" McCOY
Place of Birth: Smokey Corners, West Virginia.
Age: 22 when the series begins.
Maiden Name: Kate Purvis.
Nickname (by Luke): Sugar Babe (Honey Babe in the pilot).
Affiliations: The Charity Clothing Drive, the Ladies Auxiliary.
Secondary Jobs: Salesgirl at the Knit Shop; sewing (mending clothes, making dresses from home).
Character: Famous for her cooking (she won the Prize Foods of California Home Baking Preserves Contest with her piccalilli, wherein she received a blue ribbon) and a $50 gift certificate for winning the Mrs. Homemaker Contest at the Carter Brothers General Store. She is a hardworking farm wife and mother and wishes, at times, that she could live a more "citified" life. Kate looks after the household finances and insists that the money earned be used for only important purchases. In high school, Kate starred in school plays and received a scholarship to the Whelan, West Virginia, Actors' School but turned it down (she and Luke were dating, and she believed marriage was more important).

Luke's parents are deceased. He and Kate care for Luke's sister Hassie and his younger brother Little Luke (Luke's parents were so excited when the baby was born that they named him Luke—forgetting they already had a son named Luke). Kate is not one for fancy clothes; she has four special dresses (as Luke says, "One for each season of the year") and often makes her and Hassie's clothes. Her only relaxation appears to be reading *Happy Housewife* magazine.
Relations: Lurene Tuttle as Gladys Purvis, Kate's mother; Audrey Randolph as Isabel, Kate's aunt (Gladys's sister); Harry Snowden as Kate's Uncle Dave.

TALLAHASSEE "HASSIE" McCOY
Age: 13 years old when the series begins.
Middle Name: Ethel May.
Education: Valley High School (where she pledged Alpha Beta Sigma sorority). In her senior year at Valley High, Hassie joined the "in crowd" of teenage girls called the "Bunch."
After-School Hangout: The Malt Shop (later the Soda Fountain).
Jobs: Babysitting, counter girl at the Malt Shop.
Favorite Colors: Red and silver.

Trendsetter: First one in her school to have her hair set in the latest craze from France: the Bouffant Beehive (acquired at Armand's Beauty Parlor at a cost of $3.50).

Character: Hassie, as she is called, is typical of girls her age and like Kate wishes she too were living a more "citified" life. Although she is very pretty, Hassie sometimes finds resistance from Grandpa when her tastes in clothes go from "fully covered up" and dungarees to a bit more revealing dresses. Hassie is not a go-getter and often finds herself getting in trouble for following the lead of others at school. She is very respectful to Kate and Luke but often finds herself siding with Kate when the male family members have what she believes is the wrong attitude toward a woman's role in the home (no jobs, just cooking, cleaning, and caring for the man in her life). She always kisses Grandpa on the cheek, and Grandpa considers her "a great hog slopper; one of the best."

LITTLE LUKE McCOY

Education: Valley Elementary School (although he has a tendency to play hooky).

Job: Newspaper delivery boy (earned $10.24 in his first week), stock clerk at Clark's Department Store.

Pets: Mack (dog), Homer (frog).

Character: The only McCoy to be born in a hospital. He is a member of the Valley Town Tigers little league team (jersey 4). Little Luke enjoys fishing at "The Pond" (sometimes cutting school to do so) and holds the record as Champion Corn Eater of the Valley. He is also an expert marble shooter and a member of the Imperial Demons Club (his initiation was to enter the Haunted Hubbard House). When Little Luke has nothing to say, it means something is bothering him. He believes Hassie is "a sweet sister as long as you gotta have a sister." While Little Luke attends Valley Elementary School, it was originally called "That school that Little Luke attends" (Grandpa believes "it is a prison with all those rooms"). He plays the bass drum in the school band.

PEPINO GARCIA

Character: Grandpa considers Pepino, the Mexican hired hand (earns $4, then $15, a week; later $40 a month), to be a McCoy until he does something wrong and "is fired from the family." Pepino lives in "the room in the barn" and calls Amos "Señor Grandpa." He tries to help solve family problems, but Amos always tells him to "shut his big floppy mouth." Pepino believes in superstitions and potions (which he acquires from "The Owl Lady" [played by Jeanette Nolan]), and rattlesnake with beans is his favorite meal.

Relatives: Lee Bergere as Fernando Garcia, his cousin, a famous bullfighter in Mexico.

OTHER REGULARS

George MacMichael (Andy Clyde) is Amos's best friend (they play checkers every Wednesday night). He runs "the farm up the hill" from the McCoys with his sister Flora (Madge Blake). Amos says, "George is a cranky old bachelor who ought to be put out to pasture."

Note: At the start of the 1962–1963 season, viewers see Hassie leaving home for college. Little Luke is said "to be at camp," and Luke has been a widower for a year and a half (no mention is made as to how Kate "died"). George and Pepino are given featured roles, and Luke becomes involved with various women as he seeks a wife. He is often featured dating his new neighbor, Louise Howard (Janet DeGore), a widow from Cleveland with a young son named Gregg (Butch Patrick). Louise's aunt, Winnie Jordan (Joan Blondell), a former stage star, tries to spark a romance between Luke and Louise. In the first non-Kate episode, the McCoys' cousin Tilda (Tina Louise) appears to help Amos, Luke, and Pepino care for the house (the backwoods Tilda is amazed by electric lights, running water, a gas oven, and having her own room).

The Rebel
(ABC, 1959–1961)

Cast: Nick Adams (Johnny Yuma).
Basis: A bitter ex–Civil War soldier (Johnny Yuma) travels an unknown road seeking to find his own identity.

It is the post–Civil War West of 1867, and Johnny Yuma, an embittered, leather-tough ex–Confederate soldier, has begun a journey west not only to erase the nightmare of war but also to seek his own identity. Johnny wears his gray Rebel uniform proudly wherever he goes; his saddle is his pillow, and he never stays in one place long enough to call home—"The things I gotta learn about aren't here, just another stop in an off place." He keeps a diary of his travels, his "book," as he calls it, and he helps people in trouble—his strong sense of justice forces him into violent confrontations with those who oppose his beliefs.

Johnny was born in the town of Mason. He yearned to be a writer and work for the town newspaper, the Mason *Bulletin,* but he could never stay put. He ran away from home several times when he was 15 years old and joined the Confederate army as a means of running away. Johnny's mother passed away when he was very young, and he was raised by his father, Ned Yuma. He now rides his late father's horse and carries a scattergun (Ned, the town sheriff, was killed in the line of duty).

The Civil War may be over, but hatred around the country still exists. "Maybe I'll find my place one day," he says. Until that time, he wanders, and he "packed no star as he wandered far, where the only law was a hook-and-a-draw, the Rebel, Johnny Yuma." In the opening theme, the left-side profile of Johnny is branded on a piece of wood.

Johnny Cash sings the theme, "The Rebel—Johnny Yuma." It is not widely known that Elvis Presley recorded the original theme for the pilot episode, which for unknown reasons was replaced by the Johnny Cash version.

Richard Diamond, Private Detective
(CBS, 1957–1959; NBC, 1959–1960)

Cast: David Janssen (Richard Diamond), Mary Tyler Moore, Roxanne Brooks (Sam), Regis Toomey (Lieutenant Dennis McGough), Russ Conway (Lieutenant Pete Kile), Barbara Bain (Karen Wells).

Basis: The cases of New York (later Los Angeles)–based private detective Richard Diamond.

RICHARD DIAMOND

Occupation: Private investigator.

Business Address (New York): Office 306 at West 45th Street in Midtown Manhattan.

Business Address (Los Angeles): Office 117 at McDonald Street.

Mobile Phone Number (New York): ZM1-2173 (later ZM1-2713).

Home Address (New York): The Savoy Hotel.

Character: Richard is a former detective with the 5th Precinct of the New York Police Department. When he became disgusted with the limitations with which he was permitted to apprehend criminals, he resigned to do things his way as a private detective. Richard's fees are rather high for the time ($100 a day plus expenses), but, being a ladies' man, if a case involves a beautiful woman, he will lower his price (usually to $50 a day). Richard reads the New York *Chronicle* and doesn't come to the office on Tuesdays. He claims that "a private eye is only as good as his snitches" and pays such people as much as $10 for information (which he charges to the client). Richard dines at the Lunch Counter (a diner in Midtown Manhattan) and often finds going undercover the best way to solve a case ("Because people are allergic to my profession"). In New York episodes, his former superior, Lieutenant Dennis McGough, is his police department contact; Lieutenant Pete Kile (who calls Richard "Rick") is his Los Angeles contact. It is also in Los Angeles episodes that Richard acquires a girlfriend, Karen Wells.

SAM

Sex: Female.

Occupation: Telephone answering service operator.

Business Name: The Hi-Fi Answering Service.

Answering Service Phone Number: Murray Hill 4-9099 (when Mary Tyler Moore played the role); Olympia 4-1654 (with Roxanne Brooks as Sam).

Bra Size: 38-B (the then famous "Torpedo Bra").

Stocking Size: 10 (medium length).

Character: "The only thing I know about her is what she tells me—and that ain't much" is what Richard says about the sexy-voiced Sam (whom he sometimes calls "Samuel"). Richard does not have a secretary and relies on communication with Sam for client information.

Sam (no other name given) is as mysterious as Richard said. She is situated in a dimly lit room that displays her shapely legs, slim waist, and well-developed bust. Her face is never clearly seen, and she wears tight blouses and sweaters and slit (on the side) skirts or dresses raised just high enough for that "cheesecake" effect. Richard also acquires clients from Sam— "Richard, I have a friend who needs help—a female friend." Sam answers Richard's office calls on the fourth ring. When she speaks with Richard, she says, "It's me, Mr. D." Richard concludes his conversations with Sam with, "As usual, Samuel, thank you."

Note: The program is also known as *Call Mr. D.* (its title when first syndicated in 1960).

The Rifleman
(ABC, 1958–1963)

Cast: Chuck Connors (Lucas McCain), Johnny Crawford (Mark McCain).

Basis: A widower (Lucas McCain) with a young son (Mark) struggles to begin a new life in New Mexico during the 1860s.

Following the death of his wife, a rancher (Lucas McCain) and his young son (Mark) leave their home in the Indian Nations (1860s) and head west to begin a new life in the town of North Fork, New Mexico. Lucas, known as "The Rifleman" (the fastest man with a .44-40 hair-trigger Winchester rifle with a special hoop lever), purchases the 4,100-acre Dunlap Ranch, and he and Mark attempt to maintain their own empire in an era of lawlessness. Lucas rides a horse named Razor; Mark's horse is called Blue Boy, and his first job was as a stable boy.

Lucas's rifle allows normal firing when a special screw is loose and rapid firing when the screw is tightened. In the opening theme, Lucas fires 12 successive times; the rifle can fire eight times in two and a half seconds. While Lucas did serve with the Union army during the Civil War, he has learned to respect life and never shoots to kill. Although he uses a rifle (and never a holstered gun), he will aim to wound if possible. While he likes to keep to himself and run his cattle ranch, circumstances will rarely allow him to do so, as helping the town marshal, Micah Torrance (Paul Fix), maintain the law always takes precedence. Sweeney (Bill Quinn) runs the town saloon, the Last Chance Saloon; Millie Scott (Joan Taylor) owns the General Store; Eddie Holstead (John Harmon) runs the Madera House Hotel (later replaced by Patricia Blair as Lou Mallory, the owner of the Mallory House Hotel. She was born in Ireland, orphaned at

Johnny Crawford and Chuck Connors as Mark and Lucas McCain.
© ABC ABC/Photofest

14, and worked in a potato field by day and a bar at night. She saved her money and traveled to America to make something of herself. She first begins by buying unclaimed land in North Fork, then the hotel).

Gloria DeHaven played Eddie's daughter, Lillian Holstead; Cheryl Holdridge was Sally Walker, Millie's niece; Jerome Courtland played Lucas's brother-in-law, Johnny Gibbs; and Thomas Gomez was Artemis Quarles, Lucas's cousin on his wife's side.

Rocky and His Friends
(ABC, 1959–1961; NBC, 1961–1964)

Voice Cast: June Foray (Rocky/Natasha), Bill Scott (Bullwinkle), Paul Frees (Boris), William Conrad, Paul Frees (narrators).
Basis: Animated adventures of a flying squirrel (Rocky) and his dim-witted friend, Bullwinkle the Moose.

Frostbite Falls is an extremely small town in Minnesota. It is populated by 29 people, two of whom are a heroic flying squirrel (Rocket "Rocky" Squirrel) and Bullwinkle J. Moose, his dim-witted companion. For some unknown reason, Frostbite Falls has become a battleground between good and evil and Rocky and Bullwinkle's headquarters as they battle the most nefarious of villains, the evil Boris Badenov and his lovely and deadly companion, Natasha Fataly.

Frostbite Falls is serviced by the Union Pathetic Railroad (a spoof of the Union Pacific Railroad), and when the town's only movie theater, the Bijou, opened, the first picture screened was *A Trolley Named Tallulah*. Rocky and Bullwinkle attended Frostbite Falls High School and then Frostbite University (where Bullwinkle was a "B.M.O.C."—"Big Moose on Campus." He was also tricked into playing football against his own school by the rival Wossamotta U). Purple and red are the Frostbite U school colors.

Each year, Rocky and Bullwinkle vacation on an island called Moosylvania ("The wettest, soggiest, dreariest place on Earth") for one simple reason: after two weeks, any place on Earth looks like Heaven. Moosylvania is located between the United States and Canada and has the distinction of being ignored by both countries (the United States believes Canada owns it; Canada believes it belongs to the United States).

Rocky, "The All-American Squirrel," wears an aviator's cap and says, "Hoakie Smokes," when something goes wrong; his hero is Bullwinkle, a moronic moose. Bullwinkle's claim to fame is an antigravity metal called Upsadasium (which was found by his uncle, Dewlop D. Moose on Mount Platten). Bullwinkle, sometimes called Bullwinkle J. Moose, believes comic books are real life ("If you can't believe what you read in a comic book, what can you believe? It's enough to destroy a young moose's faith") and frequently asks the narrator for help with an episode ("It's difficult to follow the plot and be in it at the same time"). Bullwinkle also believes that he is the greatest actor since Elmo Lincoln (the movie screen's first Tarzan). His hero is Rocky. The biggest event in Frostbite Falls is the yearly celebration of the Flotilla Festival (when all the kids go down to frolic at Veronica Lake and let the town's old-timers enjoy a day of peace and quiet).

Boris Badenov, "International Bad Guy" and "the world's lowest snake in the grass," is, in some episodes, an international spy (from the country of Pottsylvania) and in others the vice president of Crime Syndicate. He is a member of both the Fetish of the Month Club and Local 12 (the Villains, Thieves, and Scoundrels Union). He and Natasha operate from a house called "The Old Bleakley Place." Their superiors are Mr. Big (a midget who casts a giant shadow) and Fearless Leader. Boris reads *Crime* magazine, and his hero is Fingers Scarenose, a notorious criminal.

Bullwinkle also appeared in a filler segment called "Mr. Know-It-All," where he displayed his knowledge (his "bird's eye view with a brain to match").

Other show segments include *Dudley Do-Right of the Mounties* (a dim-witted Royal Canadian Mounted Policeman attempts to capture a notorious criminal named Snidely Whiplash), *Peabody's Improbable History* (an intelligent dog, Mr. Peabody, and a young boy, Sherman, travel through time via the Way Back Machine), and *Fractured Fairy Tales* (Edward Everett Horton relates slightly warped versions of famous fairy tales).

Rocky Jones, Space Ranger
(Syndicated, 1954)

Cast: Richard Crane (Rocky Jones), Sally Mansfield (Vena Ray), Scotty Becket (Winky), Robert Lyden (Bobby), Jimmy Lydon (Biff), Maurice Cass (Professor Newton), Charles Meredith (Secretary Drake).

Basis: It is the 21st century, and the Space Rangers has been established to protect the planets of the United Worlds of the Solar System from evil.

Rocky Jones pilots the ship *Orbit Jet* (radio code XV-2), then the *Silver Moon* (code XV-3). He is the chief of the Space Rangers and is assisted by Vena Ray, Winky, and Bobby. Biff later joins the crew, and Secretary Drake is the head of the Space Rangers.

Rocky, who was officially called "Rocket Jones" in one episode, is fearless and will risk his life if it means saving the lives of others. Vena Ray, a very attractive young woman, is Rocky's scientific adviser (and assistant to Professor Newton). She weighs 118 pounds and wears a relatively short skirt (for the time) and a cape. Winky is Rocky's navigator (possibly nicknamed as such for his habit of sleeping or napping on the job), and Bobby, a young boy, is possibly a junior ranger cadet (not stated exactly what a preteen is doing accompanying Rocky on dangerous missions). When something goes wrong, he exclaims, "Roaring Rockets." Professor Newton, the elderly scientist, conducts business from his elaborate headquarters, Newton's Observatory. The channel 17W-157 allows visual communication seen through his atomic powered telescope via a TV monitor.

Overall, very little information is given. The setting is mentioned as the year 2054. Transport TR-14 and OW-9 are two of the refueling stations established in space. The United Worlds of the Solar System delegates responsibility to each member planet with the overall intent to benefit all members. The Visograph, operating on positive rays, allows visual observance of space. Astro-phones permit audio communication from planet to planet. The Mechanical Canary tests the atmosphere of other planets (indicating with a "chirp chirp" sound that the environment is breathable).

Aliens were also featured. Patsy Parsons played Cleolanta, the enchanting queen of the planet Ophischus; Dian Fauntelle was Yarra, ruler of the planet Medina; Walter Coy played Zorvac, king of the planet Fornax; and Patsy Iannone appeared as his daughter, Volca.

Rod Brown of the Rocket Rangers
(CBS, 1953–1954)

Cast: Cliff Robertson (Rod Brown), Bruce Hall (Frank Boyle), Jack Weston (Wilbur Wormser), John Boruff (Commander Swift).

Basis: Members of the futuristic (22nd century) organization, the Rocket Rangers, protect the United Solar System from alien invaders.

ROD BROWN
Character: Commander of a space ship called the *Beta* (which blasts off from Orbit 4). Rod joined the Rocket Rangers fresh out of college, as he felt an urgent need to keep the world safe. While he is a high-ranking official, Rod also finds himself becoming a diplomat, undercover agent, fighter, and peacemaker—whatever it takes to accomplish a mission. Rod sees each mission as a challenge and is a bit reluctant to use force (weapons) if a situation can be resolved through a nonviolent confrontation. He was born on the planet Earth in the year 2165 and is the son of George and Margaret

Brown. He has two siblings (a younger sister, Eileen, and an older brother, James) and became interested in outer space at an early age when he studied the history of the United Solar System (comprises the planets Earth, Mars, Jupiter, Mercury, and Venus), which was formed in the late 21st century to repel threats from the uncharted regions of outer space. As Rod grew, he studied the history and lifestyles of all the known planets in the solar system and hopes to one day explore the mysteries of the uncharted planets (Uranus, Pluto, and Saturn). Frank Boyle often serves as Rod's second in command on missions.

WILBUR WORMSER

Character: Rod's chief navigator (who plots the *Beta*'s course from Omega Base). Wilbur is a bit mishap prone and is called "Wormsey" for his sometimes cowardly actions (he hates confrontations and does what he can to avoid situations that pose a personal threat). Wormsey (as he most often called) was born in 2159 on Earth and is the only child of Elizabeth and Jonas Wormser. Unlike Rod, Wormsey had become fascinated by the early stages of flight (Amelia Earhart and Wilbur and Orville Wright were childhood idols) and entered school with a determination to one day become a pioneer and go down in history as the man who revolutionized space flight. While Wormsey is brilliant at what he does, he is easily upset, has a tendency to lose his temper and is known for exclaiming "Oh Great Jupiter" in times of stress. When referring to Commander Swift, the head of the Rocket Rangers, Wormsey calls him "The Old Man."

PROGRAM INFORMATION

Rod and other Rangers have no special weapons, and a ray gun appears to be the only weapon the Rangers use. There are also no special codes—a transmission sequence plays as "Control tower to *Beta*." "*Beta* here, over." After the message is received by Rod, he would simply sign off with "Check. Over and out." If Rod had to contact headquarters, he would simply say, "Rocket ship *Beta* calling Ranger Headquarters, Earth" (apparently no security measures were taken to encrypt messages to prevent the enemy from learning Rod's plans).

The program, broadcast on Saturday mornings, was geared to children and incorporated "The Code of the Rocket Rangers." At the end of an episode, Rod would begin reciting the code with "On My Honor as a Rocket Ranger, I Pledge That I Shall" (then state its 10 articles):

1. Always chart my course according to the Constitution of the United States of America.
2. Never cross orbits with the rights and beliefs of others.

3. Blast off at full space speed to protect the weak and innocent.
4. Stay out of collision orbits with the laws of my state and community.
5. Cruise in parallel orbit with my parents and teachers.
6. Not roar my rockets unwisely and shall be courteous at all times.
7. Keep my gyros steady and reactors burning by being industrious and thrifty.
8. Keep my scanner tuned to learning and remain coupled to my studies.
9. Keep my mind out of free-fall by being mentally alert.
10. Blast the meteors from the paths of other people by being kind and considerate.

The code, like the program, never caught on, as competition from other already established space shows (like *Tom Corbett, Space Cadet, Space Patrol,* and *Captain Video*) featured more action and more compelling stories. The program opened as follows: "CBS Television presents *Rod Brown of the Rocket Rangers.* Surging with the power of the atom, gleaming like great silver bullets, the mighty Rocket Rangers' space ships stand by for blastoff. Up, up, rockets blazing with white hot fury; the man-made meteors ride through the atmosphere breaking the gravity barrier, pushing up and out, faster and faster and then outer space and high adventure for the Rocket Rangers."

The Roy Rogers Show
(CBS, 1952–1964)

Cast: Roy Rogers, Dale Evans, Pat Brady (themselves).
Basis: Modern-day western wherein a rancher (Roy Rogers) battles injustice in and around the community in which he lives.

ROY ROGERS
Horse: Trigger.
Dog: Bullet:
Character: Owner of the Double R Bar ranch. Occasionally seen as the sheriff, acting sheriff, and forest ranger. Called "King of the Cowboys." He is also the blood brother (called "Rising Sun") of Gray Eagle, chief of the local (unnamed) Indian tribe. Roy is fast with his guns but will never shoot to kill. Rather than just stumbling on a crime, he often pokes his nose into other people's business and takes it on himself to resolve the situation he uncovered. While he is capable of taking care of himself, he often gets the worst in beatings from outlaws.

DALE EVANS

Horse: Buttermilk.

Occupation: Ranch owner and operator of town's Eureka Café and Hotel.

Character: Roy's assumed girlfriend (although not specifically stated). Dale, called "Queen of the West," is an expert shot and is the only character who lives in a modern-day ranch house in an area not reminiscent of the Old West. While pretty, Dale never uses her looks to achieve a goal and can handle herself in virtually any situation (although she too occasionally finds herself outwitted by an outlaw).

Relations: Alfalfa Switzer as Bob, Dale's nephew.

PATRICK "PAT" BRADY

Occupation: Roy's ranch foreman and Dale's diner cook and dishwasher.

Car: Nellybelle (license plate 355-388), a temperamental Jeep.

Horse: Phineas.

Character: "Roy's comical side-kick" who sometimes uses his middle name of Aloysius. He is quite naive and easily taken advantage of (he is the perfect target of schemers seeking to make an easy buck). When Pat is made a deputy (by Roy), Nellybelle becomes the town's only police car (with two large "Police" insignias on each side of the windshield). Pat claims, "There ain't no posse complete without Pat and Nellybelle—even if the Sheriff doesn't think so." He also owns a worthless, flood-prone ghost town called Lucky Springs, which he bought at a land auction.

Relations: Mary Ellen Kay as Pat's cousin, Mary Meriwether; Myron Healey as Jim Meriwether, Pat's uncle.

THE TOWN

Mineral City in Paradise Valley is an Old West–like 1860s community wherein the good guys and the bad guys ride horses, carry guns, and live in typical Old West–style wooden homes and cabins. Banks are robbed, outlaws plague the area, cattle are rustled, and gunplay is frequent (there are no police, only the local sheriff). Cars are seen (but no gas stations), telephones are used (although they represent early incarnations), roads are unpaved, and modern buildings are not seen. Stagecoaches are used as a means of transportation (in some episodes, a station wagon is seen as Arrow Stage Lines).

Note: Roy Rogers and Dale Evans are the first stars of a TV series to sing their own theme song ("Happy Trails").

77 Sunset Strip
(ABC, 1958–1964)

Cast: Efrem Zimbalist Jr. (Stuart Bailey), Roger Smith (Jeff Spencer), Richard Long (Rex Randolph), Edd Byrnes (Kookie), Jacqueline Beer (Suzanne Fabray), Louis Quinn (Roscoe), Robert Logan (J. R. Hale), Byron Keith (Roy Gilmore).

Basis: Case investigations of Stuart Bailey and Jeff Spencer, owners of Bailey and Spencer, Private Investigators, at 77 Sunset Strip in Hollywood, California. They sometimes work for the Pacific Casualty Insurance Company in San Francisco and Pacific Orient Insurance in Los Angeles.

STUART "STU" BAILEY
Character: Occupies office 101. He was a former OSS (Office of Strategic Services) agent during World War II and now lives in Apartment 301 at the Sunset DeVilla; Olympia 1-3792 is his office phone number. He drives a convertible with the license plate number PAZ 184, later AVE 424, JPN 300, RTU 020, and NPO 614. Stu is a bit reluctant to use force and relies on his intelligence training to accomplish his goals during a case.

JEFF SPENCER
Character: Jeff occupies office 102, and Olympia 6-1116 is his home phone number. He lives in Apartment 517 of an unidentified building and drives a car with the license plate PYB 767, later GBC 101. He reads *Playboy* magazine (surprisingly "not for the articles"), and $50 is the top price he pays a snitch for information. Jeff and Stu have an eye for the ladies, and girls often tell Jeff, "You're too cute to be a snoop." Jeff is more adept at physical heroics than Stu, who he sometimes calls "The Professor" for his intelligence and ability to speak several languages.

GERALD LLOYD KOOKSON III

Character: Better known as Kookie, he is the parking lot attendant at Dino's Lodge, the supper club next to 77 Sunset Strip. Kookie lives at 18026 Valley Hart Drive with his unseen mother, Helen Margaret Kookson, a public stenographer; his father is deceased. Kookie drives a hot rod with the license plate JOY 038, later K-3400, and uses hip talk, for example, "Squaresville, Man," "Like Man, let's get out of here," and "I don't dig it." He refers to Jeff and Stu as "Hey, Dad," and pretty girls are "Dreamboats." Trouble is "Troublesville." The Cool Dragon Cafe and the Chez Paulette Coffeehouse are his favorite hangouts. Kookie had a way of combing his hair that drove teenage girls in the viewing audience crazy; the song "Kookie, Kookie, Lend Me Your Comb" became a hit. In fourth-season episodes, Kookie left Dino's to become partners with Jeff and Stu. J. R. Hale replaced Kookie as the new parking lot attendant at Dino's. Chic Hammons (Sue Randall), a beautiful college girl studying art, became, as Kookie said, "The only girl to appeal to my intellectual side." Kookie is usually seen with gorgeous girls who are a bit kookie— today referred to as "airhead" or "bimbo."

SUZANNE

Character: A gorgeous French girl who operates the Sunset Answering Service from office 103 at 77 Sunset Strip. She is also a public stenographer, as seen

Edd Byrnes, Efrem Zimbalist Jr., and Roger Smith. © ABC ABC/Photofest

in printing on the left side of the door, and lives in Apartment 217 at 152½ North Maple Street, later address given as 236 North Maple, Apartment B; 354-4567 is her phone number. Suzanne's switchboard phone number for Bailey and Spencer is Olympia 4-0992, later Olympia 5-1656. Kookie gives Suzanne two donuts and a cup of coffee each day "to refuel her energy." Suzanne works occasionally for Stu or Jeff in an undercover capacity (when a beautiful girl is needed in a sting).

ROSCOE

Character: A stool pigeon who provides information to Stu and Jeff. He was born in the Bronx, New York, and is addicted to gambling. He calls Suzanne "Frenchy" and bets on horses at Hollywood Park. He owned a greyhound racing dog named Genevieve, which he purchased for $500 in a claiming race, and calls girls "Fillies." Bourbon and ginger ale is his favorite drink.

ROY GILMORE

Character: Called Gil, he is a lieutenant with the Homicide Bureau of the Los Angeles Police Department. He sometimes regrets the job and says, "I should have taken my father's advice and studied air conditioning instead of Nick Carter books."

ADDITIONAL INFORMATION

Dino's Lodge closes at 2:00 a.m. The Frankie Ortega Trio provides the music at Dino's Lodge. Kookie keeps a spare dinner jacket in the hatcheck room at Dino's for emergencies. In the back of the lodge is Dino's Poodle Palace, where the pampered poodles of patrons stay.

How did Stu and Jeff come to 77 Sunset Strip? It's all a matter of whom to believe. According to Jeff, it began when he arrived in Los Angeles and opened a successful detective agency in Beverly Hills. While driving one afternoon, his car experienced a flat tire, and he received help from a kid in a hot rod named Kookie. In gratitude, Jeff gave him his business card and said, "If I can ever repay the favor, let me know." A short time later, a struggling detective named Stuart Bailey was hired by Pacific Orient Insurance to crack an auto theft ring. During his investigation, Stu meets Jeff, who is also on the case to help Kookie, whose friend has been kidnapped by the ring. Kookie suggests that Jeff and Stu work together. With Kookie's help, the trio breaks up the ring. When Kookie realizes that Stu and Jeff would make a good team, he tells them that offices are for rent at 77 Sunset Strip.

Stu tells a slightly different version. In his scenario, Stu is successful—Bailey, private investigator—while Jeff, owner of Jeff Spencer Investigations, is struggling to stay in business. Here, it was Stu who gets the flat tire, and it was he who gave the good Samaritan, Kookie, the business card. Pacific Orient hired Jeff to crack the auto theft ring, while Stu agreed to help Kookie.

Kookie tells it a bit differently. "If it hadn't been for me, they wouldn't have made the scene at all. It all started when my wheels went out on the blink. I was makin' with the tools when Jeff just happened to be driving by and stopped to help." Kookie said, "If you ever need help, just ask." When Kookie's friend is kidnapped by the auto theft ring, Kookie figures to help Jeff and his struggling private eye business by letting him crack the ring. Pacific Orient had hired Stuart Bailey, a down-on-his-luck investigator, to do the same thing. The three meet and together break up the ring. Kookie tells Jeff and Stu, "You make a great team and I've got just the place for you to get started—77 Sunset Strip."

Note: In 1963 (to 1964), the format changed to focus on Stu Bailey as a private detective on his own. Although the title remained unchanged, Stu now had an office in downtown Los Angeles in a building called both the Bradbury Building and the Bedford Building. The theme also changed from a snappy vocal composed by Mack David and Jerry Livingston to a musical composition by Bob Thompson. Stu now had a secretary named Hannah (Joan Staley), and stories were told in a flashback manner. As Stu talked to Hannah, a flashback was used to tell the story. When the flashback ended, Stu and Hannah returned to sum up the case.

SGT. BILKO. SEE *The Phil Silvers Show*

Sheena, Queen of the Jungle
(Syndicated, 1956–1957)

Cast: Irish McCalla (Sheena), Christian Drake (Bob Rayburn).
Basis: A beautiful white jungle queen (Sheena) defends her adopted homeland of Africa from evil.

SHEENA
Age: 28 (born in Los Angeles on June 6, 1928).
Measurements: 39½-24½-38.
Hair: Blonde.
Height: 5 feet, 9 inches.
Weight: 141 pounds.
Costume: Conservative but leg-revealing leopard skin dress with a black belt (the symbol of a lion appears in the center of the belt). Sheena also wears a metal

band (embossed with the symbol of a lion) on each arm above her elbow. She also wears a necklace that has a seashell-like pendant (difficult to distinguish, as she never talks about it) and leather-like sandals. Her waist belt has an attachment that allows her to hold her ivory horn (which she uses to summon animals for help).

Weapons: A spear and a knife.

Character: At the age of five, a young girl (later to be known as Sheena) and her parents are aboard a private plane when it develops engine trouble and crashes into the African jungle. The young girl survives and, after wandering away from the plane wreck, is found by Logi (Lee Weaver), a member of the Inoma tribe. When Logi discovers that the girl's parents have been killed, he raises her as one of his own. He names her Sheena and teaches her the ways of the jungle: how to hunt for food, never kill animals unless absolutely necessary, and, most importantly, protect her homeland from the evil men (and women) who are seeking to destroy its serenity. As Sheena grows, she acquires a pet chimpanzee (Chim) who becomes her traveling companion, and, as her legend as a mysterious protector of the jungle grows, she becomes known by superstitious natives as "The White Jungle Goddess."

Sheena lives in a desolate and dangerous area of Africa known as LaMista. It is here that Sheena has established her stronghold and where only a few natives know its location. In a way, Sheena has adopted the traveling ability of chimpanzees, as she prefers to "move through the trees" (as she says) as opposed to walking through the jungle ("Faster my way," she says). Chim is a bit mischievous and curious (patterned after Cheeta from the Johnny Weissmuller *Tarzan* films) and often complicates situations for Sheena. Chim likes to fish (he has his own string on a stick fishing pole), and Sheena claims he is hoping to catch "The Big One."

BOB RAYBURN

Occupation: First said to be a big-game hunter then a white trader.

Place of Birth: Connecticut.

Character: As a big-game hunter, Bob also worked for the Kenya (East Africa) commissioner to ensure the safety of the native tribes and people on safaris. He is later a white trader (deals with the Evans Trading Post) who made Kenya his home after becoming dissatisfied with life in the United States.

He originally dressed in a black shirt and white pants and carried a handgun and knife; he later dresses in all white and arms himself with a rifle. Bob befriended Sheena after she rescued him from quicksand. Bob does help Sheena battle evil, and when Sheena leaves her ivory horn behind, it is an indication to Bob that she needs help.

PROGRAM INFORMATION
Filmed in Mexico with inserted animal stock footage shot in Africa. Irish McCalla originally performed her own stunts until an arm injury made her incapable of swinging through the trees on vines. She was replaced, for stunt sequences, by Raul Gaona, a male Mexican acrobat (who dressed in a leopard skin and blonde wig. Scenes were shot from a distance, and it is impossible to tell that it is not Irish).

Note: The original 1955 pilot episode (shot in color; the series is in black and white) featured Anita Ekberg as Sheena. Feature-film commitments forced Anita to decline the role, and it was recast with Irish. In 2000, Gina Lee Nolan played Sheena in an update of the series called simply *Sheena*.

Smilin' Ed's Gang
(NBC, CBS, ABC, 1950–1955)

Cast: Ed McConnell (Smilin' Ed), Arch Presby, Frank Ferrin (voice of Froggie), June Foray (Midnight/Grandie), Jerry Marin (Buster Brown), Bud Tollefson (Tige, Buster's dog).
Basis: Children's program where a jovial host (Smilin' Ed) entertains with songs, stories, skits, and adventure serials.

"Hi ya kids," host Smilin' Ed McConnell would say as the program opened, "You better come running, it's old Smilin' Ed and His Buster Brown Show." The gang (the studio audience) would then join Ed in singing the show's theme (built around its sponsorship by Buster Brown shoes): "I got shoes, you got shoes, everybody's got to have shoes, but there's only one kind of shoe for me— good old Buster Brown shoes" (the gang cheers with Ed addressing the home audience): "Thank you buddies and sweethearts, good old Buster Brown shoes are on the air out here in Hollywood for another good old Saturday hullabaloo."

Children of all ages were then led into a world where the unreal became real. The set resembled a clubhouse, and Ed would begin each show seated in a large easy chair. He opened a rather big book called *Smilin' Ed's Stories*, and various filmed segments were shown to illustrate the stories (most often the serial-like adventures of "Ghanga Rama, the Elephant Boy," which told of Ghanga Rama [Nino Martel] and his friend Charmer [Harry Stewart], who lived in Bakore, India). Other segments were the antics of Midnight the Cat and Squeaky the Mouse (usually Squeaky attempting to play a song on his fiddle while Midnight accompanied him on a drum), Grandie the Talking Piano, the Buster Brown Jug (jingles sent in by viewers), and the most popular segment, Froggie the Gremlin, the mischievous, magical frog (a rubber toy that was eventually marketed). Froggie's segment began with Ed standing next to a grandfather clock with Ed saying, "Plunk your magic twanger, Froggie" (at which time Froggie would become visible and say, "Hi ya, kids, hi ya, hi ya, hi ya"). After a brief conversation between Froggie and Ed, the show's weekly guest would appear and proceed to converse with (and be driven crazy by) Froggie and his antics. Buster Brown and his dog Tige appeared only in commercials. The well-known catchphrase was Buster saying, "That's my dog Tige, he lives in a shoe. I'm Buster Brown, look for me in there too" (referring to the label inside the shoe).

"Well kids, old Smilin' Ed and the gang will be on television again next week at this same time. So be sure to invite your little pals over to see it. Now don't forget Church or Sunday School. Now once again, we leave the air with this little song: The happy gang of Buster Brown now leaves the air. . . . Watch for us Saturday when Buster Brown is on the air."

The program is based on the radio series of the same title. It was originally called *The Buster Brown TV Show with Smilin' Ed McConnell and the Buster Brown TV Gang* and is also known as *Smilin' Ed McConnell and His Gang* and *Smilin' Ed's Buster Brown Gang*. SEE ALSO *Andy's Gang*.

Space Patrol
(ABC, 1950–1955)

Cast: Ed Kemmer (Buzz Corry), Lyn Osborn (Cadet Happy), Nina Bara (Tonga), Virginia Hewitt (Carol Carlisle), Ken Mayer (Major "Robbie" Robertson), Bela Kovacs (Prince Baccarrati), Norman Jolley (Agent X), Jack McHugh (Major Sova).

Basis: The 30th-century organization Space Patrol protects the United Planets from the evils that still exist in the still vastly unexplored regions of deep space.

BUZZ CORRY

Position: Commander in chief of the Space Patrol.

Rocket Ships: Battle Cruiser 100, Tera IV, Tera V. The *Tera V* was equipped with a time drive and a paralyzer ray; Star Drive was used for deep-space travel.

Relations: Kit Corry (Glenn Denning), Buzz's brother, the original chief of the Space Patrol.

Character: The son of Virginia and David Corry, Buzz was born on Earth in the year 2265. He attended Space Patrol Academy and graduated at the top of his class. He is courageous and quick to take action and as a cadet saved the life of his shipmates during a dangerous mission. This moved him up in rank, and he soon became head of the Space Patrol. He is fascinated by

Carnacan history (a lost civilization of the planet Mars) and enjoys his vacations at the Red Lake Winter Resort on Jupiter and at Space Port at Lake Azure on Venus.

CADET HAPPY

Character: Buzz's copilot. His exceptional grades in high school earned him the Corry Scholarship (set up by Buzz's family), which enabled him to attend college and enter Space Patrol Academy. His interests range from photography to rocket construction, and "Holy Smokin' Rockets" is his catchphrase (which he utters when something goes wrong). While Cadet Happy displays a mild, easygoing persona, he is always ready for a fight if the situation warrants.

TONGA

Character: A Space Patrol ally who was originally a master criminal before she was reformed (she made a career out of robbing passengers on sightseeing ships and was called "The Lady of Diamonds"). As part of her rehabilitation, she was assigned to Space Patrol and eventually became the assistant to Major Robertson, the security chief (in some episodes Tonga is mentioned as being the first secretary to the secretary of the United Planets). Tonga is also not one to sit around and let others "have all the fun" (missions). She often becomes a part of Buzz's assignments, and her past criminal knowledge and abilities are often helpful in completing a mission.

CAROL CARLISLE

Character: The daughter of the secretary-general of the United Planets (Paul Cavanaugh). Carol, a brilliant scientist, is responsible for many of the devices used by Space Patrol. These include the Agra-Ray (brings plants to full maturity in a few hours; if used in reverse it can turn cities into stone) and the *Galaxy*, a magnetic ship shaped like a metal sphere that is capable of traveling at the speed of light. With Tonga, she developed Randurium, a synthetic drug capable of treating radiation and cosmic burns. Carol (and Tonga) wore uniforms designed to show their legs and were very capable of defending themselves (but were most often depicted as "damsels in distress" who needed rescuing by Buzz).

MAJOR ROBERTSON

Character: Called "Robbie," he is not only a leader but a scientist as well. He invented the formula for the Zeta Ray, a machine that can cure any illness and stop the spread of infection. As a leader, he is quick to act but often questions his decisions and worries about the consequences of his actions.

PRINCE BACCARRATI

Character: An evil alien, also known as the Black Falcon, who seeks to rule the United Planets by destroying Space Patrol. He is based in his castle on Planet X.

OTHER VILLAINS

Mr. Proteus (Marvin Miller), the man of many faces whose knack for disguises made him difficult to apprehend; Agent X (Norma Jolley) and Major Sova (Jack McHugh).

PROGRAM INFORMATION

Earth, Mars, Jupiter, Mercury, and Venus make up the United Planets (they span seven and one-third billion miles in diameter; it would take light, which travels at 186,000 miles per second, 11 hours to span its length). Space Patrol is based on the man-made city of Terra (also the location of the Medical Science Center and the United Planets Communications Commission Control Room). Space Patrol agents communicate with each other via Space Phones, and 20th-century weapons, such as guns, are displayed in the United Planets Museum. Jack Narz does the announcing. The program opened as follows: "High adventure in the wild, vast regions of space. Missions of daring in the name of interplanetary justice. Travel into the future with Buzz Corry, commander-in-chief of the *Space Patrol.*"

Sugarfoot
(ABC, 1957–1960)

Cast: Will Hutchins (Thomas "Tom" Brewster).

Basis: The travels of a young man (Tom Brewster), labeled a Sugarfoot (a cowboy working his way up to becoming a tenderfoot), as he wanders across the western frontier.

Tom is peaceful, laid-back, idealistic, and romantic—and looked on as a gullible coward by the more roughneck cowboys. Despite their belief, Tom is skilled with his gun, his fists, and his knife—"Once you get his dander up, ain't no one who's quicker on the draw."

Tom was born in Oklahoma. When he was a child, he was inspired by Judge Henry Davis (Harry Holcombe) to become a lawyer (the judge made decisions to help change the country, deciding, for example, that the Indian is a person as defined by the Constitution). He was a man who personified the law to Tom. When the program begins, Tom is a law school correspondence student who roams the West of the 1870s. He signed up "for some of them correspondence courses from Kansas City" (he is up to lesson 7 in the pilot and carries the law book *Blackstone's Commentary*, Volume 9). Tom's future plans include hanging up a shingle in a place that needs him and that he needs.

According to Tom, "guns are tools of the devil." He wears his father's gun and believes that "shootin' ain't always the answer." He drinks sarsaparilla ("with a touch of cherry") and carries a "Home Sweet Home" plaque with him as he wanders from town to town "tryin' to earn a little livin' money." While Tom struggled to avoid gunplay (he wanted only to study his law books), trouble was all that he found—whether as the sheriff of Blue Rock (his first job in the pilot, "Brannigan's Boots"), a substitute teacher in the town of Morgan, or the ramrod of a cattle drive. His knowledge of the law and strong sense of justice helped him overcome difficult situations when defending clients.

In the town of Casa Grande, Arizona, Tom meets Toothy Thompson (Jack Elam), "a man with a face people distrust." When Tom gets Toothy acquitted of an attempted-murder charge, he finds himself with a new friend and occasional companion on the trail. Toothy, described as "kinda spooky-looking, always smiling," was so grateful for what Tom had done for him that he made himself Tom's best friend.

In the episode "MacBrewster the Bold," three of Tom's Scottish relatives appear: Douglas MacBrewster (Robin Hughes), Angus MacBrewster (Tudor Owen), and Wee Rabbie MacBrewster (Alan Caillou). Will Hutchins also played his outlaw double, the Canary Kid, in several episodes.

SUSIE. SEE *Private Secretary*

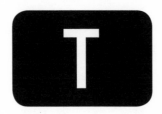

The Thin Man
(NBC, 1957–1959)

Cast: Peter Lawford (Nick Charles), Phyllis Kirk (Nora Charles), Nita Talbot (Blondie Collins), Jack Albertson (Lieutenant Harry Evans), Stafford Repp (Lieutenant Ralph Raine).

Basis: A beautiful wife (Nora) who believes she is an amateur sleuth helps her former detective husband (Nick Charles) solve crimes.

NICHOLAS "NICK" CHARLES

Address: An apartment on Waverly Place in New York's Greenwich Village (in second-season episodes, they appear to live in a brownstone).

Telephone Number: Regent 4-4598.

Place of Birth: England.

Former Occupation: Private detective (owner of Nicholas Charles—Private Investigations).

Current Profession: Mystery editor for an unnamed publishing house in Manhattan.

Car License Plate: NICK 1.

Nora's Pet Names for Nick: Nickie; but when he eyes other girls, it's Nicholas!

Character: Smartly dressed, suave (has a roving eye for the ladies despite the fact that he is married). Fell in love with Nora at first sight; bought her a dog (Asta) to impress her when she continually ignored his attempts to date her. They married in 1950 and stayed at the Ambassador Hotel (room 3-C) on their honeymoon (locale not stated).

    Nick had retired to find a more peaceful life but constantly finds that a dream when Nora constantly stumbles on crimes and involves him in her efforts to solve them. He uses what he calls "The Laundry List" method to solve crimes (Nick relates the facts; Nora writes them down).

If someone takes a shot at Nick, he falls down so as not to disappoint the shooter—"it also prevents them from taking another shot." Nick reads the New York *Chronicle* and hates to have his sleep disrupted. He works first with Homicide Detective Ralph Raine, then Harry Evans, of the New York Police Department.

NORA CHARLES

Place of Birth: San Francisco.
Maiden Name: Nora Clairdon (heir to the Clairdon business empire).
Pet Dog: Asta (wirehaired terrier).
Dress Size: 8.
Bra Size: 32-A.
Charity Affiliations: Junior Matron's Breakfast Club, the Junior Guild.
Nick's Pet Name for Nora: Tiger.
Character: Always fashionably dressed and the bell of the ball at charity functions, Nora believes her intuition is better than Nick's experience when it comes to solving crimes (she also never thinks in emergencies—"I only have hunches"). Nora is overly protective of their dog Asta. She babies him and considers him "their child" (she gave the male dog a girl's name based on her Uncle Harry's theory that a sissy name will make a man out of a boy). When Asta wants to go for a walk, he most often brings his leash to Nick. While Nick accepts Nora's affection for Asta, he sometimes regrets her creation of "Asta Day" (on the 28th of each year [month not mentioned], she and Nick celebrate the day Asta brought them together).

BLONDIE COLLINS

Character: A small-time, gorgeous blonde con artist who has been arrested by Nick on several occasions (she usually serves time at the Elmsville Prison for Women). She dislikes her given name of Beatrice Dean and feels that her alias makes her more criminal-like. While Nora dislikes Blondie (as she arouses her jealous streak when Blondie "makes goo-goo eyes at Nick" and perhaps also because she is somewhat bustier [36-D bra] and more of a flirt), she accepts her as Nick's friend (but can't wait until she is again arrested for some petty crime and out of their lives). She calls Nick "Nickie Lover" and "Nickie Darling" and Nora "That Woman" because she feels Nora "is trying to horn in on me and Nickie." Nora can sense when trouble (Blondie) is coming—"I can feel it in my bones." Blondie attributes her larcenous life to being the victim of a broken home—"I had no mother to guide me."

Tom Corbett, Space Cadet
(CBS, 1950; ABC, 1951–1952;
NBC, 1951, 1954–1955; DuMont, 1953–1954)

Cast: Frankie Thomas Jr. (Tom Corbett), Al Markim (Astro), Jan Merlin (Roger Manning), Margaret Garland, Patricia Ferris (Dr. Joan Dale), Jackie Grimes (T. J. Thistle), Ben Stone (Major "Blastoff" Connell), Edward Bryce (Steve Strong).

Basis: Solar Guards of the 24th century battle evil as they protect the colonized planets of the Solar Alliance (Earth, Mars, Jupiter, and Venus).

TOM CORBETT

Character: Assigned to training on the rocket ship *Polaris*. Although he appeared to be a cadet at Space Academy, he acted more like an official (giving orders, charting flights, and booking space maneuvers). Tom is quick-thinking, assertive, and popular with fellow cadets. Early episodes find Tom as a storyteller. He is seated in an office and welcomes viewers to relate an adventure he shared with fellow cadets (mostly Roger and Astro). A flashback sequence follows with Tom returning at its conclusion to relate a moral and signing off with "So long for now and spaceman's luck to all of you."

ASTRO

Character: The alien member of Tom's crew. He was born to Terron parents on Venus during its early colonization years; he is considered Venusian by his colleagues. He is an engineer and responsible for overseeing the rocket motors on the power deck of the *Polaris*. He has a quick temper and frequently acts without thinking first. He is often picked on by Cadet Roger Manning, and the conflict between the two often causes trouble for Tom.

ROGER MANNING

Character: A practical joke player who is also a wise guy, sarcastic, and constantly causing trouble for Tom and his crew (why he was not expelled is a mystery). While Roger did work on the radar bridge (near the nose of the *Polaris*), he also believed he was better than everyone else and always boasted of his own accomplishments while demeaning those of his colleagues. Despite his faults, in times of emergency he became helpful but always gave into temptation to belittle others. When Roger became annoyed with someone, he would utter, "Blow it out your jets"; when something didn't go his way, he would say, "Aw shucks." In final-season episodes, Roger (assigned to Space Academy on Mars) was replaced by

T. J. Thistle, a cadet with a chip on his shoulder (he believed his shorter height prevented him from achieving success).

DR. JOAN DALE
Character: The only female presence at Space Academy. She is not depicted as a "femme fatale" (a beautiful girl always in need of help). She is intelligent and capable of defending herself in any adverse situation (being the early 1950s, she is one of the first role models for girls in the viewing audience). She teaches at Space Academy (science courses) and is also an inventor and researcher. She invented the Academy's rocket-powered space suits, rocket fuel, and the Hyper Drive (which allows rocket cruisers to reach nearby stars). While Joan may sound like she is all work, she was not. She had a human side and often worried about her superior, Captain Steve Strong, and Tom and his crew when they were assigned a dangerous mission. Joan was attired in a calf-length dress that was based on the military-style dress uniform worn by the male cadets.

OTHER CHARACTERS
Commander Arkwright (Carter Blake) is the stern principal of Space Academy. Cadet Eric Rattison (Frank Sutton) headed the crew of the rocket ship *Vega*. Major Caldwell (Ben Stone), called "Blastoff" by cadets, is the roughest, toughest, and meanest teacher at Space Academy. Rex Marshall played Lieutenant Saunders in commercials for the show's longtime sponsor Kellogg's cereals (it was also sponsored by Kraft Foods and Red Goose Shoes).

PROGRAM INFORMATION
It is the year 2350 when the series begins, and the Solar Guards are attached to a training school called Space Academy, U.S.A. War, as we think of it, no longer exists, and guns have been outlawed. Men no longer wear suits (their everyday clothes are one-piece outfits), and women wear short skirts. Navigators have been replaced by Astrogators, and engineers have been replaced by Nucleonics Officers. Cadets use tele-receivers for visual communication with Space Academy, and visual exploration is accomplished through the Strato-Screen. The Paralo-Ray (which causes temporary paralysis) is the most commonly used weapon.

Not only has space travel been accomplished, but science has also advanced greatly. Blood pills heal the deepest wounds. Personal telephones are worn on the belt and are capable of calling anyone on any planet. Light sticks (tubes that contain a material that shines constantly) provide light (like a flashlight), while a special paint that absorbs light during the day illuminates rooms at night.

Schoolwork has also advanced greatly: the Study Machine allows one to absorb knowledge while sleeping. Phone numbers, however, haven't changed; they reflect the 1950s (a 1950 episode gave the phone number Andover 3-7800 as a means by which futuristic kids could order the Study Machine).

While not readily explained, women are not permitted to be Solar Guards. Space Academy enlists only men of high school and college age as cadets. Women can train as Auxiliary Cadets to assist Solar Guards in times of emergency. Space Week is a tradition at the Academy wherein various spaceship crews (each of which consists of three members) vie for top honors by competing in space races. The Academy's Electro-Scope (an electronic telescope) permits cadets to view the vast regions of outer space without leaving the academy. The Servo Unit automatically oversees academy spaceships (which include the *Polaris*, the *Falcon*, the *Orion*, and the *Ceres*). There is also the Rocket Graveyard, an eerie sight on a distant, uncharted planet where the remnants of lost rocket ships have accumulated over the past 200 years.

Jackson Beck announces the program's most recognizable opening: "Space Academy, U.S.A., in the world beyond tomorrow. Here the space cadets train for duty on distant planets. In roaring rockets they blast through the millions of miles from Earth to far-flung stars and brave the dangers of cosmic frontiers, protecting the liberties of the planets, safeguarding the cause of universal peace in the conquest of space."

Topper
(CBS, 1953–1955)

Cast: Leo G. Carroll (Cosmo Topper), Robert Sterling (George Kerby), Anne Jeffreys (Marian Kerby), Lee Patrick (Henrietta Topper).

Basis: A droll banker (Cosmo Topper) finds his life changed when he becomes haunted by the ghosts of George and Marian Kerby, the former owners of the house in which he now lives.

COSMO TOPPER
Wife: Henrietta.

Address: 101 Yardley Avenue in New York (635 Yardley in the pilot; the address is later given as 101 Maple Drive).

Occupation: Bank vice president (said to be with the following banks: National Security Bank, City Bank, Gotham Trust Company, and City Trust and Savings Bank).

Place of Birth: Boston.

Date of Birth: October 5, 1898.

Education: Lindfield High School, Boston University.

First Girlfriend: Harriet Miller.

Bank Account Balance: $3,500.27.

Favorite Restaurant: Club 22.

Car License Plate: 2K 6308.

Invention: The Seven Cent Dime (a coin to battle inflation: "If an increase in the price of sugar causes a nickel candy bar to cost a dime, the maker can use my new dime and only raise the price to seven cents").

Nickname: Called "Topper Darling" by Marian; "Old Man" by George.

Character: Always dressed in a suit and tie, Topper is also henpecked and finds his life plagued by the ghosts of George and Marian Kerby, who appear and talk only to him. He "inherited" his ghosts when he purchased the former Kerby home (Henrietta felt a change was needed from living in an apartment and convinced Cosmo to invest in a house). The house was listed at $27,000, but when the real estate agent tried to cheat Topper (saying it was worth $28,000), George and Marian stepped in and made the home look like it was falling apart, and the agent was happy to unload it for $16,000.

Anne Jeffreys and Robert Sterling as the ghosts of Marian and George Kerby haunt Cosmo Tooper, played by Leo G. Carroll. © *CBS CBS/Photofest*

HENRIETTA TOPPER

Place of Birth: Boston.

Education: Boston University.

Age: "A gentleman doesn't ask that of a lady" (she appears to be in her early 50s).

Character: Henrietta, whom Cosmo met at college, appears to be a woman from a wealthy family and accustomed to the high-society life. She is a member of the Ladies Drama Committee and married Cosmo despite the fact that her parents felt he was not good enough for her (not from a wealthy family). She and Cosmo love each other, but of late (when they moved into the Kerby home), Henrietta feels that Cosmo is overworked, as he imagines seeing three ghosts, although she too witnesses strange happenings (like the front door opening and closing by itself when it is actually George and Marian exiting and entering the house).

GEORGE AND MARIAN KERBY

Character: George is a former playboy (apparently wealthy) who met a young socialite (Marian) at a party and fell in love at first sight. They married shortly after (in 1948) and purchased their first home in 1949. In 1953, on the occasion of their fifth wedding anniversary, George surprised Marian with a trip to Switzerland. While skiing, "fifty miles from nowhere," Marian's ski broke. While contemplating what to do, a drunken St. Bernard (with a supply of bourbon attached to his collar) came to rescue them. However, before anything could be done, an avalanche killed all three of them. George and Marian, however, have much more living to do and return as ghosts—and decide to take up residence in their former home. It was when Cosmo began measuring the floor for a new carpet that Marian decided to reveal herself—by displaying first her shapely legs and then the rest of her alluring figure. George then materialized, and Cosmo became their haunt—not to scare him but, as Marian says, to "bring some fun into his dull life." Their antics do bring excitement into his life—but Topper's attempts to deal with the unusual occurrences (ghostly happenings) make him appear a bit unstable to others as he tries to explain them.

George and Marian are not Topper's only problems—the St. Bernard that also perished in the avalanche has returned as a ghost as well. Marian has named the dog Neil because of his resemblance to George's cousin. Neil is a boozer, and, as Marian says, "Neil is crazy about bones and beer. By ten a.m. he has had four martinis, two old-fashioneds and a can of beer." George and Marian are lively ghosts and survive (able to show themselves) through their supply of ectoplasm—which becomes depleted if they materialize and dematerialize too often in one day. When alive, George and Marian were the toasts of the town; they partied day and night and never had a worry. Dinner to them was inviting themselves to some-one else's home (even though Marian is an excellent cook). They were, in a way, reckless, as they never gave a thought to really settling down or even starting a family. They were young and in love, and having fun was the only thing that mattered. Now that they are ghosts, they are attempting to live their former life through Topper—but changing him into a swinger is their biggest challenge.

OTHER CHARACTERS
Humphrey Schuyler (Thurston Hall) is Topper's boss, the bank president (for all listed). He is rather uptight and appears all business (although he relaxes by raising chickens on his upstate New York farm; Hildegarde is his prize-winning hen). Vilma (who appeared in the pilot but without a credit) was the Toppers' first maid. She was replaced by Katie (Kathleen Freeman), a maid from the Abba Agency, then by Maggie (Edna Skinner).

Trouble with Father
(ABC, 1950–1955)

Cast: Stu Erwin (Himself), June Erwin (Herself), Ann Todd, Merry Anders (Joyce Erwin), Sheila James (Jackie Erwin), Willie Best (Willie).

Basis: Life with a mishap-prone high school teacher (Stu Erwin); his wife, June; and their daughters, Joyce and Jackie, who live at 413 Medvale Avenue in the town of Hamilton.

STU AND JUNE ERWIN
Stu and June have been married 19 years when the series begins. Stu, a former English teacher at Alexander Hamilton High School (always called Hamilton High), is now its principal. He is a member of the University Club (where he goes for peace and relaxation). Stuart, called Stu, and June were students at Hamilton High when they first met. They dated through high school, and after Stu acquired his teaching certificate, he and June eloped in 1931 ("We were young and romantic and it was spring," Stu says). On their honeymoon, June made golden-crust fried chicken—a tradition she still observes once a year (when they were dating, Stu was addicted to June's guava jelly sandwiches). Four years later, they became the parents of Joyce (in 1935), and in 1941, their second daughter, Jacqueline (called Jackie) was born.

Stu is a rather laid-back principal, and although he is faced with only minor problems from students, he manages to solve them without much dif-ficulty—it is solving problems at home that proves more difficult. At his time in high school, Stu was active in sports (captain of the Hamilton High football team) and, while not the best student, did keep up his grades. June, more academically inclined than Stu, was a member of the school's literary club and debate team. Although she and Stu married rather abruptly, June did hold a job as a secretary before giving it up to raise a family. As part of his duties as principal, Stu substitutes when necessary and has established a civics night class (which he teaches) for adults. Stu mentioned that he studied Latin and also taught it for a short time. June, who pays $2 for a pair of nylon stockings, is a member of the Women's Club (which sends packages to CARE once a month) and has the family's clothes cleaned at Ling Ying's Laundry. Stu, who enjoys playing golf, reads a newspaper called the *Daily Star*, and his car license plate is IT 2N 514; June reads a magazine called *Woman's Home Companion*. Stu and June were stars of sorts when they were chosen by a producer to play bit parts in a movie called *High School Life*.

JOYCE AND JACKIE ERWIN

Joyce and Jackie share a bedroom. Joyce first attends Hamilton High School (where she was a cheerleader for the football team), then State College (in 1954, when Merry Anders took over the role). Joe's Ice Cream Parlor is her after-school hangout. She is very pretty and is described as "The Perfect Lady" (but, as Joyce says, "I wasn't always. I was a tomboy and got into fights with boys. I was the terror of the neighborhood. It all changed when I fell in love. I was eleven. His name was Freddy. All I remember about him is that he had big ears"). Joyce wears a perfume called Divine Scent. Her allowance is first 50 cents, then $1 a week, and an undisclosed amount when she began college. Her favorite dinner is fried chicken and candied yams. Biff's Ice Cream Parlor is her favorite after-school hangout.

Jackie first attended Hamilton Elementary School, then Hamilton High (1954). She receives an allowance of 50 cents a week, collects stamps, and is a tomboy. She also collects "bugs, bottles and butterflies." "There are a lot of nice little girls for her to play with," says June, "but she doesn't want to." Stu wishes she would change her ways—"But she just won't," he says. Jackie has off-camera fights with boys—"Mostly sticking up for Joyce," she says, "when they tease her about mooning over boys." Jackie has a pet frog named Elmer ("He's trained. He can do somersaults and everything"). Her bedtime is 9:00 p.m., and she became a cowgirl for a short period of time when TV stars Dale Evans (*The Roy Rogers Show*) and Gale Davis (*Annie Oakley*) became her heroines. Freshly made strawberry jam is her favorite dessert, and she likes eating dinner in the kitchen—"It's closer to second helpings." Jackie is president of the Secret Six Club and also developed a fascination with wrestling programs on TV.

In high school, Jackie joined the boys' basketball team when the coach discovered she was "a natural-born sharpshooter" (while Jackie did have the ability to sink every shot, she actually joined to be near a fellow student named Glen [Dwayne Hickman]). Five years later, Sheila James and Dwayne Hickman would become famous as Zelda Gilroy and Dobie Gillis on the CBS series *The Many Loves of Dobie Gillis*.

OTHER CHARACTERS
Willie is a Baptist and was born in North Carolina. He works both as the school's custodian and for Stu as a handyman. Drexel Potter (Martin Milner) is Joyce's boyfriend (also a student at Hamilton High). They appeared together on *The TV Amateur Hour* in an elopement skit written by Drexel.

Note: The program is also known as *Life with the Erwins*, *The Stu Erwin Show*, and *The New Stu Erwin Show*.

The Untouchables

(ABC, 1959–1963)

Cast: Robert Stack (Eliot Ness), Jerry Paris (Martin Flaherty), Paul Picerni (Lee
   Hobson), Abel Fernandez (William Youngfellow), Steve London (Jack
   Rossman), Peter Leeds (Lamar Kane), Eddie Firestone (Eric Hanson),
   Nicholas Georgiade (Enrico Rossi), Walter Winchell (Narrator).
Basis: Chicago during its turbulent years (1920s–1930s) provides the setting
   for an elite team of federal agents (The Untouchables) and its leader (Eliot
   Ness) as they seek to end the rule of mobsters such as Al Capone.

ELIOT NESS
Age: 26.
Place of Birth: Chicago.
Occupation: Prohibition agent turned leader of the Untouchables.
Office Phone Number: Superior 7-599.
Romantic Interest: Betty Anderson (played by Patricia Crowley).
Betty's Phone Number: Superior 2-198 (she and Eliot married in November 1929).
Character: To battle the crime and corruption of the Chicago mob, the U.S.
   district attorney assigned Ness the daunting task. There are 300 federal
   agents in Chicago—"Some can be bought. But what if you have a special
   squad, small, operating on its own; every man thoroughly investigated,
   brought in from all parts of the country. Men who will spit on Capone's
   graft; just a few he can't buy." Ness was then given full access to agents'
   files and chose a team who were reliable, courageous, dedicated, and
   honest—"Six or seven of the most honest men." On July 5, 1929, in
   office 208 of the Federal Building in Washington, D.C., Ness chose his
   team (see below) to become the Federal Special Squad, dubbed "The Untouchables" by a newspaper called the Chicago *Bulletin* with the headline
   "Untouchables Defy Capone."

The Untouchables: Enrico Rossi (Nicholas Georgiade), Lee Hobson (Paul Picerni), Eliot Ness (Robert Stack), and William Youngfellow (Abel Fernandez). © ABC ABC/Photofest

Many episodes relate the conflict between Ness and Capone. Capone (Neville Brand) had established an illegal bootlegging operation in Chicago with headquarters in a room above the Montmarte Café. It took Ness 18 months to nail Capone on an income tax evasion charge (he was sentenced to 11 years in the Atlanta Federal Penitentiary, Cell 39, Block D; his prison number: 40886). Ness fought corruption for many years and completed the book version of *The Untouchables* shortly before his death in 1957.

THE UNTOUCHABLES TEAM

Martin Flaherty: A former Boston police officer with an outstanding police record of arrests. Commended for his relentless dedication to duty and risking his life to save a fellow officer.

William Youngfellow: A full-blooded Cherokee Indian, decorated for breaking up the Oklahoma alcohol trafficking ring. Relentless in his pursuit of justice; unable to be bribed by the local mob.

Jack Rossman: A former New York telephone lineman turned wire-tap specialist for the federal government.

Lamar Kane: An agent with the Richmond, Virginia, bureau of the justice department. A law school graduate, married, and the father of two children.

Eric Hanson: A former agent with the San Francisco bureau; previously worked as a guard on death row at San Quentin prison.

Enrico Rossi: A former barber who became an agent after testifying against the mobster Frank Nitti (Rossi became obsessed with bringing down the mob when he witnessed a hit that claimed the life of an innocent 17-year-old girl).

Lee Hobson: A Harvard graduate and a former district attorney before joining the Treasury Department.

Note: The pilot episode also featured agents Tom Kopka (Robert Osterloh) of the Sacramento Bureau, a former Pennsylvania State Trooper and World War I hero, and Joe Fuscelli (Keenan Wynn), a man who speaks the Sicilian and Neapolitan dialects, spent five years in prison for robbery, and knows every street and alley in the city—the best driving hands in Chicago.

Wanted: Dead or Alive
(CBS, 1958–1961)

Cast: Steve McQueen (Josh Randall), Wright King (Jason Nichols).
Basis: An Old West bounty hunter (Josh Randall) and the situations he encounters tracking down wanted outlaws.

On March 7, 1957, "The Bounty Man" aired on the CBS series *Trackdown*. The episode introduced viewers to an Old West bounty hunter named Josh Randall and spawned the successful *Wanted: Dead or Alive* series. While millions of people saw the episode, only potential sponsors saw the show's sales pitch (which played right before the closing theme song; replaced for the aired version by a commercial). It went as follows:

> "Hi, my name is Steve McQueen. I hope you liked what you saw. Kind of a new approach to Westerns. I hope you liked Josh Randall. Oh, he's not a lawman, but he's got a lot of friends who are. And they like him because he respects them and their jobs. Since Josh doesn't wear a badge, he can take the shortest distance between two people. On these occasions, his lawmen friends kinda turn their heads and wish they could use the same methods. The stories on *Wanted: Dead or Alive* are about the people of the times, their dreams, their problems, their happiness. . . . There are a lot of stories on *Wanted: Dead or Alive* and they all have one thing in common—they all happen to people. . . . Anyway you slice it, *Wanted: Dead or Alive* is a good show, full of action and adventure. Good entertainment for the whole family—and that's what'll sell any product. . . . See y'all now."

The time is the 1870s, and being a bounty hunter "wasn't a bad way to live. You got to see a lot of the country and meet a lot of people. It was a living and now and then a good one. Josh Randall liked the life and it seemed to like him."

Although the world may be big and outlaws can easily hide from the law, Josh finds that is not a problem—"He's a man, there's nowhere he can lay down his feet that I can't walk—I'll find him." Josh's motto—"If he's got a price on his head, I've got an empty pocket."

Josh Randall was born in the town of Cameron and is not like other bounty hunters (who seek outlaws only for the offered reward and care nothing for the person they seek). Josh is a compassionate bounty hunter and sometimes finds himself in the position of protector, struggling to safeguard his prisoners from the less scrupulous bounty hunters. Josh carries a .30-40 caliber sawed-off carbine he calls his "Mare's Leg." "It's kinda like a hog's leg but not quite as mean. If I have to use it, I want to get the message across."

Josh's occasional assistant is Jason Nichols, a former deputy turned sheriff turned bounty hunter who travels with a dog he calls "Hey Dog." The first person Josh tracked was Nate Phillips (George Niese), a killer with a $500 price tag who was wanted for murder in Texas. In the 1959 episode "Legend," Josh finds the tables turned when Sam McGarrett (Victor Jory) puts out a $1,000 wanted-dead-or-alive poster on him (as it was the only way Sam knew to find Josh and bring him to him—to lead him into the desert to find hidden Mexican gold).

Yancy Derringer
(CBS, 1958–1959)

Cast: Jock Mahoney (Yancy Derringer), X Brands (Pahoo), Kevin Hagen (John Colton), Frances Bergen (Mme. Francine).

Basis: An undercover agent (Yancy Derringer) for New Orleans attempts to ferret out the crime and corruption that is now a part of his beloved city.

In a hotel room in New Orleans, Louisiana (1868), John Colton, the city administrator, meets with Marchancy "Yancy" Derringer, a former Confederate soldier and the owner of both a plantation and a riverboat. "Since becoming administrator of this city, I've come across a very astonishing fact. In the highest to the lowest places, particularly the lowest, your name has always been spoken with the greatest respect. I want you to work for me. The [Civil] war is over. New Orleans has become a treasure chest; the fortune hunters of the world are here. I want a man who loves this city, loves the South, who will work without pay, without prejudice, without protection as my personal agent. I want a black angel who will be on the inside before something happens, a man who will do anything for law and order—anything and get away with it. Because if that man were caught, I might be compelled to hang him." In response, Yancy says, "What you want is a rogue, scoundrel, gentleman, smuggler, gambler and fool. . . . Well, Mr. Colton, I guess I'm your Huckleberry."

Yancy's adventures as he helps Colton institute a system of law and order are depicted. Yancy is assisted by a nonspeaking Pawnee Indian named Pahoo-Ka-Ta-Wah ("Wolf Who Stands in Water"). Pahoo saved Yancy's life at some point within the last eight years. He went against his faith by saving a white man and is now responsible for Yancy's life. Pahoo carries a shotgun with him at all times.

The only background information on Yancy is that he was born in New Orleans. He left in 1860, joined the Confederacy, was shot during the Battle of Cold Harbor, and spent one year in a Yankee prison. When he was released (possibly 1865), he traveled west to strike it rich (as a gold miner) but failed (it was probably at this time that Pahoo saved Yancy's life). Yancy then returned to New Orleans to pick up where he left off. Old Dave is Yancy's dog, the *Sultana* is his riverboat, and Waverly Plantation is the place of his birth. Yancy does carry a derringer—in his hat, up his sleeve, in his belt, and in his boot. He owns a silver mine in Virginia City, Nevada, and buys his fancy clothes (his "duds") at Deveraux's Gentleman's Apparel.

Mme. Francine is Yancy's love interest; Mai Ling Mandarin (Lisa Lu), Yancy's friend, runs the Sazarack Restaurant, and Captain Billy (J. Pat O'Malley) is the skipper of the *Sultana*. The General Pacific Railroad was mentioned as just laying track in New Orleans.

Noreen Marsh played John's sister, Agatha Colton; Victor Sen Yung was Hon Lee, Mai Ling's cousin, the owner of the Green Dragon Café in San Francisco.

Zorro
(ABC, 1957–1959; 1960–1961)

Cast: Guy Williams (Don Diego de la Vega/Zorro), Britt Lomond (Enrique Monasterio), Gene Sheldon (Bernardo), George J. Lewis (Don Alejandro de la Vega), Henry Calvin (Sergeant Demetrio Lopez Garcia), Peter Adams (Captain Arturo Pollidano), Penny Santon (Cresencia), Jolene Brand (Anna Maria Verdugo), Richard Anderson (Ricardo Delano), Annette Funicello (Anita Cecilia Isabella Cabrillo and Constansia de la Torres), Arthur Space (Don Miguel Cabrillo).

Basis: A mysterious figure, dressed in black and known only as Zorro, battles the evils of a tyrant (Commandante Monasterio) in his quest to protect the people of his beloved community in Monterey, California (1820).

DON DIEGO/ZORRO
Date of Birth: 1794, Monterey, California (Old Los Angeles).
Home: The de la Vega ranch.
Horse: Tornado (when Zorro), Phantom (when Don Diego).
Trademark (as Zorro): The sign of the "Z" (which he carves with his sword).
Servant: Bernardo (a deaf-mute).
Relations to Don Diego: Don Alejandro, his father.
Don Diego Character: A Spanish nobleman, expert with a sword (possesses trophies), three years of study at the University of Spain. To conceal his identity as Zorro, he pretends to be a coward, inexperienced at swordplay and the lazy son of a wealthy rancher. He has an eye for the ladies but never lets his guard down when learning of injustice (he pretends to be passive and thus suspicion never falls on him as being Zorro).
Zorro Character: Don Diego's creation as a way to battle evil as a mysterious figure for justice. He chose the name "El Zorro" (The Fox) to deal with a powerful enemy (the Commandante) as someone who is cunning but not

obvious (he based it on an old proverb: "When you cannot clothe yourself in the skin of a lion, put on that of a fox"). Because Don Diego cannot stand by and do nothing in a troublesome situation, he also devises a way to convince others that he is perfectly harmless: "Instead of a man of action, I shall be a man of letters, an innocent scholar interested in only the arts and sciences." His creation of a black mask, costume, and whip completes his Zorro disguise (as Don Diego, he appears in a maroon jacket with gold braid and a walking stick). He carves his first "Z" on a sheet of music on his piano.

The de la Vegas are the most important family in Old Los Angeles. As a child, Don Diego discovered a secret cave beneath his hacienda. It is located behind the fireplace, and Don Diego believes it was built by his grandfather as a means to escape Indian raids. He now uses the cave as his base of operations as Zorro. Although Zorro helps people, he is considered criminal by the authorities, and wanted posters have been issued: "Reward. 100 Pesos will be paid for the capture—Dead or Alive—of the bandit who calls himself Zorro." Zorro has also left a message for the Commandante: "My Sword is a flame, to right every wrong. So hold well my name—Zorro." Zorro is called "A Friend of the People," "The Defender of the Oppressed," and "The Champion of Justice."

PROGRAM INFORMATION

Captain Enrique Monasterio is the real threat to Zorro (he is based in the Pueblo de Los Angeles, which was founded in 1781). He is assisted by a somewhat bumbling sergeant, Demetrio Lopez Garcia, a soldier of the king of Spain (the King's Lancers). And how did one so inept become a sergeant? "It was easy. I was a private for a long time. Then one day I saw the Commandante kissing the Magistrato's wife and the next thing you know, I am a sergeant." Garcia frequents the Pasada de Los Angeles (a pub), believes he possesses the natural qualities of leadership, and, like other lancers, is paid every six months.

When the viceroy (John Dehner) arrives to inspect the Pueblo and discovers that Enrique is corrupt (keeping tax money unjustly acquired from citizens), he arrests him and replaces him with Captain Arturo Pollidano, an honest soldier of the king who also sought to capture Zorro.

Cresencia is the de la Vegas' maid; Anna Maria Verdugo is Don Diego's romantic interest; Ricardo Delano is Don Diego's rival for Anna Maria; Anita Cecilia Isabella Cabrillo is the beautiful girl from Spain who has come to Los Angeles to find her long-lost father, Don Miguel Cabrillo; Constansia de la Torres is a girl whom Don Diego and Garcia have known since she was a child; she has now become of age and seeks to marry Miguel Serano (Mark Oamo), a scoundrel whom Zorro exposes as a fortune hunter seeking Constansia's money.

Index

About the Author

Vincent Terrace has worked as a researcher for ABC and is currently the TV historian for BPOLIN Productions, LLC (for which he created and wrote the pilot episode for a projected TV series called *April's Dream*). The author of 37 books on television and radio history, Terrace has teamed with James Robert Parish for the *Actors' Television Credits* series of books for Scarecrow Press. He has also written such books as *The Encyclopedia of Television Programs, 1925–2012*, *The Encyclopedia of Television Pilots, 1937–2012*, *Television Specials, 1936–2012*, *The Encyclopedia of Television Subjects, Themes, and Settings*, and *Television Introductions: Narrated TV Program Openings since 1949* (Scarecrow, 2013).